The Effects of Mass Immigration on Canadian Living Standards and Society

The Effects of **Mass Immigration** on Canadian Living Standards and Society

edited by Herbert Grubel

Fraser Institute
www.fraserinstitute.org
2009

Date of issue: August 2009
Printed and bound in Canada

Library and Archives Canada Cataloguing in Publication Data

The effects of mass immigration on canadian living standards and society / edited by Herbert Grubel.

Includes bibliographical references.
ISBN 978-0-88975-246-7.

Contents

About the authors ◆ v

Acknowledgments ◆ xiii

Introduction and policy implications ◆ xv
Herbert Grubel

Overview and International Perspectives

1 The current state of Canadian immigration policy ◆ 3
James Bissett

2 Immigration's impact on public coffers in the United States ◆ 29
Steven A. Camarota

3 Immigration and its impacts in France ◆ 41
Jean-Paul Gourévitch

Economic Issues

4 Immigration policy in free societies: Are there principles involved or is it all politics? ◆ 57
Vernon M. Briggs, Jr.

5 Is Canadian immigration too high? A labor market and productivity perspective ◆ 73
Patrick Grady

6 Recent immigration and Canadian living standards ◆ 97
Herbert Grubel

Demographic Issues

7 Immigration's impact on the growth and age structure of the Canadian workforce ◆ 121
Robin Banerjee and William Robson

8 The immigration option to population aging in Canada ◆ 145
Marcel Mérette

Social Issues

9 The creation of a global suburb and its impact on Canadian national unity ◆ 171
Stephen Gallagher

10 Immigration and multiculturalism undermine culture and security in Canada ◆ 197
Salim Mansur

Political Issues

11 The politics of Canadian immigration policies ◆ 213
Gordon Gibson

12 The challenges of reforming immigration policy in Britain ◆ 225
Sir Andrew Green

About this publication ◆ 233

Supporting the Fraser Institute ◆ 234

About the Fraser Institute ◆ 235

Editorial Advisory Board ◆ 236

About the authors

Robin Banerjee

Robin Banerjee is a former policy analyst at the C.D. Howe Institute. He has a B.A. in economics from the University of Toronto and an M.A. in economics from both the University of Guelph and the University of Maryland, College Park. His research at the Institute ranged over a number of areas, including monetary policy, environmental policy, pensions, demographics, and economic growth.

James Bissett

Former Executive Director, Canadian Immigration Service

Mr. Bissett is a former Canadian Ambassador with 36 years of service in the government of Canada. He was the Canadian Ambassador to Yugoslavia, Bulgaria, and Albania, and High Commissioner to Trinidad and Tobago. From 1985 to 1990, he was the Executive Director of the Canadian Immigration Service. During this period, he served on the Prime Minister's Intelligence Advisory Committee.

Upon leaving the Public Service in 1992, he was employed by the International Organization of Migration as their Chief of Mission in Moscow. He worked in Moscow for five years helping the Russian Government establish a new Immigration Service and draft new Immigration legislation and a new *Citizenship Act*. During this period, he was in Chechnya helping evacuate and find accommodation for refugees fleeing the civil war there in 1994.

Since his return to Canada in 1997, Mr. Bissett has acted as a consultant to the Government on a number of immigration issues. He was a regular panelist on the now-defunct Public Broadcasting System (PBS) TV Program, *The Editors*, and is a regular contributor of articles to Canadian newspapers.

Vernon M. Briggs, Jr.

Emeritus Professor of Labor & Human Resource Economics, Cornell University

Mr. Briggs is an Emeritus Professor of Labor and Human Resource Economics at Cornell University in Ithaca, New York. Before joining the faculty at Cornell, Mr. Briggs taught at Michigan State University and the University of Texas at Austin.

Mr. Briggs is widely regarded as an expert in the field of human resource policy and has written extensively on the subject. Aside from his published articles, he was also the author of *The Chicano Worker, Immigration Policy and the National Interest.*

In addition to serving on numerous editorial boards of professional journals, he was a member of the National Council on Employment Policy and served a term as Chairman. He has also sat on the Board of Directors for the Center for Immigration Studies, located in Washington, D.C., and has presented before numerous committees of the US Congress.

Steven A. Camarota

Director of Research, Center for Immigration Studies

Mr. Camarota is Director of Research at the Center for Immigration Studies in Washington, D.C. He holds a Ph.D. from the University of Virginia in public-policy analysis, and a Masters degree in political science from the University of Pennsylvania.

In recent years he has testified before Congress more than any other non-government expert on the economic and fiscal impact of immigration. He is currently under contract with the Census Bureau as the lead researcher on a project examining the quality of immigrant data in the American Community Survey.

His research has been featured on the front pages of the *New York Times*, *Washington Post*, and *USAToday* as well as many other media outlets. He has written academic articles for such journals as the *Public Interest* and *Social Science Quarterly.* He has also written general interest pieces for such publications as the *Chicago Tribune* and *National Review.*

He appears frequently on radio and television news programs including CNN, MSNBC, Fox News Channel, *NBC Nightly News,* and *ABC World News Tonight, CBS Evening News,* National Public Radio, and the *NewsHour with Jim Lehrer.*

Some of his most recent works published by the Center for Immigration Studies are: *Immigrants in the United States 2007: A Profile of the America's Foreign-born Population; 100 Million More: Projecting the Impact of Immigration on the U.S. Population, 2007 to 2060; Illegitimate Nation: An Examination of Out-of-Wedlock Births among Immigrants and Natives; The High Cost of Cheap Labor: Illegal Immigration and the Federal Budget; Back Where We Started: An Examination of Trends in Immigrant Welfare Use since Welfare Reform; Dropping Out: Immigrant Entry and Native Exit from the Labor Market 2000–2005; Births to Immigrants in America: 1970 to 2002; Immigration in an Aging Society: Workers, Birth Rates, and Social Security.*

Stephen Gallagher

Program Director (Montreal),
Canadian International Council

Dr. Stephen Gallagher is Program Director of the Montreal Branch of the Canadian International Council and a lecturer in Political Science. He has taught at McGill University, Carleton University, and the University of Manitoba.

Dr. Gallagher has published widely on Canadian and European migration policy, has appeared as a witness before Parliamentary Committees, and has been interviewed on such media sources as *BBC World Report,* CBC, CBS *60 Minutes*, and CTV.

Gordon Gibson

Senior Fellow, Fraser Institute

Gordon Gibson is a Senior Fellow in Canadian Studies at the Fraser Institute. He received his BA (Honours) in Mathematics and Physics from the University of British Columbia and his MBA from Harvard Business School. This was followed by research work at the London School of Economics. His current areas of study include federalism, governance, and relations between aboriginals and non-aboriginals.

Mr. Gibson has written books and monographs for the Fraser Institute that include: *Plan B: The Future of the Rest of Canada; Thirty Million Musketeers: One Canada for All Canadians; Fixing Canadian Democracy; Comments on the Draft Nisga'a Treaty; A Principled Analysis of the Nisga'a Treaty; Principles for Treaty Making; Challenges in Senate Reform: Conflicts of Interest, Unintended Consequences, New Possibilities;* and, his most recent study, *A New Look at Canadian Indian Policy: Respect the Collective—Promote the Individual.*

In 2002, he was commissioned by the BC Government to design the Citizens' Assembly on Electoral Reform. His report was substantially adopted (with amendments as to size) and the Assembly process is now successfully completed. The Assembly architecture is currently the subject of extensive world-wide study as an innovative technique in tackling difficult public-policy problems. His columns appear frequently in the *Vancouver Sun*, *Winnipeg Free Press*, and *Globe & Mail.*

He served as Assistant to the Minister of Northern Affairs, then Executive, and later Special, Assistant to the Prime Minister, and ran in three federal elections. In addition, he was elected twice to the BC Legislature and served as both MLA and Leader of the British Columbia Liberal Party. He is currently on the Board and Chair of the Audit Committee of the Westshore Terminals Income Fund.

Jean-Paul Gourévitch

International expert on immigration;
Academic, Université Paris XII

Jean-Paul Gourévitch is an international expert on human resources, specializing in migrations and in Africa, where he has conducted missions since 1987 for various organizations: the French Department of Foreign and European Affairs, the European Union, UNESCO, the World Bank, and a range of companies and NGOs.

His most recent books in this field are *Les migrations en Europe* (Acropole, 2007), *La France en Afrique* (Acropole, 2008), and *Les Africains en France* (Acropole, 2009) as well as a monograph on *Le coût réel de l'immigration en France* (Contribuables associés, 2008). His report on sub-Saharan migrations was adopted by the Council of Europe parliamentary assembly on April 18, 2008.

He has also taught in French universities on political imagery (Paris XII), the informal economy (Paris II), and the history of youth literature (Bordeaux IV). A number of his books, *L'image en politique* (Hachette Littératures, 1998), *L'économie informelle* (Pré aux Clercs, 2002), and *La littérature de jeunesse dans tous ses écrits 1529–1970* (CRDP Créteil-Argos, 1999) have become reference works.

In addition, he has written detective novels (*Maux Croisés*, Archipoche, 2008) and children's novels, including *Pompei.com* (Belin, 2008) and *Ulysse.com* (Belin, 2008) as well as the *Barbares* saga (Bayard Poche Jeunesse) recounting the lives of street children revolting against society in nineteenth-century Paris. He has also written, for Le Pré aux Clercs, the text of illustrated anthologies on writers who spoke of their childhoods (*Mémoires d'enfances*, with Jacques Gimard, 2004) or of love (*Plaisirs d'amour*, with Dominique Marny, 2006).

Patrick Grady

Co-Founder, Global Economics Ltd.

Mr. Grady is an economic consultant with Global Economics Ltd. He is a former senior official in the federal Department of Finance and Bank of Canada. Dr. Grady obtained his B.A. in political science from the University of Illinois and a M.A. and Ph.D. in economics from the University of Toronto. He has written many articles and five books and on economic and fiscal issues.

As a consultant, he has worked for most of the departments and agencies of the federal government concerned with economic and fiscal matters as well as many for provincial and territorial governments and some private companies. In addition, he has completed assignments for international financial institutions and aid organizations in more than 30 countries in Eastern Europe, Asia, Africa, Latin America, and the Caribbean.

Sir Andrew Green

Chairman, Migrationwatch UK

Sir Andrew Green was a professional diplomat for 35 years. He studied Natural Sciences and Economics at Cambridge before taking a three-year Short Service Commission in the Royal Green Jackets.

On joining the Diplomatic Service in 1965, he studied Arabic in Lebanon. Thereafter, he spent half his career in the Middle East where he served in six posts. The remainder of his service was divided between London, Paris, and Washington. He was Ambassador in Syria (1991–1994) and then Director for the Middle East in the Foreign Office before serving for four and a half years as Ambassador in Saudi Arabia. He retired in June 2000. He has since devoted his time to voluntary work.

In late 2001, he founded Migrationwatch UK, an entirely independent organization that accepts no funds from the government but relies entirely on donations from the public. Its purpose is to set out the facts in a comprehensible form so that the political system can respond.

Herb Grubel

Senior Fellow, Fraser Institute

Mr. Grubel is a Senior Fellow at the Fraser Institute and Professor of Economics (Emeritus), Simon Fraser University. He has a B.A. from Rutgers University and a Ph.D. in economics from Yale University. He has taught full time at Stanford University, the University of Chicago, and the University of Pennsylvania; and has had temporary appointments at universities in Berlin, Singapore, Cape Town, Nairobi, Oxford, and Canberra.

Herbert Grubel was the Reform Party Member of Parliament for Capliano-Howe Sound from 1993 to 1997, serving as the Finance Critic from 1995 to 1997. He has published 16 books and 180 professional articles in economics dealing with international trade and finance and a wide range of economic policy issues.

Salim Mansur

Associate Professor, Department of Political Science,
University of Western Ontario

Mr. Mansur is an Associate Professor in the faculty of social sciences, University of Western Ontario, London, and teaches in the department of political science. He is the co-editor of *The Indira-Rajiv Years: The Indian Economy and Polity 1966–1991* and has published widely in academic journals such as *Jerusalem Quarterly*, *Journal of South Asian and Middle Eastern Studies*, *American Journal of Islamic Social Sciences*, *Arab Studies Quarterly*, and *Middle East Quarterly*.

Mansur writes a weekly column for the *Toronto Sun* and his *Sun* columns are published across Canada in newspapers owned by Sun Media. He also writes a monthly column for the magazine *Western Standard* (Calgary) and the *PajamasMedia.com* in the United States.

Mansur was born in Calcutta, India, and moved to Canada where he completed his studies, receiving a doctorate in political science from the University of Toronto. Before joining the University of Western Ontario he worked as a Research Fellow at the Canadian Institute for International Peace and Security in Ottawa and was a candidate on record for the Canadian Alliance in the riding of London-West in the Canadian federal election of November 2000.

Mansur is a member of the Board of Directors of the Center for Islamic Pluralism located in Washington, D.C., an academic consultant with the Center for Security Policy also based in Washington, D.C., and Senior Fellow with the Canadian Coalition for Democracies in Toronto. Mansur was presented in September 2006 with the American Jewish Congress's Stephen S. Wise "Profile in Courage" award.

Marcel Mérette

Associate Professor, Department of Economics,
University of Ottawa

Mr. Mérette is currently the Vice-Dean of Research in the Faculty of Social Sciences and Associate Professor in the Department of Economics at University of Ottawa. He received his Ph.D. in Economics from the Université de Montréal (1993). His past positions include Postdoctoral fellow and Visiting Professor at Yale University (1993–1995), Economist at the Canadian Department of Finance (1995–1999), Assistant Professor (1999–2003) and Associate Professor (since 2003) in the Department of Economics as well as Vice-Dean of Research in the Faculty of Social Sciences (since 2005) at the University of Ottawa.

Mérette's recent papers include: Demographic Changes and the Gains from Globalisation: A Multi-Country Overlapping Generations CGE Model (2009); Population Ageing, Time Allocation and Human Capital: a General Equilibrium Analysis for Canada (2009); Population Ageing in Canada: A Sectoral and Occupational Analysis with a CGE Overlapping Generations Model (2007); Population Ageing and the

Effective Rate of Retirement in Canada (2005); The Bright Side: A Positive View on the Economics of Aging (2002).

William B. P. Robson

President and Chief Executive Officer, C.D. Howe Institute

Bill Robson took office as President and CEO of the C.D. Howe Institute in July 2006, after serving as the Institute's Senior Vice President since 2003 and Director of Research since 2000. He has a B.A. from the University of Toronto and an M.A. from the Norman Paterson School of International Affairs at Carleton University.

Mr. Robson has written extensively on government budgets, pensions, healthcare financing, and on inflation and currency issues. His work on demographic change and health care financing won an award from the federal Policy Research Secretariat, and his work on monetary policy with David Laidler has won prizes from the Canadian Economics Association and the Donner Canadian Foundation. Mr. Robson chairs the C.D. Howe Institute's Monetary Policy Council. He writes a regular column for the *Globe and Mail*, and is a familiar commentator on economic issues in the media.

Mr. Robson serves as an advisor to, or director of, several education-related and public affairs organizations. He lectured on public finance and public policy at the University of Toronto from 2000 to 2003. Before joining the C.D. Howe Institute in 1988, he held positions as an economist with Wood Gundy Inc. and the federal Department of Energy, Mines and Resources.

Acknowledgments

The papers in this volume were presented on June 3–4, 2008 at a conference in Montreal entitled "Canadian Immigration Policy: Reassessing the Economic, Demographic and Social Impact on Canada." The Fraser Institute sponsored this conference. Martin Collacott, Alexander Moens, and Herbert Grubel, Senior Fellows at the Fraser Institute, were responsible for the designing the program and selecting speakers and session chairs. Grubel is grateful to his colleagues for relieving him of most of his responsibilities for the four-month period in the Spring of 2008, when he held a teaching position at the Johns Hopkins School of Advanced International Studies in Bologna, Italy.

Financial support for the conference came from the Barbara & Mark Mitchell Fund and the Aurea Foundation. It is acknowledged with gratitude. The Conference program included a formal presentation by the Honourable Diane Finley, Minister of Immigration in the federal government. It also included a lively panel discussion among members of the parliament and government of Quebec: Yolande James, Minister of Immigration and Cultural Communities; Catherine Morissette, Official Opposition Critic for Immigration and Cultural Communities, Action démocratique du Québec; and Martin Lemay, Second Opposition Group Critic for Immigration, Cultural Communities and Citizenship, Parti Québécois.

The views expressed by these politicians contributed much to the informal discussions among the over 100 members of the public who attended the conference and participated energetically in formal question-and-answer periods. They also are reflected in the papers in this volume that were revised by the authors after their initial presentation.

The many logistic and organizational details of the conference were handled superbly by the staff of the Fraser Institute. In Vancouver, these included: Heather Corbett, Event Coordinator; Ashley Astells, Events Assistant; Arby Yeo, Event Coordinator; Leah Costello, Director of Special Projects; Bill Ray, Art Director; and Dean Pelkey, Director of Communications. A large part of the responsibilities were shouldered very competently by the staff in the Montreal office of the Fraser Institute: Sébastien Côté, Manager, Events and Development; Johana Křížová, Events Assistant; Tasha Kheiriddin, Director, Quebec and la Francophonie, and Julie Lajoye, Communications Officer.

The Fraser Institute and organizers of the conference and the editor of this volume are very thankful to all of the many persons who have made this project successful.

Herbert Grubel, editor

Introduction and policy implications

Herbert Grubel

Since 1990, Canada's annual rate of immigration has been extremely high—the highest in the world, averaging 0.75% of the population—and has had a significant impact on the size of the population, adding, between 1990 and 2006, 3.9 million (14.2%) to the 1990 level of 27.4 million. Such mass immigration has profound effects on economic, demographic, social, and political conditions in Canada that affect the well-being of all Canadians, including past immigrants. Unfortunately, Canadians are insufficiently aware of these effects partly because a code of political correctness tends to identify any examination of immigration policies with racism and partly because Canada's electoral system rewards politicians who are in favor of the current high intake. As a result of these conditions, during the 2008 federal election, politicians typically promised to maintain or even raise this rate of immigration without any public discussion of the consequences of such policies or any significant input from Canadians affected by them.

The papers in this volume provide the Canadian public with analytically sound and well-documented empirical information about the significant positive and negative effects mass immigration has on their well-being and that of their offspring. It is hoped that this information will mobilize public opinion, lead politicians to engage in debate of the issues, and ultimately result in an improvement in official immigration policies.

The chapters are organized into five sections. The first presents an overview of the issues and some international perspectives. The three papers in this group deal with Canadian, American, and French immigration policies and the economic and social effects they have on the residents of those countries. The second part contains three papers focusing on the economic effects of mass immigration in Canada.

In part three, two papers are dedicated to the analysis of the demographic effects of immigration and the relief from the financial troubles of Canada's social programs that immigration is alleged to bring. The fourth part contains two papers that examine the social challenges brought on by mass immigration, such as threats to national identity, culture, unity, and security. Part five comprises two papers that analyze the political and other obstacles that prevent changes to existing immigration policies in Canada and Britain.

Overview and international perspectives

James Bissett, the author of chapter 1, has been a Canadian ambassador and has much practical experience with immigration policy as a former executive director of Canada's Immigration Service. For readers in a hurry, his chapter provides a succinct summary of many of the issues discussed in more detail in the other papers of this volume.

Steven Camarota is the Director of Research at the influential Center for Immigration Research in Washington, DC. His careful analysis of conceptual issues surrounding all attempts to measure the fiscal impact of immigrants sets the stage for a review of the most important existing studies of these costs. The results of these studies leave little doubt that recent immigrants to the United States have imposed significant costs on taxpayers. They mirror the findings for Canada presented in the next part of the study.

Jean-Paul Gourévitch has written a number of books and reports on immigration issues facing France. The paper in this volume reveals that in France recent immigrants have problems in the labor market and suffer from low average incomes and high unemployment rates. There are high net financial costs for the government in dealing with the needs of immigrants. Social integration is inadequate and has led to civil unrest, with militant Muslims playing an important role. He documents that recent immigrants have relatively high crime rates but that they have also made significant contributions to French sports and society.

The French are more aware of these problems than are Canadians partly because some of them are more severe in France and partly because of the publicity and political upheaval that over recent years have accompanied incidents of civil unrest involving immigrants. Gourévitch's studies on immigration and his involvement with government agencies in France and international organizations around the world are well known and discussed widely in his country and Europe.

Economic issues

The second part of this volume contains papers by economists Vernon Briggs, Patrick Grady, and Herbert Grubel. They analyze the economic impact of mass immigration on labor markets, productivity, and the living standards of Canadians. All three economists stress the fact that this analysis needs to focus on per-capita incomes of people resident in the country when the immigrants arrive, which is in contrast to the measure of aggregate national income used widely by politicians and immigration advocates to justify mass immigration.

The most fundamental proposition advanced by all three authors (as well as by Camarota) is that the immigrants' contribution to the nation's output is equal to their pay, which they use to claim goods and services. This analysis is based on economists' widely accepted theory that wages equal the marginal product of workers, which leads to the important conclusion that immigrants do not raise the incomes of other Canadians, even though they increase aggregate national income.

However, this analysis and conclusion are based on a number of simplifying assumptions. The first of these is that immigrants do not give rise to economies of scale in the operation of public and private investments. These benefits occurred in the past when Canada's population was small and international trade was limited by high transportation costs and international protectionism. In recent times, however, Canada's large population caused the development of diseconomies of scale and increased the cost of output produced by public infrastructure investments. Low transportation costs and free trade have allowed private investment at optimum scale and least-cost output without having to rely on a large domestic market.

A second simplifying assumption is that government does not tax and provide public services. In fact, of course, Canada operates a welfare state characterized by progressive taxation of personal income and universal social programs, resulting in a substantial redistribution of income from the rich to the poor. Official statistics show that recent immigrants on average earn substantially lower incomes than Canadians, so that the system provides them with subsidies through taxes paid by high-income earners. Grubel estimated that immigrants who arrived in the 12 years before 2002, in that year imposed a fiscal burden of $18.5 billion on all Canadians.

These chapters also discuss the view that immigrants are needed to fill job vacancies that Canadians allegedly do not wish or are unable to accept and note that filling job vacancies through immigration serves the interest of employers but keeps the wages of Canadian workers competing with them lower than otherwise would be the case. These lower wages are inconsistent with Canadians' desire to have their government create a more equal distribution of income and reduce the level of poverty. It also has the important effect of reducing employers' incentives for the introduction and development of labor-saving capital, which raises productivity and wages and allows employers to pay higher wages without reductions in profits.

For these main reasons, the three authors conclude that job vacancies should not be filled by immigrants but by allowing wage increases for Canadians. The higher wages will cause the supply of labor to rise and the demand for labor to shrink until vacancies are eliminated. The process of adjustment to the higher wages induces employers to use more labor-saving capital and technology, so that in equilibrium wages equal productivity and there is no necessary increase in the cost of production undertaken by these workers.

Grubel also notes that, when monetary and fiscal policy are neutral and result in stable wages and prices, there tend to be no overall labor shortages. Changes in technology, demand by consumers and from abroad, and similar events can produce temporary shortages of labor and skills in some industries but they tend to be matched by surpluses in other industries. Internal migration removes these imbalances of the domestic labor market. Ironically, if overall excess demand for labor is met through immigration, because of the demand for goods, services, and infrastructure created by the immigrants, the shortages tend to persist or can even get worse. The elimination of such overall labor shortages requires the pursuit of appropriate monetary and fiscal policies.

The chapters in this section discuss other negative effects that mass immigration has on the living standards of Canadians, including increased pollution and crowding, higher real-estate prices, and longer commutes. They conclude that the effects of mass immigration on the average living standards of Canadians have been significantly negative and that present immigration policies should be changed correspondingly.

It should be noted that some of the economic problems associated with immigration from abroad also arise from the migration of Canadians from one province to another. However, because the average incomes of all Canadians are very similar, there is much less effect on the distribution of income in the receiving provinces than there is when migrants come from abroad.

The discussion of the effects of international migration in this study is justified by the fact that internal migration is guaranteed constitutionally and recipient provinces have to deal with the problems as best they can, while the number of foreign immigrants is determined by the federal government.

Demographic Issues

One argument in favor of immigration heard often in Canada is that it is needed to cover the unfunded liabilities of the country's social programs, especially pensions, welfare, and health care. The unfunded liabilities of these programs are very large because their financing was based on the pay-as-you-go model that envisaged a growing number of young people being taxed to pay for those no longer working. In fact, however, the number of young people has been growing much more slowly, and the number needing social benefits has been growing more rapidly, than had been expected when the financing of the social programs was planned.

The chapter by Marcel Mérette and that by Robin Banerjee and William Robson use sophisticated computer models to examine the feasibility of financing these unfunded liabilities through immigration. They used projections for Canadian fertility and life-expectancy rates produced by Statistics Canada to estimate the number of immigrants needed to keep the ratio of recipients of benefits to tax payers at the present level of 0.2, which implies that, on average, five taxpayers pay the benefits received by one recipient.

Both authors found that, to achieve this objective, the number of immigrants would have to rise so much above present levels that Canada's economy and society could not deal with them successfully. One estimate is that by the year 2050, Canada's population would have to be 165.4 million to meet this objective and that the intake of immigrants that year alone would be 7 million. The basic reasons for this outcome are that immigrants age at the same pace as everyone else and, like other Canadians, are eligible to receive social benefits in retirement.

The authors use their computer models to investigate the effects of some other immigration policies. One of these involves having only immigrants aged 20 come to Canada. They found that, even under this assumption, the number of immigrants required to deal with the financial problems of the social programs would be reduced only minimally.

The authors analyze how a gradual increase in the average age of retirement would solve the financial problems of the social programs without the large costs associated with their resolution through immigration.

Social issues

Stephen Gallagher and Salim Mansur are political scientists who in their chapters analyze the impact that mass immigration has had on a range of social conditions in Canada. Gallagher considers the implications of the fact that increasing numbers of recent immigrants have retained their loyalties and attachments to their native countries. Many of them have done so to the extent that they live in their native countries while they are citizens of Canada and enjoy all of the privileges that come with that status, including a Canadian passport and protection while abroad. The extent of this phenomenon became clear during the hostilities between

Israel and Hezbollah in 2006, when thousands of Canadian passport holders living in Lebanon demanded that the Canadian government evacuate them on the basis of their rights as Canadian citizens. Gallagher suggests that immigrants with Canadian passports living abroad have turned the country into a "global suburb," a home away from home, to which one returns when conditions abroad warrant.

He analyzes how Canada reached this condition, moving from a "nation of immigrants" to one in which multiculturalism is central to its national identity. He blames the policy of multiculturalism and the electoral system for these problems. The latter gives much influence to interest groups and prevents the creation of political parties in Canada seeking to place limits on immigration. Such parties in some European countries have played important roles in reshaping immigration policies.

One reason for this development is that Canada's tradition of tolerance, which is rooted in history and its experience with past immigration, fosters these problems by sanctioning under the protection of multiculturalism the refusal of some immigrants to assimilate or integrate.

Other reasons for expecting future troubles in Canada are that immigration levels bear no relationship to the demand of the domestic labor market so that immigration causes unemployment to rise cyclically above levels prevailing otherwise, potentially causing social tensions. At the same time, the promotion of preferential hiring and the failure to deter the entry or secure the removal of criminals and terrorists result in resentment and tensions between Canadians and groups of immigrants from other countries.

Salim Mansur's paper focuses on the way in which mass immigration and the policy of multiculturalism are undermining Canada's culture, national identity, and security. He paints with a broad brush, considering how liberalism has resulted in widespread self-loathing of Western societies, preparing the ground for the relative ascendency of different cultures and values with stronger beliefs in their own merits. This shift feeds on the declining fertility rates in the West combined with high fertility rates in Muslim countries.

He foresees the development of conflicts between Canadian society and values and those of large numbers of immigrants from different countries and cultures. The presence of Islamic extremists in Canada offers support for this expectation. The efforts by the citizens of Hérouxville to protect their culture are also indicative of a growing conflict and efforts to resist the undermining of Quebec and Canadian culture and tradition by the growing number of immigrants from very different cultural backgrounds.

Political issues

Gordon Gibson is the author of the first chapter in this section. He has been heavily involved in politics through much of his life, for a time serving as a member of the British Columbia legislature as head of one of the major political parties. He is also well known as a newspaper columnist and author of a study that led to the creation of a citizens' assembly to examine the merit of changing the existing electoral system in British Columbia.

His background has shaped the contents of his paper. He articulates well the idea that there exists a political market place in which politicians buy the votes of groups of immigrants in return for monetary and regulatory favors for them. He laments, much like several other authors in this volume, the way in which the operation of this political market place has in recent years prevented any changes in immigration policies that would have limited the ability of both political parties to benefit from the present system.

Gibson offers some suggestions on how this situation can be changed. One of them involves changes to the electoral system that would allow the entry into parliament of political parties whose platform is based on single issues. In some European countries that elect legislators based on the proportion of votes received by their parties, parties concerned about issues of immigration and integration have had a degree of electoral success, which eventually forced the broad-based parties to address the issues through open public debate and actual changes in policies.

A second way to change the present market for the votes of immigrants is to inform all voters of the detailed costs and benefits of immigration. This information can bring electoral success to a party that proposes reforms of immigration policies with surprising ease. This is so because immigrant groups tend to represent only a small percentage of voters, so that only a small percentage of the majority of voters who otherwise would not cast their ballot in favor of such reforms need to be persuaded to vote for desirable changes.

Sir Andrew Green was a British diplomat who served as ambassador to Syria and to Saudi Arabia. After his retirement in 2001, he founded Migrationwatch UK for the purpose of producing and distributing information about the economic, social and security effects of Britain's immigration policies. In his chapter, he describes the challenges and tactics used to make the work of his organization credible and public. Through his efforts, he has indeed succeeded in making it a source of information used by the media to discuss immigration issues and for politicians to use in their work.

However, the influence of this information on policies was relatively limited until fairly recently, when Britain received large numbers of immigrants from Eastern and Central Europe, which were added to earlier waves of immigrants from the former colonies, and have created problems with security, housing, the labor market and stress on the health-care system, traffic congestion, and so on. These problems have now become so important to the public that it has become receptive to the view that immigration is one of the main contributing factors. The Select Committee on Economic Affairs of the House of Lords took note of these public concerns and has issued a report that flatly condemns present immigration policies as inimical to the economic interests of the people of Britain on grounds that are discussed in the above section on the economic effects of mass immigration.

Both Gibson and Green expect the fight to change immigration policies to remain difficult and lengthy. The creation and communication of information about the effects of immigration on the well-being of the public is a necessary condition for bringing about such change. Not only must this information be readily available to the public but also they must appreciate its importance through personal experience if they are going to demand changes from the political system.

Possible policy changes

The basic conclusion of the papers in this volume is that recent mass immigration has affected the living standards of Canadians negatively and is challenging the country's existing national identity, culture, and social fabric. Added to this list of negative effects of immigration are the problems with internal and external security that were discussed at the 2007 conference on immigration organized by the Fraser Institute and summarized in the volume of papers from that conference titled "Immigration Policy and the Terrorist Threat in Canada and the United States." Given these findings, it is clear that it would be in the interest of Canadians to change the present immigration policies. There are broadly two ways to change the policies.

The first involves a better process of selecting immigrants since the costs and problems documented in the volume are the direct consequence of the present system used to select immigrants. Ideally, the new selection process would make the average incomes of immigrants and the distribution of incomes around the average equal to those of other Canadians. Under these conditions, the taxes paid by the immigrants with high incomes are sufficient to pay for the public benefits absorbed by those with lower incomes, just as is the case with other Canadians. The fiscal costs to other Canadians, which arise under the present system, would disappear.

One step in this direction towards the ideal is suggested by Bissett. It involves the elimination of the family class of immigrants, whose earnings and attachment to the labor force are low and who tend to be of an age where they absorb high levels of public services. Another method proposed by Grubel involves the placement of the responsibility for the selection of immigrants into the hands of private employers, taking it away from civil servants and the present points system. Under his proposal, immigrants and their immediate families would be admitted only if they have a work contract issued by a Canadian employer. To avoid employers issuing employment contracts to immigrants with low skills and wages, who would continue the fiscal burden, the government would have to set a minimum pay for the potential immigrants. Such a minimum might be the average wage paid to workers in the region where the employer operates.

The second class of changes to existing immigration policies involves reductions in the number of immigrants. Grady suggests that the present level of about 250 thousand be reduced to 100 thousand. Bissett's suggestion that the family class be eliminated also implies a lowering of the numbers. It is clear that any reduction in the number of immigrants would lower the economic costs and social problems that exist presently. However, these costs can be minimized or possibly eliminated only by setting immigration levels that match the rate of emigration, so that the international movement of people does not change the country's population level. This policy of zero net immigration is proposed by Green and Grubel. In the year 2007, it would have resulted in the immigration of 45,000 foreigners in contrast with the 250,000 that actually immigrated.

It is important to realize that under this proposal the important freedom of Canadians to migrate is preserved. At the same time, the country's population size is determined by the free decisions of Canadians, whose fertility may be presumed to be the outcome of deliberate considerations of what they consider to be the optimal number of children in the light of many personal, practical, ethical, moral, and religious considerations. Politicians have no right to interfere with the outcome of the fertility decisions made by their constituents.

It is not known what population growth would be under this policy. If it turns out to be zero or negative, it would result in economic and social problems that Canada has not faced in modern times and that raise fears in the minds of many about the ability of society to deal with them. These fears are misplaced. The problems would develop gradually and could be tackled through appropriate economic and social policies. We need only consider the experiences of Japan that has had a few years of near zero population growth and an aging population for many years. Resources have been reallocated successfully between industries that serve the needs of the elderly and of the young. This process has worked well and smoothly in Japan. The experience of some European countries with rapidly aging populations has been similarly positive.

Another important unknown associated with the adoption of a policy of zero net immigration is the influence it has on the fertility decisions of Canadians. Lower taxes, less pollution and crowding, and lower land prices could easily induce them to have larger families.

The adoption of the proposed move to balanced immigration will give rise to many issues involving the selection of immigrants and fairness in the transition from one policy regime to another. Thus, the government of Canada should honor the promises, implicit or explicit, made to recent immigrants that they can have their families join them. Canada should continue to meet its international and moral obligations to receive refugees, whose number should be counted as part of the number of immigrants admitted to maintain net zero immigration.

It remains to be seen whether the analysis of the effects of mass immigration in Canada found in this volume and the policy recommendations made will influence politicians' attitudes and actions. The paper by Gibson contains a note of pessimism on this issue, a sentiment shared by many who have studied immigration issues before and have seen their views ignored.

On the other hand, it is also difficult to predict circumstances like recessions, high unemployment rates, fiscal deficits, and protests by Canadians who wish to defend their culture, as did the people of Herouxville in Quebec. Such circumstances could lead to public demand for the discussion of the role played by immigration policies in the development of these problems. While everyone hopes that such calamities will not afflict Canada in the future, the facts and ideas found in this volume are good to have as a basis for possible rational public discussions, just in case the problems do develop.

Overview and international perspectives

Chapter 1

The current state of Canadian immigration policy

James Bissett

We are led to believe that Canada's immigration policy serves the national interest and is essential for economic growth, to fill our labor shortages, and to offset an aging and diminishing population. We are also told that most of our immigrants are selected because they possess the education, trades, skills, and training essential to meet our labor-force demands. These assertions need to be challenged because they do not bear up under examination. They have become myths, used by governments and pro-immigration advocates to justify unreasonably high immigration levels.

As will be documented below, there is a strong body of evidence indicating that immigration does not contribute significantly to the economy, is not essential to the labor force, and does not help with the problems stemming from an aging population. Less than 20% of the immigrants coming to Canada are selected because of their skills and training. Most of the immigrants admitted are sponsored by their relatives already in Canada, or enter as refugees, or for humanitarian reasons. These immigrants do not have to meet any economic selection criteria to be accepted. It should not be surprising, therefore, that immigrants arriving since the 1990s are not faring as well in their new country as did previous immigrants.

Canadians are conditioned to accept immigration as a natural phenomenon. It is part of our national heritage. The romantic idea that we are all descendents of immigrants remains strong and is embedded in our national consciousness. All of the political parties favor large scale immigration and insist that our economic growth depends on it. In this they are supported by much of the media and special-interest groups who repeat the arguments that Canada must rely on immigration if it wishes to prosper. Government policies advancing multiculturalism and diversity reinforce this view.

Until the mid-1980s, the immigration movement to Canada was regulated in accordance with economic conditions. When there was a buoyant economy and a strong demand for labor, the intake was increased; at times of economic down-turn and rising unemployment, the tap was turned off and immigration was reduced. This was the system that had governed the flow of immigrants since the end of the Second World War and it had served Canada and the immigrants well.

However, in 1985 the newly elected Progressive Conservative government of Prime Minister Brian Mulroney raised immigration levels despite evidence of an economic down-turn. This was the signal that the Conservative party was determined to win ethnic votes by supporting high immigration levels. In 1990, the then Minister, Barbara McDougal, convinced her cabinet colleagues to raise the levels to 250,000, by arguing that higher levels would help the party to establish stronger ties with ethnic communities. Later, the Minister said in an interview that a political party was not doing its job if it failed to reach out to ethnic groups (Windsor, 1990, October 24). There was political capital to be gained by high numbers whether they were needed or not.

This change in policy marked a significant turning point in the way the immigration program was to be managed in the years ahead. The numbers to be admitted were no longer to be governed primarily by economic factors. Immigration had become "politicized" and immigrants were to be seen by all political parties as potential voters. The two political parties that have subsequently shared power now compete with each other in raising the immigration levels and even the New Democratic Party advocates high levels. Numbers have become the primary consideration.

For the past 20 years or so, we have been accepting close to 1% of our population as immigrants each year. This is a very high number to absorb and on a per-capita basis is more than is accepted by any other immigrant-receiving country. The United States, for example, admits less than half the number of legal immigrants per capita that Canada does (Stoffman, 2002).

It is important to realize that the immigrants arriving in Canada are not distributed equally across a population base of 33 million people. They are for, the most part, settling in the three major urban centres of Toronto, Vancouver, and Montreal. These centers have a combined population base of approximately nine million people. As David Ley, a professor of geography at the University of British Columbia has pointed out, "[t]his is a huge country but immigration, especially visible minority immigration, is extraordinarily concentrated in just a few square miles" (Ley, 2006: A11).

The result is that these cities are experiencing serious infrastructure and environmental problems: traffic congestion, garbage disposal, rising crime, sky-rocketing welfare, education and health costs. Yet seldom are these problems attributed to, or associated with, the extremely high numbers of immigrants entering these cities every year. In his 2000 annual report, Gord Miller, Ontario's Environmental Commissioner, expressed concern about the Province's plan to accommodate an additional 4.4 to 6 million people in the next 25 years. He warned that any plan based on continuing population growth and consumption of resources is not sustainable (Miller, 2000). Unfortunately Mr. Miller's warning has not been taken seriously.

Another issue that is seldom discussed is that most of the newcomers are coming from Asian countries and consequently are transforming the demographic content of our major urban areas. The latest census figures show that 5 million or 16% of Canada's population is made up of visible minorities but that 60% of these live in the two metropolitan areas of Toronto and Vancouver (Ley, 2006). It seems likely that if immigration intake continues at the present level these two cities of Canada will over time become predominately Asian. Already Metro Toronto's foreign-born population has reached 46% and Metro Vancouver has 39.6% foreign born (Statistics Canada, Immigration and Citizenship, 2006). This may or may not be desirable but surely it is something that should be discussed openly and done so without accusations of racism. In other words, there are important implications involved when the traditional demographic and cultural nature of a city or country is subject to sudden change. If our immigration policy is designed to encourage more diversity and to promote multiculturalism, then we should be told that this is one of its objectives. What guarantee do we have that diversity in itself is a desirable objective? At what point does diversity mutate into a form of colonization?

These are issues that should be at the center of public-policy discussions about immigration, but they are not. Immigration policy is rarely debated in the Parliament of Canada, it has not yet been raised by any of the political parties—all of whom support high immigration levels—and the parties clearly do not want immigration policy to be debated. The House of Commons Standing Committee on Citizenship and Immigration focuses on operational issues but does not question the overall policy objectives or the high immigration levels.

The witnesses called before the Committee are usually those who have a vested, and often a monetary, interest in high levels of immigration. They are immigration lawyers or consultants, ethnic organizations, non- governmental organizations that receive government funding to help in the settlement of newcomers, other support groups, and immigration activists arguing for another amnesty or for open borders. Over time, these hard-core lobbyists have developed a symbiotic relationship with governments to the extent that they are no longer referred to as lobbyists but are looked upon, and dealt with, as "stakeholders."

Many of the reasons with which Canada justifies its high immigration intake are simply not valid and the economic and social costs are not open to discussion or debate. The policy is out of control and desperately in need of reform. We may not yet have reached the tipping point but, if we continue to sleepwalk into the twenty-first century and ignore this issue, we may find out too late that Canada has been unalterably changed without either the consent of its people or a full awareness on their part of what is happening.

A program out of control

A government that cannot control or regulate the numbers of immigrants permitted to enter its country has lost control of the program. Canada now finds itself in that position. The problem dates back to the passage of the 2001 *Immigration and Refugee Protection Act* (Bill C-11). The new

Act left out a key element of any immigration legislation—a mechanism for managing or limiting the numbers to be admitted annually.

In the past, the numbers admitted had been controlled by changing the selection criteria either by adjusting the numbers of points awarded to specific occupations or by raising or lowering the pass mark. Because economic conditions changed rapidly, it was necessary to be able to make adjustments quickly. Therefore, the necessary changes were normally achieved by amendments passed by Regulatory means rather than by changes to the Act, a much more cumbersome and time-consuming exercise. The 2001 Act contained a provision that stated that, if any applicant met the selection criteria and other requirements of the Act, a visa "shall" be issued (Bill C-11, cl.11(1)). This was the core of the problem. That section of the Act overlooked the reality that there will always be many more thousands of people able to meet the selection criteria and who want to come to Canada than can either be processed or satisfactorily absorbed by the economy. Within months of the passing of the Bill, a backlog began to grow.

One year after the new Act was enacted, the Liberal government realized the problem and tried to correct it by introducing retroactively a more stringent passing mark for those in the backlog who had already been accepted. This attempt was struck down by the courts and the backlog has continued to expand since then. In June 2008, the backlog had reached the 950,000 mark and the Department estimated it would reach 1.5 million by 2012. In addition, the backlog at the Refugee Board had reached 62,000 and was expected to be 84,000 within two years. Most of these refugee claimants will eventually end up as landed immigrants in Canada.

To these extraordinary numbers must be added another 100,000 to 150,000 temporary workers who will in all probability, based on past experience, remain in Canada. Recent changes in immigration rules now permit certain categories of temporary workers to apply for permanent residence from within the country. Moreover, it has become extremely difficult to remove people from Canada without a prolonged and expensive investigation and litigation process.

Nevertheless, in the face of such extraordinarily high numbers, the Government was forced to act and did so in February 2008, by incorporating amendments to the immigration Act in Bill C-50, the *Budget*

Implementation Act. These amendments were designed to restore to the government the power to decide the numbers and the categories of immigrants to be admitted annually. The amendments, it should be noted, did not apply to the backlog and all those currently waiting in it are guaranteed eventual entry.

The opposition parties in Parliament, immigration lawyers, and other "stake holders," assailed this attempt to regain control of the immigration program. The government was accused of having a hidden agenda and of giving the Minister of Citizenship and Immigration too much power to pick and choose the types of immigrants to be selected. In any event, the Bill passed into law on June 9, 2008, with most of the Liberal members absenting themselves from the vote.

It remains to be seen if these new measures will enable the government to regain control of immigration. The numbers in the backlogs and the intention of the Minister to admit between 240,000 to 265,000 new immigrants in 2009 present an almost impossible challenge. Whatever course the government might take, it is difficult not to conclude that the current immigration system is out of control. In the face of what appears to be a serious global recession, immigration reform is badly needed. This will not be easy to do since our political leaders do not seem to be impressed by the facts of immigration. They seem interested only in numbers.

Does immigration help the economy and the labor force, or reduce the problems stemming from an aging population?

The short answer to each of these questions is "No." Curiously, about the only people who *do not* believe that immigration benefits the economy and the labor force and reduces problems stemming from an aging population are those whose business it is to research and study these questions. It is the economists, the demographers, the statisticians, and the academics who find the answers.

Most economists consider the question of whether immigration helps the Canadian economy is essentially settled. That is to say, they do not believe immigration contributes significantly to our economic prosperity or our per-capita income. Studies done in Canada looking at the economic costs and benefits of immigration reach the common conclusions that there is little gain to the economy from immigration and that costs appear to outweigh any benefits.

One of the first extensive studies of this question was the 1985 report by the Macdonald Royal Commission on *The Economic Union and Development Prospects for Canada.* This report concluded that immigration did not contribute to economic growth but in fact caused a decline in per-capita income and real wages of Canadians (Macdonald, 1985). In December 1989, the Department of Health and Welfare published the results of a comprehensive three-year demographic study entitled *Charting Canada's Future: A Report of the Demographic Review* (Demographic Review Secretariat, 1989). This study also concluded there was no economic argument for increased population growth and stressed that immigration was not an answer to the aging of the population. Later in 1991, two studies by the now defunct Economic Council of Canada, *New Faces in the Crowd* (Economic Council, 1991) and *Economic and Social Impacts of Immigration,* arrived at similar conclusions (Swan, Auer, et al., 1991).

Professor Alan Green of Queen's University, in a paper entitled *What Is the Role of Immigration in Canada's Future* (2003), suggested that although immigration had been useful to Canada in the past, the economic argument for it had "largely disappeared. The current political posture of using immigrants to solve economic problems is no longer valid" 2003: 42). Frank Denton, of McMaster University, and his colleagues, Byron Spencer and Christine Feaver, have produced a long list of studies of aging and the labor force showing that immigration cannot significantly affect the aging of our population.

A more recent study by Professor Herbert Grubel of Simon Fraser University entitled *The Fiscal Burden of Recent Canadian Immigrants* has shown that in the year 2002 alone, the costs in services and benefits received by the 2.5 million immigrants who arrived between 1990 and 2002 exceeded the taxes they paid by $18.3 billion. As he points out in his study, $18.3 billion represents more than the federal government spent on health care and twice what it spent on defence in the fiscal year 2000/2001 (Grubel, 2008). That amount is also approximately what Canada has spent so far on the Afghanistan campaign. Typically, Professor Grubel's study received little media coverage and elicited no comment by government spokespeople.

In January 2007, Statistics Canada released a report entitled *Chronic Low Income and Low Income Dynamics among Recent Immigrants* (Picot, Hou, and Coulombe, 2007). This study revealed that, despite the emphasis placed on the educational qualifications of the "skilled worker" category of immigrants, their earnings in relation to native Canadians were significantly lower and continue to deteriorate. In other words, the hard evidence shows that the immigrants selected for their value to the labor force are not performing nearly as well as in previous years. In this context, it is useful to remember that approximately 80% of our immigrants are not in the "skilled worker" category but enter, or are allowed to stay, for humanitarian reasons or because they have been granted refugee status. They do not have to possess education, skills, or work experience.

The studies referred to above raise serious questions about the economic value of our current immigration policy. Similar studies done outside Canada also have concluded that immigration does not help the economy, nor does it result in any appreciable increase in the per-capita income of the receiving country. In the United States, George Borjas of Harvard University, perhaps the world's most renowned immigration economist and an immigrant himself, has demonstrated in numerous studies that it is wrong to say that immigration benefits the economy. He argues that any net gain is so small as to be insignificant.

Borjas points out that, while some large companies might earn more profit because of the added supply of labor, this is offset by the losses suffered by native workers whose wages are reduced by immigration. In his book, *Heaven's Door,* he recommends the annual immigration flow into the United States be cut in half because the levels are not helping economic growth (Borjas, 1999).

In Britain, a report by the House of Lords in April 2008, warned that the Government's plan to admit 190,000 immigrants per year would achieve little benefit but would seriously affect the availability of housing and have an adverse impact on public services. The report added that record numbers of immigrants entering Britain were bringing no economic benefits to the country. The report sharply criticized the Government for using "irrelevant and misleading statistics" to justify the high immigration levels of the past decade. It concluded there was no economic benefit from the present high levels of immigration and that immigrants were not needed to fill labor shortages or help fund the state pension fund for retiring Britons (Winnet, 2008, April 2).

Unfortunately, it is highly unlikely that many of our political representatives have read any of the economic studies listed above or, if they have, they are not paying attention to them. The 2007 *Annual Report to Parliament on Immigration* (Citizenship and Immigration Canada, 2007) bewailed the fact that, unlike the situation in the past, Canada is seeing more and more competitors for immigrants entering the field and observed that China and India are beginning to offer opportunities for their own skilled workers. Section one of the *Report*, bearing the impressive but misleading title of Making Immigration Work for Canada, went on to say that "[i]mmigration will play an increasingly important role in supporting Canada's economic prosperity and competitiveness. In a few short years, given our aging population, Canadians who leave school for the workplace will only offset the number of retirements. Immigration will be a key source of labor force growth in the future" (Citizenship and Immigration Canada, 2007: 1).

Here we have the same old myths being advanced to support higher immigration levels: that we need it for the economy, the labor force, and to replace our aging population. There is no acknowledgement that only 17% of the principal applicants in the selected worker category are chosen for their potential to enter the labor force. There is no mention that despite years of high immigration levels the incomes of Canadian workers with more than a university undergraduate degree declined by 7% between 1980 and 2000 (Statistics Canada, Family and Labour Studies Division, 2007). Statistic Canada's study concluded that immigration played a role in this drop in wages and pointed out that if labor supply increases by 10% then wages decline by 3% or 4%. The hardest hit are the young native-born males and immigrants.

In an article in the *Globe and Mail* about the 2006 census results, Michael Valpy points out that wages being paid to well-educated workers are in decline, "largely because there are so many of them—bad news for both the highly educated immigrants Canada vacuums up from the developing world and its own well educated native-born." He goes on to question the morality of admitting more than 200,000 immigrants, "who are struggling—with declining success—to find jobs commensurate with their knowledge and experience, good incomes and decent, affordable housing" (Valpy, 2008, April 26: 11).

Daniel Stoffman in his excellent book, *Who Gets In* (2000), warned that there seemed little justification for raising immigration levels at a time when a large group of younger Canadians were just beginning to enter the labor force. These he described as the "echo generation," the children of the "baby boomers" born between 1980 and 1995. They are the second-largest population cohort in Canada after that of their parents and they number 6.5 million potential workers. As the author rightly asks: "Why make their entry into the labor force more difficult by bringing in armies of competing workers from abroad" (Stoffman, 2002: 102).

Concern is frequently expressed that as our birth rate declines our labor force will inevitably shrink and therefore it is only through immigration that Canada will be able to see an expansion of its labor force. The assumption here is that we need a larger labor force to guarantee economic viability. Yet the size of the labor force is not a guarantee of economic success. Many countries with small labor forces have vibrant and strong economies. The Netherlands, Switzerland, Finland are three examples and there are many more.

Canada has historically relied on immigration to bolster its labor force and will continue to do so but there is a downside to relying on foreign workers unless they are carefully selected and possess the skills that cannot be filled by domestic supply. Reliance on foreign workers can inhibit innovation and the development of labor-saving technology. Japan's answer to its shrinking labor force has not been to rely on the immigration of foreign workers but to encourage technological adaptation and innovative labor-saving devices.

Leon Bouvier in his book, *Peaceful Invasions,* calls for a reduction in the levels of immigration to the United States and points out that "unskilled immigrants can lower wages and increase profits but if workers are readily available firms are discouraged from buying machinery that can raise productivity" (Bouvier, 1992: 94). He states that it was "[t]he availability of immigrant workers that helps explain why parts of the American economy remained labor-intensive in the 1980s despite calls for business to raise labor productivity to compete successfully in the global economy" (Bouvier, 1992: 94).

Undue reliance on foreign workers may also delay and discourage other methods of resolving skill shortages such as training domestic workers or raising the age of retirement. James Knight, president of the Association of Community Colleges, told a House of Commons Industry Committee that thousands of students who, with adequate training, would be employed immediately cannot get the training needed because of a serious lack of training capacity. He quoted a study that showed that 42% of the skill shortages are in occupations that normally demand college or apprenticeship training compared to about 7% that require university education (Knight, 2008). Although there is no evidence that high immigration levels have inhibited investment in community and technical college infrastructure, it is reasonable to assume there is a relationship between the two. Why spend money on training native workers when trained workers can be supplied through immigration?

Interestingly enough, there is some question of whether Canada does in fact have a serious skill shortage. A study by the Canadian Policy Research Networks challenged the pessimistic predictions of large-scale skill shortages as unfounded and exaggerated. The study, entitled *Labour Force Ageing and Skill Shortages in Canada and Ontario,* pointed out that it is difficult to measure skill shortages and there is disagreement about the impact skill shortages are having on the Canadian labor market (McMullin and Cooke, 2004]. The study suggests Canada could help meet its labor-force demands by raising the age of retirement. Research has shown that workers between 50 and 60 years old are the most productive and the study estimated that, by raising the retirement age by one year, Canada could boost its GDP per capita by 3.5% by 2050.

The study also suggested there were a number of strategies that could be followed to meet labor demand: immigration that targets skills in demand; encouraging more aboriginals and single mothers into the work force; promoting life-long learning and training; and recruiting an "age balanced work force" for companies. The study concluded by arguing that aging is not the only significant determinant of skill shortages. It stressed that labor-market policies need to look beyond the fact of an aging work force and consider industry and occupational specific issues and the whole complex of factors involved.

The aging of our labor force is used as one of the major arguments justifying high immigration levels and the importation of temporary foreign workers from abroad. Like many of the other standard arguments used as the basis of our current policy, the aging issue does not stand up to the facts.

The refugee policy disaster

It appears clearly evident that the state of our current immigration policy is in disarray. But our asylum policy is in even worse shape. It is a cynical and costly policy, out of step with other asylum countries and working against the interests of the world's refugees. It is a policy designed to satisfy the special interests of immigration lawyers and other organizations—the "stakeholders"—whose existence depends on delivering services—paid for by the taxpayers—to the thousands of people entering Canada every year claiming to be persecuted in their own country.

Canada is the only country in the world that permits almost everyone who arrives at our borders claiming persecution to enter and to be granted a full quasi-judicial hearing to determine if the individual is a genuine refugee. In 2004, for example, citizens of 152 countries submitted refugee claims in Canada (Immigration and Refugee Board, 2004). This wide-open invitation is fully exploited by thousands of people desiring to avoid the normal immigration procedures. Our asylum system has made a mockery of the United Nations Refugee Convention and has degenerated into a "self-select" immigration flow.

The numbers are high. In the past 25 years, over 700,000 asylum seekers have entered Canada and the flow continues at about 2,000 each month (UNHCR, 2007). There is a serious backlog of 62,000 cases before the Immigration Refugee Board (IRB) so that it takes up to two years or more before a decision can be made. The costs are also high but difficult to measure because they cover a multitude of services and are diffused through different levels of government. So far there has not seemed to be any interest on the part of the immigration department to calculate or even to estimate the costs to the taxpayer of our asylum policy.

It is possible, however, by looking at the costs sustained by the British Government—the Home Office does keep track of costs—to get a fair idea of what the Canadian system is costing for services provided since they are similar in both countries. In 2001, the British spent £1,052 million for services to asylum seekers (Helper, 2002). That year Britain received 70,135 asylum claims; in the same year, Canada received 44,000 claims, a little more than half that of the British. At the 2001 rate of exchange and cutting the British figure by half, we can estimate Canada's costs at close to or more than a billion dollars annually.

It can be assumed that whatever the actual figures might be, they are high. These costs may help explain why our annual contribution to the United Nations High Commissioner for Refugees [UNHCR] of between $20 to $25 million is so woefully inadequate. After all, government budgets have limited funds to spend on asylum seekers and refugees. Canada ranks tenth out of the top ten donor countries, below such countries as Denmark, Norway, the Netherlands, and Sweden (UNHCR, 2007). The United States is the largest donor and also receives the largest number of asylum seekers of any industrial country. Despite this record, a judge of the Canadian Federal Court recently declared the United States to be "unsafe" for refugees. Happily his judgment was overruled by a superior court.

The UNHCR is responsible for looking after approximately 25 million real refugees, living in deplorable conditions in camps around the world. They are poorly housed and inadequately fed. The majority are women, children, the elderly, and the sick. They do not have the means to pay smugglers to get them aboard an aircraft destined to Canada. It would seem that, if Canada really wished to help resolve the global refugee problem, it would provide more funding to the UNHCR so that the real refugees in the camps received better care and protection and spend less on the thousands of people who arrive here only claiming to be persecuted in their own countries.

Before Canada became a major asylum country, our refugee policy was to take from camps around the world refugees whom we believed able to become established in Canada within a year and resettling them here. Our record in this humanitarian effort since the end of the Second World War was recognized in 1986 when the UNHCR awarded Canada the Nansen prize. We now only select between 5,000 to 7,000 refugees from abroad. The numbers have diminished because settling refugees or asylum seekers involve high costs and we cannot afford to do both. The refugee lobby has made it clear the preference should go to asylum seekers and the government seems to agree.

The current asylum system also plays into the hands of human smugglers who can guarantee individuals being trafficked into the country a stay of at least two or three years even if the decision on refugee status is denied. Should the decision be negative, it is unlikely the person concerned will be removed since, after two or more years in Canada, it would be considered inhumane to send the person home.

The Department conducts a humanitarian review of all those who have been found by the IRB not to be genuine refugees and also carries out a check to ensure there would not be any risk if the person were removed from Canada. Because of the findings of these reviews, many of the failed refugee claimants are permitted to remain on humanitarian grounds. The Immigration annual report of 2007 indicates that over 6,000 of these people were allowed to stay as permanent residents in 2006.

Many thousands of failed refugees who are asked to leave Canada are unaccounted for. Auditor General Sheila Fraser's latest report in May 2008 indicated there were 41,000 illegal immigrants missing whose whereabouts were unknown; most of these were assumed to be failed refugee claimants (Auditor General, 2008).

The asylum fiasco has existed since the mid-1980s when Canada began to receive more and more people arriving at our ports of entry claiming to be persecuted in their own country. Almost all of these claimants were coming from western European countries or from the United States or they were coming direct from countries that did not have a record of persecution such as Portugal, Trinidad and Tobago, Brazil, and India.

The first step in trying to stop this movement was to require a visitor visa from the citizens of the above countries and, since the 1980s, whenever Canada has received large numbers of asylum seekers from a particular country we have used the visitor visa as a means of stopping the flow. In the late 1990s, an influx of Romanians from Hungary and the Czech Republic was halted by the imposition of visas on the nationals of these two countries. Anyone suspected of being an asylum seeker is not issued a visa and without a visa legal travel to Canada is not possible.

Unfortunately, the introduction of visitor visas adversely affects our bilateral relations with the countries concerned, some of whom retaliate by imposing visa requirements on Canadians. Although the imposition of visas does help stop or slow down the flow of asylum seekers, it also inhibits tourism and may, as well, adversely impact our commercial relations with the countries concerned. Despite these negative consequences, there has been little effort to reform the system.

Accompanying the increase in the volume of asylum seekers (from 7,000 claims in 1984 to 44,000 in 2001) was a concurrent expansion in the size and influence of the "refugee" lobby. Lawyers, consultants, church groups, non-governmental organizations, and politicians rallied to the side of the "refugees." The multimillion dollar "refugee industry" was born. Any and every attempt to curtail the flow of asylum seekers, whether coming from refugee producing countries or not, produced fierce and highly organized opposition. It still does.

The problem was compounded when the Supreme Court ruled in 1985 that, to conform with the new Canadian Charter of Rights and Freedoms, asylum seekers were entitled to an oral hearing before the refugee board. Experience quickly showed that under a quasijudicial process that allowed universal access to the system, the number of asylum seekers entitled to hearings reached unsustainable levels. New legislation, therefore, was passed in 1989 containing a provision enabling the Cabinet to declare a country "safe" for refugees. The concept was not new and is in force now in the countries of the European Community. A country is considered "safe" if it is democratic, follows the rule of law, and is a signatory to the UN Refugee Convention, which obliges signatory countries to protect refugees and not to return them to a country of persecution. Under the proposed legislation, anyone coming to Canada from a "safe" country would have been denied the right to make an asylum claim and would have been removed from Canada.

The purpose of the new legislation was to restrict access to the asylum process. The integrity of the Bill depended upon the ability to ensure that only those claimants who had a credible claim for protection would have their application heard by the Refugee Board. Since most of the people claiming persecution were coming from "safe" countries, it was assumed that Canada would receive few asylum seekers eligible to submit a claim. Thus, by restricting access it was possible to construct a refugee determination process that would not be overwhelmed by frivolous claims but one that could be exceptionally fair and generous with those whose claims were credible—and this was done.

Every advantage was to be afforded the claimant. The process was to be "non-adversarial," meaning that cross examination of the asylum claimant was not permitted. In other words, the story told by the claimant was assumed to be true. A further concession was that both members of the Refugee Board had to agree on a refusal. If only one Board member believed the person was a genuine refugee that was enough to secure a positive decision. IRB members were not required to give written reasons if they accepted a claim but reasons for refusing an applicant had to be in writing. In addition, any refusal by the Refugee Board could be appealed with leave to the Federal Court.

It appeared that Canada was on the road to resolving its asylum problem. However, this was not to be. On the eve of enacting the new legislation, which was to come into effect on January 1, 1989, the Minister of Immigration issued a press release announcing that the Bill would come into effect but without enacting the "safe" country provisions. At the last minute, the legislation was emasculated. The lobbying by the "stakeholders" who had stridently opposed the Bill had prevailed. The legislation without the provision to restrict access was doomed to failure and the numbers of asylum seekers since the Bill was passed speak for themselves.

Twelve years later, when the Liberal Government passed the Immigration and Refugee Protection Act in 2001—two months after the 9/11 terrorist attack—the new legislation, astonishingly, made it even easier for asylum seekers to claim refugee status and more difficult to remove failed claimants. The definition of refugee was expanded beyond that of the UN Convention to include anyone who claimed to be persecuted and additional levels of appeal and review were introduced.

This failure to express the most elementary concern about allowing thousands of people into the country, none of whom had been medically examined or checked for criminality or security, has been the primary reason why the United States has "militarized" the border between our two countries. American authorities are very much aware that a number of identified terrorists in Canada entered as asylum seekers. The most notorious of them was the "millennium bomber," Ahmed Resam, the Algerian al-Qaeda operative who attempted to blow up the Los Angeles airport on the eve of the millennium.

There is no redeeming merit in our current asylum policy. It serves as a symbol of the willingness of successive governments to placate the selfish demands of special-interest groups at the expense of the Canadian people. The policy should have been reformed long ago. Instead, for almost 20 years and at a cost of billions of dollars, this charade of pretending to be managing a humanitarian program has been defended and indeed promoted by both Liberal and Conservative governments.

The dysfunctional Immigration Refugee Board (IRB) has been used as a pork barrel to appoint members who in many cases have not been qualified to determine who is or who is not a refugee. A special report to the Liberal Government in 1997 entitled, *Not Just Numbers,* recommended scrapping the IRB and replacing it by a Protection Agency staffed by a cadre of professional career officers to decide asylum claims both at home and abroad (Trempe, Davis, and Kunin, 1997). This sensible report, which was replete with sound recommendations, was shelved by a government clearly not interested in a change of policy. So far, there can be no doubt our politicians have placed the interests of the refugee lobbyists ahead of the public interest and the public purse.

Some concluding thoughts

Canada's immigration and refugee policies are deeply flawed and are leading the nation down a perilous road. When a policy is fundamentally flawed, it is difficult if not impossible to fix it through adjustments of the program or by operational directives. When the real objectives are to keep the numbers high without regard to economic conditions or the successful settlement or integration of the immigrants themselves, the prospects for reform are bleak. Nevertheless, pending a thoroughgoing review, there are some priority issues that should be addressed as quickly as possible by any government truly concerned with the interests of the nation rather than the "stakeholders."

Select highly skilled workers

The current selection criteria for skilled workers is not obtaining the type of workers needed by the labor force. The selection grid places too much emphasis on education and experience—46 out of 100 points—without taking into account differences in educational standards or the fact that Canadian employers as a rule do not credit foreign experience. As a result, many workers with high educational achievement in their own country and years of experience in their occupations easily meet the criteria but cannot qualify for jobs in Canada. On the other hand, many highly skilled tradesmen with low educational achievement cannot meet the requirements. Either fewer points should be allotted to education and experience or a system of educational equivalencies and assessment of foreign experience should be provided to the selection officers

Select workers for occupations in high demand

The selection criteria should contain points for occupations that are in high demand as was done in the original point system. This critical selection factor was dropped because it was found that occupational demand changed frequently and often immigrants selected for their particular occupation after they arrived, did not work in that occupation. The department should devise an improved and more up-to-date method of ascertaining the occupations that are needed by our labor force and adjust the points allotted accordingly. Possession of an occupation that is in demand is one of the key factors helping immigrants to become established in Canada. There needs to be a process to get these workers into Canada quickly while their occupations are still needed.

Interview applicants in the skilled-worker category before they are accepted

All immigrants in the skilled-worker category should be interviewed by a Canadian visa officer before being accepted. In recent years, because of pressure of numbers, the vast majority of immigrants are not seen or interviewed by a visa officer but receive their visas after a paper review only. This is not satisfactory: it is only through a personal interview that a proper assessment of an applicant can be made. The visa officers should also have the power to refuse or accept an applicant if, after a personal interview, it is apparent the points obtained in the selection grid do not adequately reflect the chances of successful settlement. This power can be carefully monitored and controlled to ensure there is not discrimination involved in the officer's decision. It would be difficult to find a business enterprise anywhere that would hire a worker without a personal interview.

Provide counseling for immigrants

Before being overwhelmed by numbers, visa officers took the time to counsel prospective immigrants, tell them about Canada, suggest the most appropriate destination for them to settle in, and provided valuable and practical advice to ease the first months after arrival. Written material was also provided and at times films about Canada were shown at group counseling sessions. Counseling was an important feature of the visa officer's job and it demonstrated that immigrants were important enough to be given personal attention before their departure and were not regarded by their new country as mere numbers. Counseling should be reintroduced in the selection procedure for the selected worker class if not for all immigrants.

Put more emphasis on ability to speak English or French

More emphasis on language ability is necessary and the criteria should reflect this requirement. The 2007 *Annual Report to Parliament on Immigration* (Citizenship and Immigration Canada, 2007) disclosed that in 2006 83,298 immigrants who arrived in Canada did not speak either English or French. The ability to speak English or French is an essential qualification for successful establishment in Canada. It should be allocated more points in the selection grid and there should be language testing for selected workers. In the case of professional immigrants, fluency in one of the official languages should be mandatory.

Control the numbers admitted each year

It is essential there be a mechanism for controlling the numbers of immigrants admitted each year. In the past, this was done by either adjusting the pass mark or by refusing any applicant whose occupation was not in demand. This is the only means of ensuring that backlogs in the skilled-worker category do not build up. With the passage of Bill C-50, the government now has regained this power to manage the numbers admitted annually. It remains to be seen how this mechanism will be incorporated in the selection system.

Restrict family class

The family class as defined in the current Immigration Act is too broad. The inclusion of parents and grandparents of any age generates the phenomenon called "chain immigration," whereby young parents sponsored by one of their children in Canada enter the country accompanied by others of their children. These latter siblings in turn later are able to sponsor their spouses or fiancé[e]s. The family class constitutes a growing portion of the immigration flow and adds to the cost of health and social services. The *Annual Report to Parliament on Immigration, 2007* (CIC, 2007) shows there were 20,006 parents and grandparents admitted in 2006. The definition of family class and the obligations of sponsors is a complex and controversial issue that needs careful review, but the existing definition means that the numbers admitted under the family class will eventually squeeze out the economic portion of the immigration program.

Do not issue visas to professional immigrants until they have met Canadian standards

Many professional immigrants who arrive in Canada find they are unable to practice their profession because they do not meet the professional licensing requirements. All professional immigrants are warned prior to their departure that they will not be able to follow their profession until they meet the necessary Canadian requirements. Many find they are unable to do so and this can create resentment and disaffection. The fact is that Canadian standards in medicine, engineering, architecture, and other professions are among the highest in the world and are difficult to meet. Canada should follow the Australian practice of not issuing visas to any professional immigrants until they have first satisfied all of the requirements.

Monitor admission of foreign temporary workers closely

The *Annual Report to Parliament on Immigration, 2007* (CIC, 2007) tells us that 112,658 foreign temporary workers were brought into Canada in 2006 and that this figure represents a 13% increase over the 99,141 admitted in 2005. These workers are allegedly permitted entry to address labor-market shortages but many of them are unskilled workers employed in low-paying jobs. Their long-term prospects of successful establishment are dim. This is an area that requires careful review and monitoring. Are the shortages primarily because the employers are not willing to pay wages that might attract Canadian workers? Is this a program designed to ensure a plentiful supply of cheap labor? These are questions that need to be asked. There are warning signs: the *Ottawa Citizen* on July 11, 2008 reported that Alberta had launched a $1.4 million pilot project to help the 23,000 foreign temporary workers there settle in the province (*Ottawa Citizen*, 2008, July 11). If they are there on a temporary basis, why do they need financial support to become settled? Germany and other European countries admitted thousands of so-called temporary guest workers in the 1970s only to find out too late that the workers did not go home. These temporary workers eventually formed a permanent and costly under-class in the countries concerned. Canada is in danger of making the same mistake.

Require government to publish the costs of immigration each year

It is difficult for the average Canadian to get an accurate idea about immigration policy. The annual reports and statistics are not helpful and are designed to present immigration in a positive light. There is never any mention of costs or of studies questioning the value of immigration. The millions of dollars spent in donations and grants to "stakeholder" groups are hidden or not revealed in public reports. The number of immigrants receiving welfare is not available or perhaps not even recorded by provincial governments. In 2006, Denmark was forced to adopt a new policy on immigration when it was revealed by their Minister for Employment that immigrants were using the welfare system so heavily that the government was in danger of becoming bankrupt (MacAllen, 2007). Our government should be required to make public each year the costs of immigration; these should include the costs of social welfare, language training, processing and settlement, and free legal services.

Track entry, residence, and exit of visitors and temporary residents

Canada is one of the easiest countries to enter and, yet, we do not have a system for recording entry or any tracking process to know where visitors or other temporary residents are residing. Furthermore, we have no exit control, so there is no way of knowing if people entering for a temporary period have left or not. We do not normally detain people who arrive with forged papers or without documents. In other words, we are operating as if these issues were not a matter of national security or a matter of common sense. Our border-control officers are more concerned about whether returning Canadians are bringing in extra tobacco or alcohol than if foreign visitors are entering illegally. At some of our ports of entry, there is no separate inspection line for non-Canadians. The examination priority is on the violation of customs and excise rules and not on the entry of illegal immigrants. This must change if Canada is to be taken seriously by our allies in combating the activities of international criminals and terrorists. A priority for the effective management of any immigration program is to keep track of the whereabouts of high-risk temporary entrants and to know whether they have left the country before their legal status has expired.

Canada has a problem with its immigration and refugee policy. The problem becomes even more serious when government camouflages its real motives by carefully designed public relations activities to convince the people that there is a desperate need for massive immigration flows. By refusing to debate policy issues in the public forum, and counting on full support from opposition parties, the "stakeholders," and the media while doing so, it affords little opportunity for sensible and informed discussion. Attempts to discuss this issue are often dismissed as the narrow opinions of those who hold to outdated and racist views. Yet immigration is changing Canada and responsible citizens have the right to challenge whether the abnormally high levels are needed.

Now is an opportune time to call for an intermission to slow down the number of new immigrants admitted each year and to reassess our immigration policy. The reality that almost one million immigrants are already at the gate and have the legal right to enter should call for a temporary moratorium on new immigrants until the backlog has been eliminated.

During this period of economic slow down, the only new immigrants to be admitted should be those who have proven skills that are critical to our economy and the spouses and minor children of Canadian citizens and legal residents. During this period, the people in the backlog would be able to enter and join their relatives or take up new jobs but it would also provide an opportunity for the thousands of recent immigrants to settle in and become integrated into Canadian society. It would be a "time-out," and a chance for a serious and non-partisan review of our policy to determine what we expect immigration to do for Canada and what benefits we expect to derive from immigration.

A review of this kind, aimed at immigration and refugee reform and a return to the days when immigration was seen as an instrument of national policy to enhance our labor force and improve our economic productivity, is long overdue but urgently needed. The real challenge will be to carry forward some of the reforms that are needed. Immigration has become such a political tool in the hands of our political parties that it has been impossible to generate any objective discussion about the subject. It is an important area of public policy and it needs attention.

References

Auditor General (2008). *Report of the Office of the Auditor General of Canada*, May 2008. Chapter 7, Detention and Removal of Individuals, Canadian Border Service Agency.

Bill C-11, *An Act Respecting Immigration to Canada and the Granting of Refugee Protection, etc.*, 1st Sess., 37th Parl., 2001, cl. 11(1). Short title: *Immigration and Refugee Protection Act.*

Bill C-50, *An Act to Implement Certain Provisions of the Budget Tabled in Parliament on February 26, 2008 and to Enact Provisions to Preserve the Fiscal Plan Set Out in That Budget*, 2nd Sess., 39th Parl., 2008. Short title: *Budget Implementation Act 2008*.

Borjas, George (1999) *Heavens Gate—Immigration Policy and the American Economy.* Princeton University Press.

Bouvier, Leon F. (1992). *Peaceful Invasions—Immigration and Changing America.* University Press of America.

Citizenship and Immigration Canada [CIC] (2007). *Annual Report to Parliament on Immigration, 2007.* Cat. No. Ci1-2007. <http://www.cic.gc.ca/english/resources/publications/annual-report2007/index.asp>

Demographic Review Secretariat (1989). *Charting Canada's Future: A Report of the Demographic Review.* Health and Welfare Canada.

Denton, Frank, Christine H. Feaver, and Byron Spencer (1997). *Immigration, Labour Force and the Age Structure of the Population.* McMaster University.

Economic Council of Canada (1991). *New Faces in the Crowd: Economic and Social Impacts of Immigration.* Study No. 22-171. Economic Council of Canada.

Green, Allan (2003). *What Is the Role of Immigration in Canada's Future?* John Deutsch Institute for the Study of Economic policy, McGill-Queens University Press.

Grubel, Herbert (2008). The Fiscal Burden of Recent Canadian Immigration. Paper presented at conference, Canadian Immigration Policy: Reassessing the Economic, Demographic and Social Impact on Canada, Montreal (June 4–5, 2008).

Helper, Roger (2002, July 1). Britain's Asylum System in Crisis. *Rutland Times* [England]. (Mr. Helper is the MP for East Midlands).

Immigration and Refugee Board [IRB] (2004). Immigration and Refugee Board's internal monthly statistics for 2004, in possession of the author.

Knight, James (2008, April 22). Shortage of Skilled Workers Remains a Problem: Study. *Ottawa Citizen*: F4.

Ley, David (2008, April 3). Integration a Challenge Professor Says. *National Post*: A7.

Macdonald, Donald S. (1985). The Report of the Royal Commission on the Economic Union and the Development Prospects for Canada. "The Macdonald Report."

MacAllen, Susan (2007). Salute the Danish Flag!—It's a Symbol of Western Freedom. <http://www.fsmarchives.org/article.php?id=1172085>.

McMullin, Julie Ann, and Martin Cooke (2004). *Labour Force Aging and Skill Shortages in Canada and Ontario.* Canadian Policy Research Networks (CPRN). <http://www.cprn.org/doc.cfm?doc=1088&l=en>.

Miller, Gord, Environmental Commisioner of Ontario (2000). *Changing Perspectives: Annual Report 1999/2000.* <http://www.eco.on.ca/eng/index.php/pubs/eco-publications/1999-2000-annual-report.php>.

Ottawa Citizen (2008, July 11). Alberta. Foreign Workers Get Help Settling In. *Ottawa Citizen* (Early Edition): A3.

Picot, Garnet, Feng Hou and Serge Coulombe (2007). *Chronic Low-Income and Low-Income Dynamics among Recent Immigrants.* Catalogue No. 11F0019MIE2007198. Statistics Canada.

Statistics Canada, Family and Labour Studies Division (2007). Impact of Immigration on Labour Markets in Canada, Mexico and the United States. *Update on Family and Labour Studies* (Winter). Cat. No. 89-001-XIE. <http://dsp-psd.pwgsc.gc.ca/collection_2007/statcan/89-001-X/89-001-XIE2007001.pdf>.

Statistics Canada, Immigration and Citizenship (2006). Census, Release no. 4, 2007. <www.statcan.ca>.

Stoffman, Daniel (2002) *Who Gets In: What's Wrong with Canada's Immigration Programme—and How to Fix It.* Macfarlane, Walter, and Ross.

Swan, Neil, Ludwig Auer, et al. (1991). *Economic and Social Impacts of Immigration: A Research Report Prepared for the Economic Council of Canada.* Cat. No. EC22-176/1991E.

Trempe, Robert, Susan Davis, and Roslyn Kunin (1997). *Not Just Numbers: A Canadian Framework for Future Immigration.* Report of the Immigration Legislative Review Advisory Group to the Honourable Lucienne Robillard (December 31, 1997).

United Nations High Commissioner for Refugees [UNHCR] (2007). *Asylum Trend; Statistics—Claims in Industrial Countries.* <www.unhcr.org/statistics>.

Valpy, Michael (2008, April 26). Wide Gap Exposes Fresh Labour Challenge. *Globe and Mail.*

Windsor, Hugh (1990, October 24) McDougal Wins Battle to Increase Immigration. *Globe and Mail.*

Winnet, Robert (2008, April 2). Limit Immigration, Warns the House of Lords. *The Telegraph.* <http://www.telegraph.co.uk/news/uknews/1583500/Limit-immigration-warns-House-of-Lords.html>.

Chapter 2

Immigration's impact on public coffers in the United States

Steven A. Camarota

Immigration's impact on public coffers has long been at the center of the immigration debate in the United States and other developed countries such as Canada. Until recently, however, we actually had very little reliable data on the subject. While there is still much that is not known, we now have some reasonably good information about immigration's impact in the United States.

There is a pretty clear consensus that the fiscal impact of immigration depends on the education levels of the immigrants. While other factors also matter, the human capital of immigrants, as economists like to refer to it, is clearly very important. There is no single better predictor of one's income, tax payments, or use of public services in modern America than one's education level.

Less-educated immigrants have lower incomes and pay less on average in taxes while at the same time they tend to make heavy demands on social services. Because such a large share of immigrants to the United States have low educational attainment, the few studies that have tried to estimate the total fiscal impact of immigrants have concluded that they pay less in taxes than they use in services. While there has been much less research on these questions as they relate to Canada, the educational level of immigrants is almost certainly a key determinate of the impact of Canadian immigrants on public coffers.

Methodological issues

The fiscal impact of immigration on a receiving society has not been as well studied as one might imagine. This is partly because of limitations in the data and partly because researchers have to deal with a number of difficult methodological questions on which there is not complete agreement. What assumptions one makes can have a significant impact on one's findings. The methodological questions are important and, when evaluating any study on this topic, it is important to understand the assumptions the authors make about the following issues.

Unit of analysis

The first question that has to be answered when studying immigration's fiscal impact is whether one will examine only the individual immigrant or the costs associated with their young children born in the receiving country. This is a critically important issue because all industrial democracies spend heavily on young children, particularly in the area of public education. Yet, most children in immigrant families are born in the receiving country and would typically not be considered as immigrants. In the American context, if a study excludes services and costs created by the US-born children of immigrants, it will tend to show lower costs than if they are included.

However, many studies use immigrant households, including the children born in the United States, as the basis of the study of costs. In its landmark study, *The New Americans*, the National Research Council (NRC) in the United States stated: "Since the household is the primary unit through which public services are consumed and taxes paid, it is the most appropriate unit as a general rule and is recommended for static analysis" (Smith and Edmonston, 1997: 255–56). In their study of New Jersey, Deborah Garvey and Thomas Espenshade also used households as the unit of analysis because, as they state, "households come closer to approximating a functioning socioeconomic unit of mutual exchange and support" (1996: 143).

Looking at households and thereby including the native-born children seems reasonable since the presence of these children in the receiving country is a direct result of their parents having been allowed to enter and remain in the country. If, for example, immigrant parents cannot provide for their US-born children and so qualify for programs like food stamps, it makes little sense to consider this as a cost caused by natives. Children are dependent on parents and thus the use of social services by children reflects the positions of their parent. Therefore, counting services used by these children allows for a full accounting of the costs of immigration.

Marginal versus average costs

In any study of immigrant costs there is also the issue of average costs versus marginal costs: Does an additional person or household using a program or service cost the same as those already using it? In some cases, they will cost more and in others they will cost less.

Consider, for example, the addition of new immigrant students to a public school that is half empty. Since the school in question has plenty of room, the costs of adding new children will be relatively low because the school is already built and no additional funding is needed for school construction. In such a situation, the marginal costs of the new students are much less than the average costs for the students already in the school.

On the other hand, an additional group of students added to an already overcrowded school may require a whole new school to be built, thus making the marginal cost of each additional student much greater than the average cost. The NRC and other researchers assume that marginal costs equal average costs because over time the two tendencies discussed above should balance out.

Public goods

Some goods provided by government are what might be termed pure public goods. That is, everyone living in the country benefits from receiving them but adding people does not raise the costs. The most important example of this type of program is national defense. Having more people in the country does not mean more will be spent on defense. Most studies of the fiscal impact of immigrants have assumed that there are some pure public goods, including defense, government-sponsored research, space exploration, and so on.

In the United States, there are more pure public goods associated with the national government than with state and local governments, which typically play a large role in providing services such as police and fire protection, education, and infrastructure maintenance. For reasons explained above in the context of education, expenditures on these projects are not pure public goods and have to expand as the population grows.

Payment on the national debt

Obviously, immigrants who have just arrived in the country have not contributed at all to past deficits or to the cumulative total of those deficits. On the other hand, if an immigrant household created a net fiscal drain in past years then it would account for a share of the nation's debt obligations.

The NRC study noted above did not count interest on the national debt as a cost for either immigrant or native households. The NRC study focused only on what it called the "primary" budget, that is, the budget excluding debt-service payments. This makes for an easier analysis but the question of payments on borrowed money remains an area that needs to be addressed in future research.

Direct versus indirect taxes

It is easy to estimate the value of taxes that have been paid by immigrants and natives, such as personal income taxes, sales taxes, and real estate taxes. It is harder to determine who ultimately pays such taxes levied on corporations and landlords. Clearly, some corporate taxes are passed to consumers in the form of higher prices, and landlords will try and recoup property taxes in the form of higher rents. However, not all such taxes can be passed on and corporations and landlords also pay some of these taxes.

In general it can be argued that households pay all of the taxes directly or indirectly because rental property or businesses are ultimately owned by individuals and those individuals pay the taxes that are not passed on to consumers and renters. Nevertheless, most studies attempt to apportion tax payment to individuals and immigrants based on whether they are workers, landlords, or owners of capital. It is also worth noting that the issue of taxes paid by persons living abroad is ignored in most studies.

Impact of immigrants on incomes

One final issue for a study examining the fiscal effects of immigrants is their impact on the level of income of Americans or, more precisely, the after-tax income of the average American household. Most economists believe this effect to be very small since the contributions to the nation's output made by the immigrants is returned to them in the form of wages. If they bring along capital, its contribution to output is similarly returned to its owners through dividend payments. For this reason, the National Research Council's study mentioned above (Smith and Edmonston, 1997) simply assumed away the effects of immigration on the incomes of Americans.

However, immigration leaving unchanged average incomes can and often does have effects on the distribution of income between capital and labor on the one hand and between workers with different skill levels on the other. Some business owners who use immigrant labour may benefit while some native workers, particularly those at the bottom of the labor market, might see their incomes decline considerably.

Some results from research on the education levels and economic status of immigrants to the United States

The column, "Median income," of table 1 shows the average levels of income of immigrants in the United States by educational attainment and compares them with the incomes of native-born Americans with the same educational attainment in the year 2006. The figures under "Overall education" show that, for all persons in the sample, the incomes of native-born Americans exceed the average level of immigrant incomes by $9,000. The rows below show that the difference in income between the two groups decreases with increasing levels of educational attainment: the annual earnings of all immigrant workers is only 77% that of native-born Americans but, once education is controlled for, immigrants earn about 90% of what native-born Americans earn. These data reveal the important fact that most of the difference in the median earnings of natives and immigrants is explained by the low educational attainment of many immigrants in the United States. Most notable is the fact that the median earnings of immigrants with a college degree is about the same as natives with a college degree.

Table 1: Socio-economic status by education level (2006)

	Nativity	Median income[1]	Welfare use by household[2]	In or near poverty[3]	Without health insurance[4]
Overall education					
	Immigrant	$31,074	33%	39%	34%
	Native	$40,344	19%	26%	14%
Less than high school					
	Immigrant	$21,176	54%	60%	51%
	Native	$24,402	41%	53%	22%
High school only					
	Immigrant	$26,459	36%	42%	38%
	Native	$31,486	23%	31%	18%
Some college education					
	Immigrant	$35,010	28%	29%	26%
	Native	$37,096	19%	23%	14%
College or graduate degree					
	Immigrant	$55,582	13%	16%	14%
	Native	$56,583	7%	10%	12%

Notes: [1] Persons who worked full time, year round, in 2006. [2] Based on nativity and educational level of household head. Major welfare programs include food, cash, and housing assistance and health care. [3] In or near-poverty defined as income under 200% of the offical US poverty threshold. Persons 18 and older only.

Source: Camarota, 2007.

Table 1 also shows that immigrants use welfare more, are more subject to poverty, and more often lack of health insurance coverage than the native-born, though these differences are smaller, the higher the education of both groups. Canadians may find it surprising to learn that one third of those without health insurance in the United States are immigrants or the young children of immigrants. Moreover, immigrants who have arrived since 1990 and their US-born children account for three fourths of the growth in the population lacking insurance in the United States. To a very significant extent, America's health insurance crisis is being driven by its immigration polices.[1]

1 ◆ Calculating the impact of recent immigrants on the growth of the uninsured is relatively simple. The March Current Population Survey (CPS) collected by the US

The current American immigration system allows most legal immigrants into the country based on whether they have a relative in the United States rather than whether they have the skills to compete in the modern American economy. This fact, coupled with widespread toleration of illegal immigration, means the foreign-born population in the United States as a whole is much less educated than the native-born population; and less educated than it would be if selection were based on educational attainment rather than family ties.

Given the nature of the modern American economy, as well as the existence of a well-developed welfare state, it seems unavoidable that less-educated immigrants will tend to have lower incomes, make heavier use of means-tested programs, and be more likely to lack health insurance than natives.

Review of research on fiscal impact of immigrants

The true fiscal impact of immigration can only be determined by examining both tax payments made by the immigrants and the costs they impose on services provided by the government. Relatively few studies have tried to calculate this total fiscal balance between tax payments and costs. However, those that have done so found that the size of the fiscal imbalance is different for immigrants with different levels of education and the higher the education of immigrants, the smaller the fiscal imbalance.

The National Research Council study

The study by the National Research Council (Smith and Edmonston, 1997) is probably the most sophisticated report ever to examine the impact of immigration on public coffers in the United States. While that report did not consider the legal status of immigrants, it did divide immigrants by education. The report found that, during his lifetime, an immigrant without a high-school education imposed a net fiscal drain (taxes paid minus services used) of $89,000. For those with only a high-school degree, the

---

Census Bureau asks all respondents if they have insurance and, if so, when they arrived in the country. The CPS is what the US government uses to determine the size of the uninsured population.

net fiscal drain was $31,000. On the other hand, the study found that, for those immigrants with more than a high-school degree, the immigrants provided a fiscal benefit worth $105,000 because they paid more in taxes than they consumed in government services.

These figures are only for individual immigrants and exclude the costs imposed on government through their US-born children. When the study included such children and examined households, it found that each year the net fiscal drain for the country as a whole from immigrant households was $20 billion. The study concluded that the primary reason for the net drain was the low education and incomes of immigrants relative to those of other Americans.

Study of New Jersey

A study published in 1997 of the state of New Jersey found that immigrant households (legal and illegal) created a net fiscal drain in the state but the drain varied by immigrant group (Garvey and Espenshade, 1996). For households headed by immigrants under the age of 65, the study estimated their annual fiscal drain in 1990 was $1,824 per household. Those with the least education, such as immigrants from Latin America, created a larger drain (–$2,844) than those with more education, such as immigrants from Europe (–$1,101) and Asia (–$1,467) (Garvey and Espenshade, 1996: 159).

It should be noted that the study assumed all businesses in the state paid more taxes than they received in government benefits, which means households in general were a net fiscal drain, with the drain that immigrant households created being larger than that of native households.

Heritage Foundation study

A 2007 study by the Heritage Foundation focused on immigrant households (legal and illegal) headed by a person without a high-school diploma (Rector, 2007). It concluded that in 2005, on average, low-skilled immigrant households in the United States created $30,160 in costs each year and paid only $10,573 in taxes for a net fiscal drain of $19,587. The study also concluded that the lifetime net fiscal drain of each unskilled immigrant household would be $1.2 million. Of course, non-immigrant low-skilled households incur costs similar to those of immigrant low-skilled households. The focus on the costs caused by the immigrant households is that they are avoidable by the use of government policies that prevent them from settling in the country.

Center for Immigration Studies

My own research considered the fiscal cost for the US federal budget imposed by illegal immigrant households (Camarota, 2004). I found that the fiscal costs stem primarily from the educational level of illegal immigrants and resulting low incomes and tax payments, not their legal status. An estimated three fourths of illegal immigrants had either failed to graduate high school or had just a high-school degree.

I found that the illegal immigrants paid in federal taxes $10.3 billion less than they cost the federal taxpayers. The net fiscal drain at the state and local level is almost certainly much larger than this sum. If currently illegal immigrants obtained legal status, the fiscal drain at the federal level would almost triple, since the previously illegal immigrants would begin to pay taxes but also begin to use government services to which they were previously not entitled.

The study highlights the fact that it was the educational level of the illegal immigrants rather than their legal status that created the net fiscal drain. In fact, being illegal tended to hold down the drain less-educated immigrants create. Immigrants with little education who are legally in the country were found to be much more costly than illegal immigrants with little education.

Other studies

Several studies by the Urban Institute have examined only tax payments by immigrants without looking at any of the costs they create. The most recent study examined the Washington DC metropolitan area (Capps, Henderson, Passel, and Fix, 2006). Among the study's findings was that the tax payments vary by immigrant group. The study concluded that those groups that had the highest average levels of education make the highest tax payments and the least educated immigrant groups make the lowest payment.

A 1994 study of the New York State also done by the Urban Institute came to the same conclusion (Passel and Clark, 1994). Several recent studies have tried to look only at illegal immigrants in the United States, an issue that is not particularly relevant to Canada.[2]

These studies have generally not included the costs associated with the US-born children of illegal immigrants and have also generally avoided including any figures for what might be called population-based costs, such as increased expenditures on roads, bridges, police, and fire protection associated with a larger population. The conclusions of these studies have varied.

Conclusion

The fiscal impact of immigrants is only one issue to consider when deciding on immigration policy. The available evidence in the United States strongly indicates that if fiscal costs are a concern, then immigrants must be selected based on their education rather than other criteria such as whether they have relatives in the United States. The evidence is clear that less-educated immigrants create significant fiscal costs, which can be avoided by the use of proper immigrant selection procedures or reductions in the number of immigrants admitted.

It is worth noting that many native-born Americans observe that their ancestors came to America and did not place great demands on government services. This view is also sometimes expressed in Canada. Perhaps these sentiments are correct, but the size and scope of government was dramatically smaller 100 years ago when both the United States and Canada experienced large-scale immigration. Thus, the arrival of immigrants with little education in the past did not have the same negative fiscal implications that it does today. Moreover, the American and Canadian economies have changed profoundly in recent decades, with education now the key determinant of economic success. The costs that unskilled immigrants impose simply reflect the nature of a modern economy and welfare state. These costs should not be interpreted as a kind of moral defect on the part of immigrants. But, if fiscal costs are to be

---

2 ◆ See Siskin, 2007, which examines several recent studies that attempted to examine the costs of illegal immigrants in the United States in particular parts of the country. CRS reports are difficult for the general public to obtain.

avoided, then immigration policy must reflect the realities of a modern post-industrial society with a well developed administrative state.

References

Camarota, Steven (2004). *The High Cost of Cheap Labor: Illegal Immigration and the Federal Budget.* Center for Immigration Studies. <http://www.cis.org/articles/2004/fiscal.html>.

Camarota, Steven (2007). *Immigrants in the United States, 2007: A Profile of America's Foreign-Born Population.* Backgrounder (November). Center for Immigration Studies. <http://www.cis.org/immigrants_profile_2007>.

Capps, Randolph, Everett Henderson, Jeffrey S. Passel, and Michael E. Fix (2006). *Civic Contributions: Taxes Paid by Immigrants in the Washington, DC, Metropolitan Area.* Urban Institute. <http://www.urban.org/publications/411338.html>.

Garvey, Deborah L., and Thomas J. Espenshade (1996). State and Local Fiscal Impacts of New Jersey's Immigrant and Native Households. In Thomas Espenshade, ed., *Keys to Successful Immigration: Implications of the New Jersey Experience* (Urban Institute Press): 139–72.

Passel, Jeffrey S., and Rebecca L. Clark (1994). *Immigrants in New York: Their Legal Status, Incomes, and Taxes.* Urban Institute. <http://www.urban.org/publications/407432.html>.

Rector, Robert (2007). *The Fiscal Cost of Low-Skill Immigrants to the U.S. Taxpayer.* Heritage Foundation. <http://www.heritage.org/Research/Immigration/sr14.cfm>.

Siskon, Alison (2007). *Cost Estimates of Unauthorized (Illegal) Immigration.* Congressional Research Services (CRS).

Smith, James P., and Barry Edmonston (1997). *The New Americans: Economic, Demographic, and Fiscal Effects of Immigration.* National Academies Press.

Chapter 3

Immigration and its impacts in France

Jean-Paul Gourévitch

To give a summary of immigration to France and an analysis of its impact that will provide lessons for Canadian immigration policy in the compass of one short chapter will require me to schematize and take shortcuts, for which I ask you to excuse me.[1] In this chapter, I will first survey the various aspects of immigration in France—demographic, economic, societal, and political-geopolitical—and then dwell more on the first two of these, which reflect my personal research. After that, I will go more quickly over the qualitative aspects, which are observations I am sharing with other specialists.

---

1 ◆ This chapter was translated by Élisa-Line Montigny from the French of the author's presentation at the conference, "Canadian Immigration Policy: Reassessing the Economic, Demographic and Social Impact on Canada, Montreal, QC (June 3–4, 2008). For a discussion in greater depth and detailed information, please see the author's recent publications: first, *Les migrations en Europe: Les réalités du présent, les défis du futur* (2007); second, an extended discussion of the same subject in a report for the Council of Europe on sub-Saharan migrations, *L'immigration en provenance d'Afrique subsaharienne* (2008, April 18), which was adopted unanimously by the deputies; third, a monograph on the true cost of immigration in France, *Le coût réel de l'immigration en France* (2008), produced by Contribuables Associés, one of the few French think tanks with the courage to raise these disagreeable topics.

The demographic approach

Who are the immigrants?

In France we have three different concepts in speaking of immigration. The term "immigrant," according to the definition given by the *Haut Conseil à l'Intégration*, our institution of reference, designates persons born abroad to foreign biological parents who have decided to settle on a long term or permanent basis in France. "Immigrant" thus stands in opposition to "native."

The term "foreigner" applies to persons who do not have their normal residence in France, who have not—or not yet—decided to settle there and who can consider returning to their countries of origin or leaving for another country. "Foreigner" stands in opposition to "French." Some immigrants have obtained French nationality. That makes them both French and immigrants. Others have not sought French nationality or have not obtained it. They are immigrants and foreigners.

"Persons of foreign origin" is a term designating the children of these immigrants, born abroad or in France. These two categories do not have the same status. Children born abroad are viewed as immigrants. Children born in France, since the time of Lionel Jospin, the Socialist prime minister (1997–2002), will automatically be French at age 13, 16, or 18 unless they ask specifically not to be.[2]

How many of them are there?

The institutes in charge of statistics in France, in particular the National Institute for Statistics and Economic Studies (INSEE, Institut national de la statistique et des études économiques) are responsible for providing a picture of the French population and the place held by immigrants in our country. But the INSEE has a very particular concept of immigration: in the under-18 group, it includes only those born abroad. It thus adds the 2% of the population who are under 18 and born abroad to the 9.5% of the population who are immigrants over 18, leading it to deem that there are 4.93 million immigrants out of a French metropolitan population estimated at 60.86 million inhabitants in 2006.

2 ◆ This is consistent with the fact that their parents or the young themselves may seek French nationality before the legal limit of 18 years.

This bit of trickery falsifies the statistics and minimizes the impact of immigration, because the children born in France to these immigrants have greater needs than the native population in education, health care, housing, and environment. Their situation is different, because French is not always the language spoken in their families. Their traditions and cultures sometimes conflict with those of the host country, and the segregation that enters into the allocation of social housing often traps them in ethnic ghettos where anger is stoked up. Using INSEE statistics, we have reconstituted complete cohorts including immigrants over age 18 and their children, whether born in France or abroad, which brings the foreign population in France to 11% (figure 3.1).

This population has been rising continuously since the 1960s for two major reasons: a positive annual migratory balance varying from 50,000 to 150,000 persons and a sharp differential in birth rates. While women in France, of whatever origin, average 1.9 to 2.1 births, almost equal to the generational replacement rate, immigrants from nearby countries (Spain, Italy, Germany) have a lower rate whereas immigrants from the Maghreb and, especially, from Africa have much higher rates, in the latter case between 3.5 and 5, close to the rates in their countries of origin.

Figure 3.1: Change in the immigrant population (1960–2007)

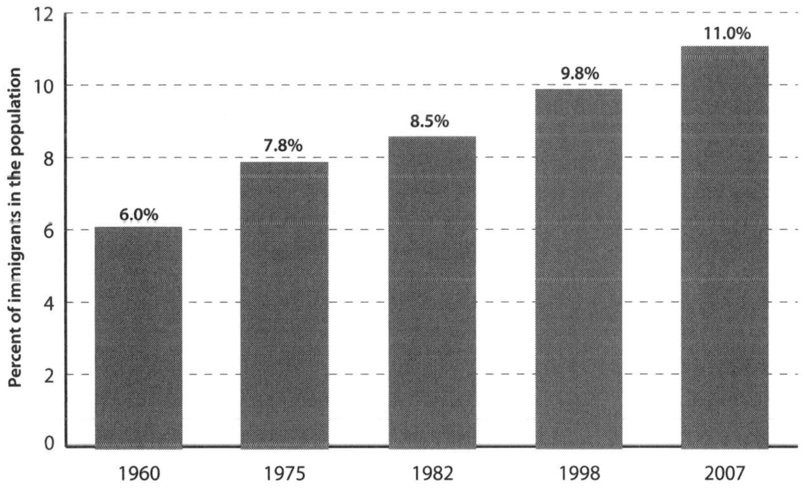

Source: Institut national de la statistique et des études économiques (INSEE), 2005a, 2005b, 2006; calculations by author.

I will add a final point. These statistics from INSEE, even if methodologically re-tallied, underestimate the immigrant population. First, INSEE produces statistics that obviously lag behind the current situation (the numbers in figure 1 are excerpted from the 2006 statistics). More importantly, they are based on censuses that count only those able or willing to be counted. Some residents do not want to be counted, were absent during the count, cannot fill out the papers, or did not receive them because they live in lawless zones that government representatives cannot enter. Researchers estimate that from 1.5% to 3.0% of the population is missed by censuses, which means the percentage of immigrants, as defined above, may be closer to 14% than to 11% and the number of immigrants and their children in 2008 may be between 8.5 and 9.0 million rather than around 6.9 million.

Where do they come from?

The composition of this immigrant population has also changed. Immigrants from the countries in the former 12-member European Community are now very much in the minority. Immigration in France is mainly from outside Europe, with origins divided approximately as follows:

- Maghreb: 3 million
- sub-Saharan Africa: 2.4 million
- Far East: 0.6 million
- Turkey and Middle East: 0.3 million
- eastern countries (former USSR + Balkans + countries recently admitted to the European Union): 0.3 million
- other countries: 0.3 million.

What are the characteristics of this population?

In this population, the number of *illegal migrants,*—which has given rise to fishy estimates that range from 180,000 (Jack Lang) to 1,500,000 (the far-right press)—is, according to the majority of researchers, somewhere between 350,000 and 700,000 and this cannot really be narrowed any further. This population is very *young*: 4.83 million of them are over 18 and 2.04 million under 18—29% of the total, compared to 23% for metropolitan France as a whole.

This population is much less likely to be in the workforce (43.7%) than French residents on average (55%) and more likely to be unemployed. Of the three million in the workforce, 600,000 are officially jobless, with some of these probably working in the informal economy.

Why did they come to France?

The main motive for migration is *family ties*. Marital or prenatal migration and reunification of families and their variants account for more than 70% of entries to France, though some migrants later seek to join the workforce.

Student migration is second in order of importance. Since it is not possible, given the absence of personalized follow-up procedures, to determine how many decide to settle permanently in France after their studies, we rely on the number of foreign students at postsecondary institutions in France, 263,000 out of 2.5 million students.

The third category, *medical and social* migration, is specifically French. France is the only country (apart from the Spanish province of Andalusia) to provide medical assistance to migrants who are there illegally. It is also generous in the various forms of assistance given to migrants in difficulty. Some of those who leave their countries for medical or social reasons naturally head for France.

In contrast, *political and religious* migration has declined recently. In 2004, with 61,600 asylum seekers, France was the most sought-after country in Europe and received more requests than the United States. Not that France is more generous than other countries but those who were refused knew they did not risk being sent back to their home countries, due to pressures from associations of undocumented persons. But right-wing governments have toughened the legislation, shortened the time for requests to be reviewed, and shown signs of firmness in the forceful repatriation of some Africans. The flow of requests has returned to a low-water mark of 35,000, which is more in harmony with those arriving in other European countries. This migration is sometimes mixed with militant political or religious migration aimed at mobilizing diasporas for the struggle against political authorities in their countries of origin, demands for rights recognized in the host country, or fundraising.

Compared with these figures, and setting aside the *star-studded* migration generated by the success stories of migrants in sport, music, or fashion, and *"charm"* migration (80% to 90% of those living from prostitution are foreigners), *labor* migration involves only 7% of all migrants. The French authorities are aware of this gap between work migration and settlement migration, and they have been working in the last few years to narrow it (by creating the "talent competence" card, setting quotas in some professions open to foreign workers, instituting "brain drain" practices, and so on).

The economic approach

A long-hidden debate

Debate over the costs of immigration has long been taboo in France despite the contributions of Pierre Milloz, Gérard Pince, and the team gathered around the *Institut de Géopolitique des Populations* (Gérard Lafay, Jacques Bichot, Yves Laulan, Gérard-François Dumont, and so on). Any approach was seen as xenophobic and most of the left and extreme left denounced these "obscene statistics." Today, the debate is somewhat less ideological, with France assuming the presidency of the European Union on July 1, 2008, and aiming to help Europeanize immigration policies. Also, debate on the deficit in public finances is pointing to a quest for savings and a reorientation of French policy. This said, costs are just one of the variables of immigration policy and cannot be viewed as the only factor in decision-making. These factors can be divided into three areas: expenditures, revenues, and long-term investments.

Expenditures

Analysis of the cost-benefit ratio of migrations has three aspects: costs for the country of origin, costs for migrants themselves, and costs for the host country. We will examine here only this last aspect. Expenditures by the French government for migrants amount to €71.76 billion (Gourévitch, 2008), allocated as in the table 3.1. *Social costs*, which account for the great majority of expenditures, consist essentially of payments for health care (€20.5 billion) and retirement (€16.56 billion). To this must be added unemployment and reintegration payments, family allowances and anti-poverty or exclusion payments, in particular the program for minimum integration income. *Fiscal and societal costs* stem mainly from shortfalls due to the informal economy, especially from illegal work, prostitution, fraud, and counterfeiting. *Security costs* result from the scope of petty crime caused by immigrants and their offspring and observed by many micro-investigations, even if ethnic statistics are prohibited in France.

Revenues

On the other hand, immigrants bring €45.57 billion to the state budget and to local communities, divided as shown in table 3.2. Many immigrant families in fact pay no income tax because of their low earnings, are exempted from some local taxes, and pay little corporate tax. Their wealth solidarity tax contributions are negligible. On the other hand, in terms of consumption, the behavior of the immigrant population differs little from that of the native French, and it can thus be considered that the government gets from them a share of taxes proportionate to their numerical proportion in France's population.

Table 3.1: Expenditures by the French government for immigration

Nature of expenditures	Amount (€ billions)
Social costs	51.9
Fiscal and societal costs	12.78
Security costs	5.24
Educational costs	1.64
TOTAL	71.76

Source: Gourévitch, 2008.

Table 3.2: Revenues of the French government from immigrants

Nature of revenues	Amount (€ billions)
Consumption taxes (VAT, oil tax)	16.7
Income tax	9.66
Local taxes	6.81
National insurance contribution	12.4
TOTAL	45.57

Source: Gourévitch, 2008.

Long-term investments

The expenditure-revenue balance from immigration, reflected in the state budget by a deficit of €26.19 billion, does not account on its own for a government's political choices. France makes what are, in effect, investments, on the one hand, to slow migratory flows by assisting developing countries, especially those to which it feels it has historical duties, and, on the other, to improve the integration of immigrants who have arrived on French territory and their children.

Part of public development assistance, €4.26 billion out of a total of €7.84 billion, is devoted to external action by the government in cancelling debts, financing co-development operations, offering scholarships to students, or paying to repatriate clandestine migrants to their countries of origin. This investment brings no immediate profit because, to give an example, a decline in the demand for asylum generates very limited savings in relation to the amounts invested. Similarly, in integration policy, government expenditures to facilitate learning of the French language by new arrivals and developing a generous policy that extends to positive discrimination in education, housing, and living arrangements, at €6.55 billion a year, bring no short-term spin-offs. Their effectiveness can be measured only over the long term. All in all, the government invests €10.81 billion for the benefit of its immigration policy without the impact being even remotely measurable.

Reducing costs

In recent years, the French government has become more attentive to growth of the public debt, threats from the European Commission in Brussels, and demands from a society worried by stagnation in purchasing power, and it is seeking to reduce the deficit in its migration policy. A partial simulation of the spending inventory in government accounting and of the cost referred to previously suggests the following conclusion: if the 11% of immigrants counted here were to pay taxes based on the national average, their annual contribution would be €81.425 billion, or as much as expenditures and investments combined. To reduce costs, action is required on three specific parameters:

- *increase the income* of this population, which is poorer than the national average and leading a precarious existence;

- *reduce unemployment* among this population to bring it to a lower level near the national average;

- *rebalance the ratio* between work migration and settlement migration, with new immigrants who come to meet labor requirements added to the incompressible stock of settlement migration and encouraging some economically inactive immigrants to seek work rather than remaining content with public assistance.

The French government has gone after these three aspects by developing a city policy (Borloo plan and Amara plan), reducing unemployment, and favoring the arrival of productive new migrants. It is too soon to judge the results, however. We have calculated that, to achieve a balance between expenditures and revenues, it would be necessary to apply, over a period of nine years, a policy resulting annually in:

- a one-point drop in unemployment among the immigrant population;
- a 1% increase in its average income in constant euros;
- the arrival on the job market of 100,000 unmarried working immigrants.

The societal, political and geopolitical approaches

Societal approach to the immigrant population

This population, described as structurally poorer and more precarious than the national average, has two basic specificities. First, it is a population with *a large Muslim majority*. There were in 2008 about seven million Muslims in France, or 11% of the population. But the forms of Islam practised are very different. Maghreb Islam is different from African Islam or Turkish Islam and, even within the Maghreb community, there is a lively antipathy between Moroccan Islam and Algerian Islam, as shown by the elections to the French Council of the Muslim Faith.

Second, this population is structured into *very active diasporas with high levels of solidarity*. Diaspora members play a long-term role in welcoming new arrivals, helping them find work or housing, or even welcoming them for a time into their own homes. They facilitate accommodation and the steps needed for those lacking regular status, showing them how best to benefit from opportunities offered by the host country, and they organize formal and informal money transfers from the host country to the country of origin. They are indispensable intermediaries in negotiating with the public authorities, even though the latter tend to short-circuit them.

Successes of immigration policy

Contrary to a widespread view abroad fed by shocking images in the media, the great majority of immigrants see themselves as *integrated and respectful of national values and culture*, and they aspire to enjoy quiet and prosperous lives in the country where they chose to settle. The era of a French football team presented as black, white, and North African, as well as the enthusiasm for Maghreb and African music and recognition for the talent of foreign-born business creators in the fashion or computer fields, plus the fact that the current government has three top officials from the Maghreb and African immigrant communities, have legitimized this immigration and shown all migrants, especially the young, that success is possible in today's France if the will exists.

At the same time, French public opinion is showing greater tolerance toward immigrant communities, accepting the differences and sometimes seeking them out, as the increase in mixed marriages proves. We are seeing a retreat in the country of *xenophobia*, as shown by the decline of the National Front in the latest national elections.

Failures of immigration policy

All the same, the many obstacles encountered both by the government and by immigrants in achieving a harmonious integration in French society must not be hidden. They are summed up below.

The *explosion of the informal economy* in all its forms, from trafficking in drugs, animals, plants, weapons, and human organs to exchange of services, and including illegal work and money laundering, amounts to 17% of national GDP and matches an onerous trend observed throughout Europe. This casts a heavy weight on French growth. What matters here is not to set out an equation between immigration and the informal economy: not all immigrants are caught up in it and the people involved are not all immigrants. But, it must be pointed out that the informal economy, which is very widespread in immigrants' countries of origin, developed in large part thanks to them and today forms an economic and societal vector of their integration.

The *increase in petty crime*, broadly attributable to a population of immigrant origin, led to urban violence in the autumn of 2005. Inner and outer suburbs, particularly in the department of Seine-Saint-Denis, where the number of persons of foreign origin is higher than that of natives, are the scene of regular incidents between "young people" and the "forces of order" that are pushing part of the population to exasperation and leading others to move elsewhere. The Marseillaise was even booed at some football matches at the Stade de France, and at some educational institutions there has been physical aggression against teachers and principals. This *rejection of the French model* is broadly advanced by radical Islamists who use the precarious state of this population to get it involved in violent actions against the state and its representatives.

Failure to control illegal immigration has led to unmanageable situations such as the Sangatte refugee centre, which was closed without the problem of clandestine movements to the United Kingdom being dealt with permanently and leaving the way open to trafficking of all sorts. From that point of view, immigrants are more often victims than agents.

Religious conflicts concerning the governance of Islam in France, the persistence of *illiteracy* and, it must be added, *discrimination* frequently suffered by immigrants in housing, education, and especially jobs prolong an unhealthy climate in places where immigrants form a sizable minority.

The political and geopolitical approach

With regard to the problem of immigration, French public opinion and its leadership are divided into several tendencies.

Immigrationists, on the left or extreme left, call for total opening of the borders in the name of free movement of goods, people and messages. Though their numbers are limited (about 15% of the population), they are well regarded in intellectual circles and the media, thanks in particular to support from publications such as *Libération* and *Le Monde diplomatique*. The immigrationists have been outflanked on the left by the *communitarians*, who challenge the secular state and want to allow immigrant communities to apply their own laws, particularly Muslim *sharia* law. Small in numbers but very active, they are influential in some housing estates where women and girls wear the veil, sometimes from conviction but more often from fear of reprisals.

Facing them are the *national-populists*, with Jean-Marie Le Pen as their emblematic figure, seeing themselves as the voices of Fortress Europe and "zero immigration." They have lost much of their audience but their ideas remain popular even if they have moved to more realistic positions and are calling today for a "zero migratory balance."

A majority of French public opinion takes more moderate positions. These run the gamut from a *muscular liberalism*—"France is a welcoming country, especially for immigrant workers, but it will take the necessary measures against clandestine immigration"—to *humanitarian republicanism*—"Yes to immigrants wherever they come from and whatever their motivation provided they respect the laws of the host country"—and including *European realism*—"France cannot act alone but must build a common immigration policy with its other partners".

It is this last tendency that prevails today but Europeanization of immigration policies is still far from reality. Even if Europeans show the same basic principles (political asylum, family reunion, access to work), the means of applying it are so different that migrants practise what is being called, for lack of a better term, "*immigration shopping,*" which consists simply in seeking the country offering the most advantages and fewest risks, especially the risk of being sent back to countries of origin.

The political approach is giving way increasingly to a *geopolitical* vision. Europe is asking itself today about its ability to conduct a single coherent immigration policy in a world where migratory flows are proliferating and diversifying. It is tempted by an overture that could be made toward French- or English-speaking sub-Saharan Africa (demanded by many African countries but rejected by most European countries), toward Turkey, the Balkans, or the countries of the former Soviet bloc, or more especially toward the Mediterranean. In this regard, the Sarkozy project of a *Euro-Mediterranean partnership*, an extension of the Barcelona agreements (1995) and the Rabat conference (2006), is no doubt viewed as the most promising even though many obstacles remain before the Mediterranean becomes an internal lake where countries on the southern and northern shores can live in peace and share together in the fruits of prosperity.

The current debate

French society remains very divided on the immigration issue, beyond the cleavages of right and left, as shown by the debates that keep erupting. *Should illegal immigrants have their status regularized*? Which ones? As a group, at the risk of causing a fuss, or discreetly, by individual preferential treatments? Or, on the contrary, should they be encouraged financially to return home and those who refuse forced to go anyway? France is currently regularizing about 30,000 migrants a year and sending home 15,000 to 20,000, most of whom reattempt the experience.

Should voting rights in local elections and, perhaps later, in national elections, be granted to foreigners, or should this be reserved for those who have chosen French nationality?

What place should be given to Islam in France? Should the state and local communities play a direct or indirect role in the building of mosques demanded by Muslims and in the training of imams? And how best to protect the majority of French Muslims from the siren calls of Islamism?

Should an apology be issued for the misdeeds committed in the slave trade and colonization to current representatives of formerly subjected peoples, or should the slave trade be placed in the context of Arab-Islamic trade, and should the positive effects of colonization be shown?

Should one preserve the purity of a language, protector of the Francophone world, or is it acceptable for it to be mixed with inputs from back-to-front slang, "ghetto lexicon," or terms borrowed from Arabic or African national languages? Along the same lines, can French culture withstand the risks posed by the existence of a culture of transgression or even of a counter-culture, with models such as hip-hop, rap, tag, and yamakasi, so esteemed by many young people of foreign origin, or must it treat them as passing fads with no major effect on national values?

Finally, *should there be systematic positive discrimination* in housing, education, and job access toward the immigrant population and its children to enable them to catch up, or should society stick to the principles of equity and promotion by merit on which French civilization is based?

Not in conclusion

It seems inappropriate to end this approach to diversity and migratory flows and the plurality of its impacts with personal positions or dead-letter recommendations. From what little we know, the effect of immigration in France may be to enable the multiracial and multicultural Gallic rooster to course ahead or to crawl and to be out of the running.

References

Gourévitch, Jean-Paul (2007). *Les migrations en Europe: Les réalités du présent, les défis du futur* [Migrations in Europe: Current realities, future challenges]. Les Éditions Acropole.

Gourévitch, Jean-Paul (2008). *Le coût réel de l'immigration en France*. Contribuables Associés. <http://www.contribuables.org/publications/les-monographies/le-cout-reel-de-l-immigration-en-france/>.

Gourévitch, Jean-Paul (2008, April 18). *L'immigration en provenance d'Afrique subsaharienne*. Report for the Council of Europe. ["Rapport établi pour le Conseil de l'Europe, présenté par Jean-Guy Branger (document 11526), adopté par la commission Migrations du 22/01/08 et voté à l'unanimité (moins 2 abstentions) par les députés le 18/04/08 (résolution 1611)."] <http://assembly.coe.int/Mainf.asp?link=/Documents/WorkingDocs/Doc08/FDOC11526.htm>.

Gourévitch, Jean-Paul (2009) *Les Africains de France*. Les Éditions Acropole.

Institut national de la statistique et des études économiques (INSEE) (2005a). *Les immigrés en France*.

Institut national de la statistique et des études économiques (INSEE) (2005b). Review *Insee première* No. 1042 (September).

Institut national de la statistique et des études économiques (INSEE) (2006). Review *Insee première* No. 1098 (August).

Economic issues

Chapter 4

Immigration policy in free societies: Are there principles involved or is it all politics?

Vernon M. Briggs, Jr.

Free societies with industrialized economies such as Canada and the United States are characterized by certain unique features. Among these is the fact that they both allow their citizens to come and go across their borders with few restrictions and they annually permit millions of non-citizens to travel, to conduct business, to visit, and to study in their countries with only minimal regulation. Both nations also allow some non-citizens to enter their countries and to work in competition with their citizen work-force for temporary periods under specific conditions. Furthermore, they regularly allow a generous number of non-citizens to immigrate or to take refuge as permanent residents and eventually to become citizens. It is primarily these latter situations, where work and residence issues arise, that pose the question whether years of experience have generated any principles that can guide policy makers when debates re-surface? Or, is it always simply a matter of political power and special interests at the moment that determine immigration policy on an ad-hoc basis?

It is not that politics can ever be entirely avoided, of course, since the *sine qua non* of all democratic societies is that policy decisions have to be filtered through political institutions before they can be validated and legitimately enforced. Rather, the issue is whether certain principles have achieved the status of quasiparameters to political dialogues when the subject of immigration policy is on the national agenda? It is understood, of course, that political discussions will necessarily lead to differences over the details of policy; but can the framework of these debates start with the recognition of certain uncontested principles?

Too often, if the United States' experience with immigration reform is instructive, the rhetoric surrounding these discussions becomes hopelessly entangled in a confusion of intentions and motivations of the participants that serve to divert public attention from the national interest to what are but crass private efforts to extract gains for special-interest groups. Policy options are endlessly re-hashed and re-debated as if they have never been discussed or tried before. Research dealing with experience with past endeavors is simply ignored. It often seems that no lessons are ever learned. The result, as one would expect, is usually stalemate in the legislative bodies as the politicians jockey for acceptable positions and widespread cynicism is generated among the populace because changes are not forthcoming while the failures of extant policies continue to fester in their local communities.

For 40 years, the United States has wrestled with attempts to reform its immigration policies after the unexpected revival of the phenomenon of mass immigration following the passage of the Immigration Act of 1965 (Briggs, 2003). In 1965, the foreign-born population totaled 8.5 million people; by 2007, the foreign-born population exceeded 39 million persons. As these unintended consequences began to emerge, the US Congress established the Select Commission on Immigration and Refugee Policy in 1978 to seek ways to respond to the unanticipated rise in immigration. Less than a decade after the Select Commission issued its final report in 1981, the US Commission on Immigration Reform was created in 1990 for the same reasons. Unfortunately, the major reforms advocated by both of these commissions have largely gone unheeded or been only half-heartedly enacted. As a consequence, immigration policy issues continue to ferment and the public is deeply disturbed by the lack of action. The troublesome issue of immigration reform is again waiting at the doorstep of the new administration and Congress that took over in 2009.

The purpose of this paper, however, is not to rehash the 40-year saga of efforts to reform immigration in the United States. It is a woeful tale too frustrating to dwell upon. Rather, the goal is to identify those parameters that, if recognized in advance as being "givens," could have allowed reform measures to proceed. But if there is continuing disagreement over these principles, it can be anticipated that discussion in the future will once more become bogged down over policy predicates and never get to the needed reform measures themselves. Likewise, if there really are such things as immigration principles for free societies, there should be some prospect that these lessons can be generalized to apply to other nations who are similarly free, industrialized, and open to immigration flows on a regulated basis. The principles identified below are all drawn from actual quotations from debates and the literature about immigration policy in the United States.

"The open society does not mean limitless immigration. Quantitative and qualitative limits are perfectly compatible with the concept of the open society." (Hesburgh, 1981: 25)

In a world of nation states, immigration is associated with the principle of national sovereignty. All governments have the authority to exercise control over the people who reside within their prescribed geographical borders. No nation state on Earth permits voluntary citizenship (Brubaker, 1989). Citizens in free societies believe that, in return for compulsory citizenship, they have certain rights and entitlements, which their governments must meet. The governments of these societies, in turn, expect their citizens to meet certain responsibilities. Non-citizens can only legally enter to live, work, study, travel, visit, or seek refuge under terms set by the national governments of these individual nation states. Otherwise, they can be denied entry or deported, if apprehended, if they enter the territory of the nation state without permission or violate the terms of a temporary visa. Sending violators of immigration laws back to their homelands is typically not considered to be punishment. It is simply a law-enforcement remedy.

Precisely because free societies believe they are "nations of laws," they reserve the right to limit the quantitative number of non-citizens who may annually enter and they can, as they usually do, also decide to specify certain qualitative features that they wish would-be immigrants to have as a condition of their admission. As such, the phenomenon of immigration in contemporary times must be recognized as being wholly a policy-driven phenomenon.

Like all public policies, the factors associated with determining the number and the characteristics of would-be immigrants are the national interests of the receiving nation state at a given time. The ensuing immigration flows, therefore, are not outcomes determined by free-market forces. They are the products of man-made decisions. And, as Napoleon once mused, "policy is destiny."

Immigration policies exist because most citizens in nation states have a sense of nationalism by which they seek to retain the integrity of national ideologies, institutions, and boundaries. But more than nationalism is involved because free societies also believe that their existence itself serves as a beacon to others, showing the "the possibilities of freedom and the potentiality for justice in a world which sees little of either" (Hesburgh, 1981: 24). Unrestrictive immigration would render this imitation ideal impossible.

"Immigration is, in its fundamental aspects, a labor problem."
(Gompers, 1925: 154)

In the handful of nation states in the world in which immigration is pursued and encouraged, immigration policy is composed of multiple components. But, regardless of the entry avenue, virtually all immigrants must work once they arrive. Usually, their spouses and, eventually, their children do as well. Hence, immigration policies always have labor-market consequences no matter what the rationale for their enactment.

Although seldom acknowledged in the political rhetoric, the scale of immigration flows, the human-capital characteristics that the immigrants bring with them (or the lack of same), and the geographical distribution of the foreign population always have economic implications for the nation's labor force. These impacts upon the labor supply affect not only the immigrant labor force but also the employment, earnings, and income opportunities of the citizen labor force (that is, the native-born work force as well as the foreign-born workers who have previously become naturalized citizens). Every change in immigration policy needs to contain an accompanying analysis of its anticipated consequences for the labor market, both in the short run and the long run.

Implicit in the recognition of immigration as being fundamentally a labor issue is the parallel acknowledgement that the enforcement of the provisions of immigration laws is part of government's duty to protect workers. In a pure sense, immigration policy is a nation's most fundamental worker-protection law: it defines who is eligible to be a member of the legal labor force subject to any other qualifications that the government might impose to refine that definition.

"Immigration policy inevitably reflects a kind of national selfishness of which the major beneficiaries are the least fortunate among us." (Reder, 1963: 227)

Although seldom acknowledged when immigration policy is under consideration, there are significant social-justice issues at stake for the most needy in the resident population and labor force. Much of the rationale for the admission of immigrants in free societies ignores the impacts of their actions upon the labor market. Family reunification considerations, refugee admissions, political asylum approvals, responses to the ever-present pleas of some business organizations for unskilled workers, and the presence of illegal immigrants usually mean that a disproportionate number of the immigrant inflow are low skilled, poorly educated, and often have problems with the prevailing national language. As a consequence, it is the segment of the citizen labor force that is itself low skilled and poorly educated (that is, workers in the "secondary labor market," to use the jargon of labor economics) and those workers who have been marginalized by various social barriers (e.g., some specific segments of the population who have confronted discrimination, as well as inexperienced youths in general) that typically sustain the greatest adverse impacts of large immigrant inflows.

Too often immigration debates focus on the beneficiaries of immigration policies (that is, the immigrants themselves, employers, and sometimes consumers) while failing to acknowledge that there are always losers too, which is especially important since the losers are disproportionately those already on the bottom rungs of society's economic ladder as well as the taxpayers in general who often are required to support or to supplement the financial needs of unskilled immigrants and refugees. One of the strongest reasons for the existence of immigration policies that limit the number of immigrants is that they protect those citizen workers who are most vulnerable to the increased job and wage competition of immigrant entry. Equity considerations are as important as efficiency considerations when immigration policy is under discussion, although the equality of these two positions is often overlooked. There are justifiable social reasons to regulate immigration entries and to seek strict enforcement of policy terms once restrictions are in place.

How significant this issue is, of course, depends on the size of the unskilled adult labor force in the country. In the case of the United States, there are over 90 million adults (that is, those persons age 25 and over in the population) who have only a high-school diploma or fewer years of educational attainment (or about half of the total adult population). Of these, over 50 million were in the civilian labor force in 2008.

Low levels of educational attainment are only part of the problem. Because so many adult immigrants are from the poorer nations on the planet, there is also reason to be concerned over the quality of the actual education many adult immigrants claim to have received during the years of schooling they did complete. Low levels of educational attainment, made worse by low educational achievement, only enhance the odds that many adult immigrants compete with the considerable pool of adult Americans who also have low educational levels and poor job skills.

This large low-skilled segment of the adult labor force consistently has the highest unemployment rates of all adult educational attainment categories. Similarly, the labor market experiences of youths who also are highly concentrated in the low-skilled labor market are typically even far worse.

Under these circumstances, an immigration policy that permits massive numbers of unskilled workers to enter the country legally and illegally and to seek work is a major threat to the economic well-being of this large segment of the labor force. Unfortunately, those who benefit from keeping the low skilled labor market in a constant state of surplus typically show little interest in the harm immigration policies can do to those citizen workers who already have the greatest difficulty finding jobs and earning livable wages. Policymakers, however, should not have that luxury of thoughtful neglect.

"Unless there is another compelling interest, such as in the entry of nuclear families and refugees, it is not in the national interest to admit unskilled workers." (U.S. Commission on Immigration Reform, 1995: 24)

Because of the aforementioned principle of social justice, the use of immigration policy to admit unskilled workers—other than in the specified cases of allowing unskilled members of nuclear families (that is, spouses, minor children, and elderly parents) and of refugees who are fleeing from persecution on specified grounds—should be off the table. No matter how hard advanced economies have tried, most have been unsuccessful in eliminating low-paid jobs for unskilled workers (the "secondary labor market").

The low-skilled labor market is a unique phenomenon. It includes not only those adult workers who are unskilled; it is also open to adults who are better skilled but, because of special circumstances (such as fluctuations in national unemployment levels or the existence of certain regional pockets of high unemployment even when the national unemployment rates are low) can do the unskilled work if they cannot find jobs at their higher skill level. Better-skilled adult workers can always do unskilled work if they must but, by definition, unskilled workers cannot qualify for skilled jobs.

Moreover, youths (16–19 years old) and young adults (20–24 years old) also are major participants in the unskilled labor markets as they seek discretionary income and begin the process of acquiring work experience and independence from their parents. Employers usually prefer unskilled adult workers to youthful workers due to their greater dependency on income. But they do hire youths for many of these same jobs if they have to do so. For most youths, it is vital that they have access to the unskilled labor market as they transition from being youths to becoming adults and from becoming part-time workers to becoming full-time workers. Persons who have trouble entering the labor force during their youth usually have continuing employment difficulties in their adulthood.

Hence, given the enormous size of the available pool of citizen adults and youths who compete for the available jobs in the unskilled labor market, it is hard to imagine the existence of genuine shortages of low-skilled workers that could not be filled by offering slightly higher wages as a cure (which, of course, is what free-market economic theory would suggest). It should not be the role of immigration policy to keep wage rates low for low-skilled workers.

Furthermore, there are few if any productivity gains for the economy if unskilled adult immigrants are encouraged (or allowed) to immigrate as long as the unemployment rates for unskilled adult citizen workers are well above the national average unemployment rate for the civilian labor force and persistently remain so, which is typically the case. If by chance in the future the unemployment rates for unskilled workers do fall below the national unemployment rate and genuine labor shortages for them do develop, there is no easier public policy problem to resolve. Experience has consistently demonstrated that, if invited to immigrate, low-skilled workers will come in droves.

"Immigration can support the national interest by bringing to the US individuals whose skills would benefit our society."

(U.S. Commission on Immigration Reform, 1995: 20)

Except for those aforementioned situations whereby there is a "compelling national interest" to admit adult persons without regard to their skill levels, legal immigration should be limited to adults who have high skill levels: persons with advanced professional degrees, persons with college degrees, and persons with specialized work skills and multiple years of on-the-job work experience. Immigration policy can, if domestic labor-market conditions warrant, supplement domestic programs of human resource development that require post-secondary levels of educations as well as those that provide specific skill training for job entry.

There should be limits on these entries, however, as immigration should never be permitted to undercut the wage and benefit levels that are needed to provide incentives to persons to invest in their own human-capital preparation and for communities to expend the tax revenues to provide such learning opportunities. But, in those occupations in which the adult unemployment rates are significantly below the national unemployment rates for all adult workers, immigration can play a supportive role to augment the need for a greater skilled labor supply. In the process, the productivity of the labor force is enhanced and economic growth for society is encouraged. But, inviting skilled immigrants to gain permanent residence and citizenship is not the preferred route to augmenting the skill levels of the labor force. It should always be considered a supplemental route to be used only when real labor shortages can be demonstrated. "Brain-draining" other countries of their highly skilled human resources should never be seen as a reliable or socially useful long-term strategy.

The number of such employment-based skilled immigrants should be flexible but the tendency always should be to reduce the number downward as circumstances change in order to encourage domestic education and training programs to increase their graduates in the shortage occupations. Hitting a legislated entry cap (such as provided in the Immigration Act of 1990) in a specific year, therefore, should not warrant a conclusion that the existing cap is too low. A cap is a cap. A shortage in the short run should not mean automatically that more skilled immigrants be admitted. First recourse should always be to allow market forces to signal the domestic education and training system to respond. If over time it is clear that these systems cannot provide more graduates or that demographic shifts such as an aging population or declining fertility rates will adversely affect future skill availability, the numbers (that is, the cap) for skilled immigrants can be raised.

"If US immigration policy is to serve this nation's interests, it must be enforced effectively. This nation has a responsibility to its people—citizens and permanent residents—and failure to enforce immigration law means not living up to that responsibility."

(Select Commission on Immigration and Refugee Policy, 1981: 12)

As the United States in 2008 has an estimated 12 to 14 million illegal immigrants living in the country (even after seven amnesties since 1986 that have legalized the status of over 6 million earlier illegal immigrants), the nation's enforcement experience can be judged to be a colossal failure of public policy. In the face of this failure, the importance of enforcing immigration laws cannot be overstated. Immigration policy is a nation's most fundamental labor law. It sets a baseline that legally defines who is eligible to be in the domestic labor force. Common sense says that nations that claim to adhere to the principle of "the rule of law" should enforce the laws they enact, especially when they involve such basic issues as the employment, income, and working conditions of its citizens.

When politicians lack the courage to enforce immigration laws, it breeds cynicism among the populace, causes unnecessary hardship for those citizen and permanent resident workers who must compete with illegal immigrant workers, and it widely opens the door to the exploitation of illegal immigrant workers by unscrupulous employers. The responsible course for public policy is to treat the enforcement of immigration laws as being as important as all of the welcoming immigrant services that are also associated with such laws. The fact that they often are not enforced represents the seamier side of some contemporary democracies.

"Except in national emergencies, guestworker programs [for unskilled workers] are bad public policy. They may meet the short term pleas of private interest groups, but they can never meet the higher standard of being policies that serve the national interest." (Briggs, 2004: 7)

No element on immigration policy has been more thoroughly researched and more consistently found to be unworthy of adoption than the proposals to admit unskilled foreign workers for temporary periods into advanced industrialized nations other than in times of national emergencies. Known more popularly as "guestworker programs," they consistently fail in practice because they cannot reconcile two strongly conflicting goals: on the one hand, the need to protect citizen workers from the competition of foreign workers who are willing to work for wages and under employment conditions that few citizens would tolerate (they are essentially "indentured servants"); on the other, the insatiable demands of some employers who rely on labor-intensive production and service techniques for a plentiful supply of low-cost workers.

Although the simplicity of the idea of using foreign workers on a temporary basis to meet an immediate labor shortage or as a possible remedy to illegal immigration makes it seem attractive, every national commission in the United States that has studied this notion has concluded from past experiences with such endeavors that they should not be included in a nation's immigration system. In a nutshell, they have been found to be hard to design, they are almost impossible to administer efficiently, they are politically difficult to end, they stigmatize certain jobs as being "only for foreigners," they depress wages for citizen workers in the same occupations and industries, they over-burden local health, housing, education, and social services in local communities, and they tend to encourage illegal immigration (especially by "visa overstayers").

To be successful, immigration policy debates must "overcome the four horsemen of parochialism, xenophobic demagoguery, 'knee jerkism', and perfectionism." (Hesburgh, 1981: 25)

The downfall of most legislative efforts to reform existing immigration policies can generally be ascribed to their falling prey to one or more of these apocalyptic "four horsemen." They can destroy the best-intended reform attempts.

Parochialism

The first obstacle to overcome is parochialism. If policymakers believe that they can design comprehensive and effective measures, without regard to lessons that can be learned by looking at the experiences of other similarly situated nations and how they have wrestled with the issue in the contemporary, international setting, they will probably fail. Furthermore, the United Nations Population Council has already warned that immigration is the "human crisis" issue of the twenty-first century (UN Population Fund, 1993: 15). It notes that with about 95% of the world's population growth occurring in third-world nations and with the prospect for proportionate job growth in most of these nations ranging from poor to non-existent, the pressures in these countries to emigrate is already immense and will only worsen.

Inclusion of proposals to address the "push" factors in these countries should be part of any truly comprehensive strategy to adopt and enforce an immigration policy for the advanced economies of the world. This does not mean that the problems of these sending nations can be solved by widely opening the doors of the advanced nations to receive the human outflow. Immigration policy alone cannot solve any of the dilemmas of these nations. But parallel efforts to provide assistance with economic development, to reduce trade barriers, to support family planning initiatives, and to link support for these programs to aggressive efforts in these countries to adhere to international human-rights standards, to adopt and to enforce labor standards, and to eliminate governmental corruption could at least reduce some of the pressures on immigration policy from refugees, those seeking political asylum, and illegal immigrants.

Xenophobic and xenophilic demagoguery

The second obstacle to overcome is xenophobic demagoguery. Although it may be impossible to "defang" (as one US senator once proclaimed) the tenor of immigration policy debates in free societies, the one issue that will kill such efforts for certain is if the debate falls prey to fear of would-be immigrants because of their race, national origins, or religions. Free societies are based on a toleration of differences and the use of diversity as an instrument of building national strength. The principle of *e pluribus unum* is no mere political slogan. Adherence to this concept by free societies serves as a beacon of hope to the world that people with different attributes can, in fact, live in harmony and prosper in the process.

Diversity, therefore, may be a laudable outcome but it should not be a goal *per se* of immigration policy because it is counter to the more basic human right that extols the virtue of the worthiness of the individual's personal characteristics and beliefs. Nonetheless, diversity itself should not be considered a negative outcome to be avoided. There are legitimate reasons that free nations have immigration policies and the restrictions that are inherent in their provisions but fear of human differences should never be one of the prompting rationales. If it does, efforts at immigration reform will be either be ignored or shunted aside into diversionary debates over the actual intentions of the proponents. Xenophobic fears strengthen prejudices and serve to stifle debate, neither of which serves the national interest.

By the same token, xenophilic demagoguery also serves no useful purpose for public discussions of immigration reforms. Immigration is, as mentioned earlier, fundamentally an economic issue in terms of its societal impacts. Exaggerated and uncritical assertions that proclaim the merits of more immigrants while ignoring their fiscal and opportunity costs on the receiving countries does little to further public debate. The mere existence of labor shortages —locally, regionally or nationally—does not mean that more immigration is necessary or desirable as a policy response. Tight labor markets can provide opportunities to direct public attention to the inadequacies of domestic training, education, and labor mobility programs, as well as being chances to re-examine the state of prevailing antidiscrimination efforts that assure that available human resource reservoirs are fully tapped. Furthermore, such efforts at human-resource development can reduce the tendency of expanded immigration to "brain-drain" skilled labor from developing nations where such supplies are always chronically short. Increasing the level of immigration is one way to meet real labor shortages; but it is not the only one or necessarily the preferred first option.

Rational creation of public policy cannot take place if the discussion is caught in a crossfire of propaganda between unloving critics (xenophobes) and uncritical lovers (xenophiles).

Knee-jerkism

The third barrier to reform is "knee-jerkism." Immigration issues are often as complicated as they are controversial. Because nations have immigration policies for multiple reasons, there are often conflicting proposals about how these multiple objectives are to be met and their terms enforced. Quick fixes that are offered as solutions usually fail to appreciate the complexities of the multiple issues involved, they overlook long-term consequences, and they can lead to unexpected consequences.

One of the most notorious examples of "knee jerkism" is the oft-cited efforts of business proponents to press for guestworker programs for specific occupations and industries at the first sign of any difficulties recruiting workers without raising wages or improving working conditions.

Perfectionism

The fourth path to policy failure is the insistence that proposed remedies be perfect in their execution or else they cannot be enacted or must be repealed. Proposals to build border walls, enhance border management techniques, develop personal-identification systems, and adopt methods to enforce sanctions against employers of illegal immigrants are especially vulnerable to such unrealistic expectations. As long as human beings are involved in the design and execution of public policies, there are going to be mistakes of judgment and inadequacies in implementation. They are to be expected. Experience is sometimes the only way to find out what works and what does not.

Predicting how people will respond to public-policy interventions in free labor markets is far more of an art than a science. Moreover, as times change and as experience is gained, even policies once deemed successful may have to be reconsidered. Like virtually all other labor-market policies, immigration policies should be reviewed on a regular basis, not just when a crisis arises.

"The credibility of immigration policy can be measured by a simple yardstick: people who should get in, do get in; people who should not get in, are kept out; and people judged deportable are required to leave."

(U.S. Commission on Immigration Policy, 1997: xvi)

This last principle states the overall performance standard for policy makers in free societies with respect to immigration policy. Adherence to this "yardstick" would assure that serving the public interest is the actual product of their efforts. It is a summary truism that requires no amplification.

The remainder—the political issues

In addition to the aforementioned general principles that might guide immigration debates, there are other uses of immigration policy about which there is less general consensus. These policies are typically justified for political reasons that vary in scope and change over time and from one nation to another even though they too have economic consequences for each nation's labor market. They involve the admission of refugees, the granting of political asylum claims, the use of temporary worker programs for skilled workers, and the creation of special entry programs such as those for foreign investors, "diversity immigrants," religious workers, employees of overseas embassies, victims of human trafficking, foreign students, visiting foreign scholars, and a myriad of others.

Concluding observation

When debating vital national issues such as immigration, democratic societies require participants who are informed, not merely citizens who are opinionated. "Too often," as President John F. Kennedy once warned his nation in 1962, "we subject all facts to a prefabricated set of interpretations. We enjoy the comfort of opinion without the discomfort of thought." Immigration policy requires thought as a predicate for action.

Countries such as Canada and the United States have now had decades of experience with the phenomenon of mass immigration. There are policy lessons that have been learned, whether or not all special-interest groups are comforted by them. These lessons—the principles described in this chapter—may not be universals that are true for all societies for all time. But they do reflect a consensus of thoughtful judgments from parties who are knowledgeable about the subject matter rather than the opinions of partisans whose views are shaped by political opportunities to gain power or private benefit. While politics does have an important and continuing role to play in the formulation of immigration policy, the range of political discourse about immigration could be narrowed considerably if politicians would concede that at least some of the issues have been resolved for the time being—and acted accordingly.

References

Briggs, Vernon M., Jr. (2003). *Mass Immigration and the National Interest: Policy Directions for a New Century*. M.E. Sharpe.

Briggs, Vernon M, Jr. (2004). *Guestworker Programs: Lessons from the Past and Warnings for the Future*. Backgrounder (March). Center for Immigration Studies.

Brubaker, William R. (1989). Citizenship and Naturalization: Policies and Politics. In William R. Brubaker (ed.), *Immigration and the Politics of Citizenship in Europe and North America* (University Press of America): 99–127.

Gompers, Samuel (1925). *Seventy Years of Life and Labor.* Volume 2. Dutton.

Hesburgh, Rev. Theodore M. (1981). *Testimony before the Joint Hearings of the Subcommittee on Immigration and Refugee Policy of the U.S. Senate Committee on the Judiciary and the Subcommittee on Immigration, Refugees and International Law of the U.S. House of Representatives Committee on the Judiciary, May 5, 1981.* U.S. Government Printing Office.

Reder, Melvin W. (1963). The Economic Consequences of Increased Immigration. *Review of Economics and Statistics* 45,3 (August): 223–30.

Select Commission on Immigration and Refugee Policy (1981). *U.S. Immigration Policy and the National Interest* (March 1).

Select Commission on Immigration and Refugee Policy (1997). *Becoming an American: Immigration and Immigrant Policy* (September).

United Nations Population Fund (1993). *The State of World Population: 1993.* United Nations Population Fund.

U.S. Commission on Immigration Policy (1995). *Legal Immigration: Setting Priorities* (June).

Chapter 5

Is Canadian immigration too high?

A labor market and productivity perspective

Patrick Grady

Canada's immigration has been continuing at a very high level since the Mulroney government opened the door more widely in the mid-1980s (figure 5.1). Over 250,000 new permanent residents and 113,000 temporary foreign workers were welcomed to Canada in 2006 (Citizenship and Immigration Canada, 2007). Bringing in such a large number of new residents has wide-ranging implications for the Canadian economy, affecting Gross Domestic Product (GDP), real incomes, the labor force, employment, the unemployment rate, and even poverty. Yet there is very little understanding of these impacts and how they affect both existing Canadian residents and the new arrivals.

This chapter presents some of the economic considerations that should underlie Canadian immigration policy and reviews the available data on the performance of recent immigrants against this backdrop. It also offers some observations on the changes to the *Immigration and Refugee Protection Act* (Bill C-11) contained in Bill C-50, the *Budget Implementation Act, 2008*. Finally, it concludes with some suggestions for the conduct of an immigration policy that would be based more on Canada's economic interests and that would establish a lower annual target for immigration more consistent with Canada's absorptive capacity.

Figure 5.1: Immigration of permanent residents and temporary foreign workers (1980–2006)

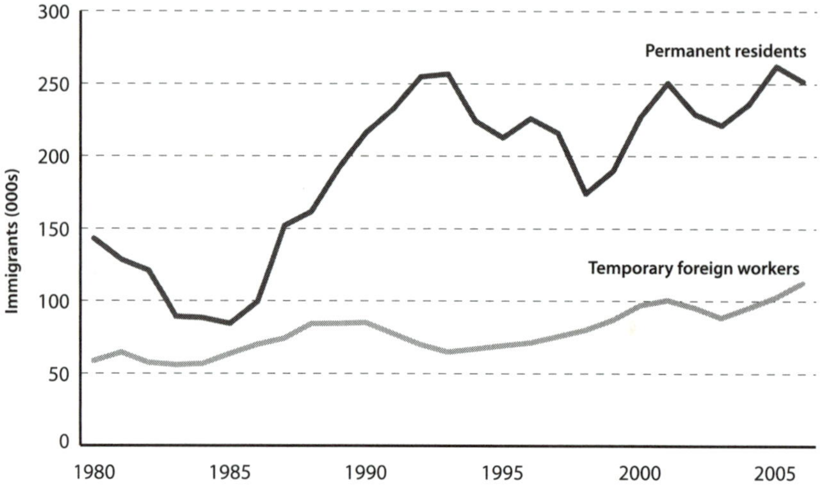

Source: Citizenship and Immigration Canada, 2007.

Economic considerations

Economic growth

All economists agree that immigration increases the population and thus the GDP of Canada. However, the impact of immigration on per-capita GDP is a matter of much controversy both on theoretical and practical grounds. There is agreement that, in the past when tariffs and trade barriers were much higher than now, immigration was important in increasing the size of the Canadian market and realizing economies of scale, which raised the income of all. However, now with the Free Trade Agreement (FTA) and the North American Free Trade Agreement (NAFTA) and globalization, it is generally agreed that there is no longer any reason to expect economies of scale. In fact, some believe that there could even be diseconomies of scale caused by urban congestion and pollution as are now evident in Toronto. In the economist's simple theoretical world described by the Cobb-Douglas production function without economies of scale and with two factors of production and a homogeneous labor force, immigration does not necessarily increase per-capita income unless it raises productivity. And for immigrants to raise aggregate productivity, they must be more productively employed than existing residents, meaning they must earn higher incomes.

There are also impacts of immigration on the country of origin that need to be taken into consideration in any overall analysis. These include the negative impact of losing some of their most productive citizens and the resulting reductions in output as well as the positive effects of increased land-to-labor and capital-to-labor ratios on per-capita output and incomes, and of remittances. However, these are not the focus of this paper as it deals with the main impact of immigration on Canada.

Productivity

Productivity has become a Canadian obsession. Immigration is said to be necessary to raise Canadian productivity and to enable us to compete internationally. The exact mechanism that produces these benefits is usually not stated other than to say that immigration opens Canada to new ideas and markets.

It must be acknowledged that there are some very prominent entrepreneurs who came to Canada as immigrants and made major contributions to the development of the economy. A partial list of some of the most important would include: Michael Lee-Chin (Chinese-Jamaican); David Azrieli (Iranian); Frank Stronach (Austrian); Arjun Sharma (Indian); Victor Li (Hong Kong Chinese); Hassan Khosrowshahi (Iranian); Terry Mathews (Great Britain); Peter Munk (Czech); and Josef Straus (Austrian).[1] The contributions to productivity made by these extraordinary individuals would certainly go well beyond their own earnings. But, on the other hand, there is a much larger group of recent immigrants who have not done so well and whose contributions can be measured by their earnings. Somewhat ironically, their earnings in Canada are usually higher than the average in their home countries but lower than average in Canada.

Growth accounting is a commonly used approach for estimating the impact on productivity of various factors such as education and the age and sex of those who make up the labor force. It involves using earnings weights to distinguish the effects of the various factors. When applied over the period from 1990 to 2004, it suggests that immigration has lowered productivity by around 1.5% or 0.15% per year (Grady, 2006). While this

---

1 ◆ Most names on this list come from List of Canadians by Net Worth, *Wikipedia*, <http://en.wikipedia.org/wiki/List_of_Canadians_by_net_worth> (last modified July 9, 2009).

is not very large, it is still significant and runs counter to the claims usually made regarding the productivity-enhancing effect of immigration.

One possible source of the gap between productivity in Canada and the United States is the lower level of capital per capita that results in Canada from immigration at least in the short run. Rao, Tang, and Wang (2003: 31) attributed 12% of the gap between productivity in Canada and the United States to the lower intensity of capital. Since immigration decreases capital intensity at least in the short run by raising labor by a larger percentage than capital, it would be fair to conclude that immigration has contributed to the decrease in productivity through this channel.

Robert Putnam (2007), the Harvard sociologist who made his name studying social capital, has recently been reluctantly forced to come to the conclusion that immigration and diversity are reducing social solidarity and social capital. It is not a long step from this to the conclusion that immigration could undermine productivity. While this type of impact would be very difficult to measure, it could ultimately turn out to be significant.

Competitiveness

Productivity and competitiveness are not the same thing. Low-wage labor can increase competitiveness, even if it lowers aggregate productivity, by complementing more highly skilled labor and lowering costs. Any such benefit in Canada, however, would be largely accidental as the government is not actually seeking to attract low-wage labor through its immigration policy. Rather, it is the result of highly educated immigrants not being able to find high-skilled jobs and being forced to take low-wage employment. Moreover, any potential competitiveness benefits from the existence of potential low-wage labor can be offset by social-welfare programs that discourage work and that must be financed through taxation. Milton Friedman warned that you can't have both free immigration and the Welfare State.

The needs of the labor market

The existing high level of immigration is usually justified on the basis of the needs of the labor market. The implication is that, if these needs are not met, the consequences for the economy will be dire. Employers are always griping about shortages of labor. But you will never hear them saying anything about the need to raise wages to attract more workers. They seem conveniently to forget that the labor market is a mechanism that has both a price and a quantity dimension. The production process can always make use of more labor if there is a surplus of people willing to work for low wages. An important reason that agriculture in California is so much more labor intensive than European agriculture is the availability of low-wage labor.

An increased foreign supply of various categories of labor will over time tend to depress the domestic supply of the same categories. If large numbers of immigrants are admitted to Canada with certain levels of education and skills, it will make it harder for young Canadians to compete in the labor markets demanding these skills and will discourage them from acquiring the same credentials unless, of course, those of the immigrants are substantially discounted or not recognized, as seems to be increasingly the case in Canada. Engineering and computer science is an example of a profession where in 2000 more immigrants were being allowed in than were graduating from Canadian universities.

The impact of immigration on the labor market

The impact of immigration on the labor market has many dimensions. It encompasses the labor-force participation rates, employment rates, and unemployment rates of immigrants. It also includes their wages and earnings. And in addition, it includes the indirect effects of increased immigrant labor supply on the labor-market outcomes of the Canadian born.

The impact of immigration can be better understood with the help of the standard textbook partial equilibrium demand-and-supply diagram (figure 5.2). If labor were homogeneous, immigration (of L1–L1′) would raise labor supply from S0 to S1. This would push the wage down from W0 to W1 and reduce the amount of existing resident labor supply from L0 to L1′.

In the real world, the situation is, of course, much more complicated. Immigrant labor is not necessarily the same as resident labor in all respects. It can be more skilled or less, more or less highly educated, and have a different occupational mix. It can also be a substitute for, or complement to, resident labor. And, over time, the demand curve for labor will shift out because of the increased demand for goods and services produced by labor and because of capital investment.

Figure 5.2: Demand and supply in partial equilibrium

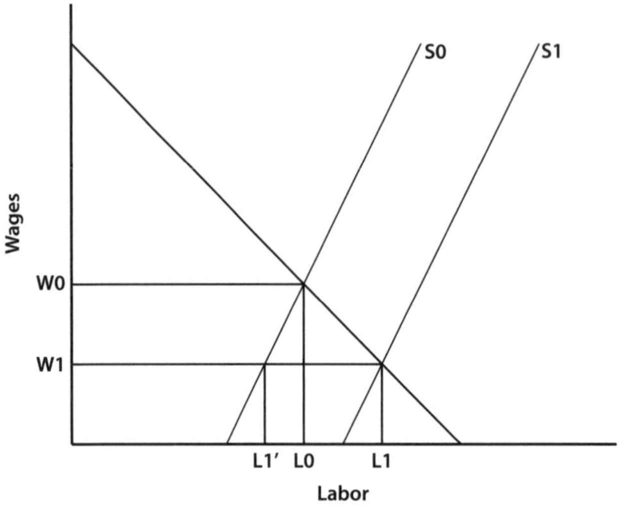

There has been much debate in the United States over the impact of immigration on wages. The early studies examined the impact of the geographic clustering of immigrants in local labor markets and found small impacts. Subsequent research by George Borjas, which considered the supply shifts across groups with different educational experience, concluded that wages fall by 3% to 4% for every 10% increase in the number of workers in a particular skill group (Borjas, 2003). David Card, who was responsible for some of the earlier studies, questioned these findings on the basis of his own subsequent research, which showed that the wages of high-school dropouts remained nearly constant relative to high-school graduates since 1980 in spite of increased numbers of immigrants without high-school education (Card, 2005: 25).

The main Canadian study of the impact of immigration on wages was done by Abdurrahman Aydemir and George J. Borjas (2006). It found that a 10% labor-supply shift caused by immigration would result in a 3% to 4% reduction in wages in Canada as well as in the United States. Interestingly, because of the different skill mix of immigrants, migration narrowed wage inequality in Canada (where the immigrants were highly educated) but increased it in the United States (where they were not).

Even though the empirical evidence on the impact of immigration on wages is not definitive, the notion that immigration lowers wages is consistent with economic theory and the textbook view that the demand curve for labor slopes downward.

Growing realization that immigration has not been working as in the past

Up until around 1980, the pattern as revealed in the census was that immigrants to Canada started out earning about 80% or so of equivalent Canadian born, but then moved up to and even beyond the average over a 10-to-20-year period. In subsequent years, at the same time as the source countries and other characteristics of immigrants such as language and job experience changed, there was a substantial deterioration in the labor-market performance of immigrants. In 1993, the point system was modified to put more emphasis on education. Selecting immigrants based on their education rather than their specific job skills has been called the "human capital" approach. It can be contrasted with the "occupational needs" approach, which attempts to identify occupational classes where workers are in short supply and to admit immigrants in these classes.

In order to improve the labor-market performance of new immigrants, the Skilled Class of immigrants was increased and the Family Class reduced starting in 1994. This move was reinforced in 2002, with more points being awarded for a trade certificate or second degree, and less for experience. The result of these two policy changes was an increase in the Skilled Class relative to the Family Class (figure 5.3) and a dramatic increase in the educational level of immigrants (figure 5.4).

While there has been some improvement since 2001 as the labor market tightened, the employment rate of recent immigrants in 2006 was still substantially lower than for the Canadian born, particularly for women (figure 5, table 5.1). The unemployment rate has come down, especially for recent immigrant men, but was almost twice as high for men and three times as high for women as for the Canadian born. The poor labor-market performance of recent immigrants is greatest for recent immigrants from Africa and to a lesser extent Asia and Latin America (table 5.2). More ominously,

Figure 5.3: Immigration of family class and skilled workers (1980–2006)

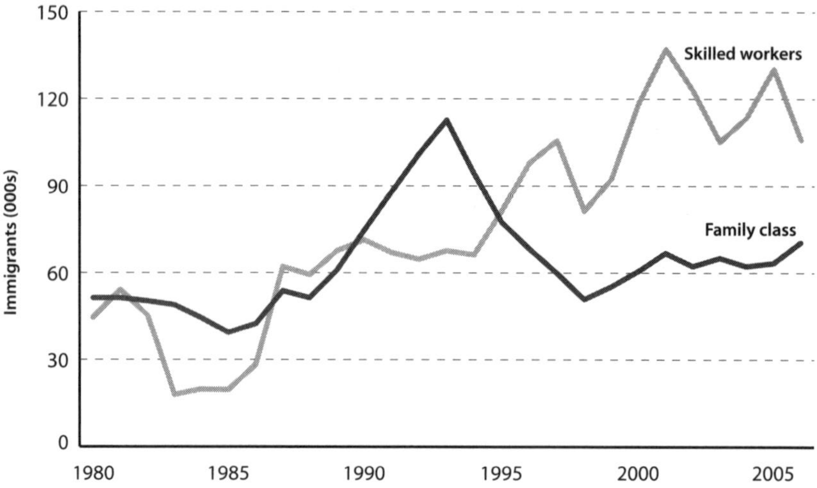

Source: Citizenship and Immigration Canada, 2007.

Figure 5.4: Immigrants, 15+ years of age, by level of education (1980–2006)

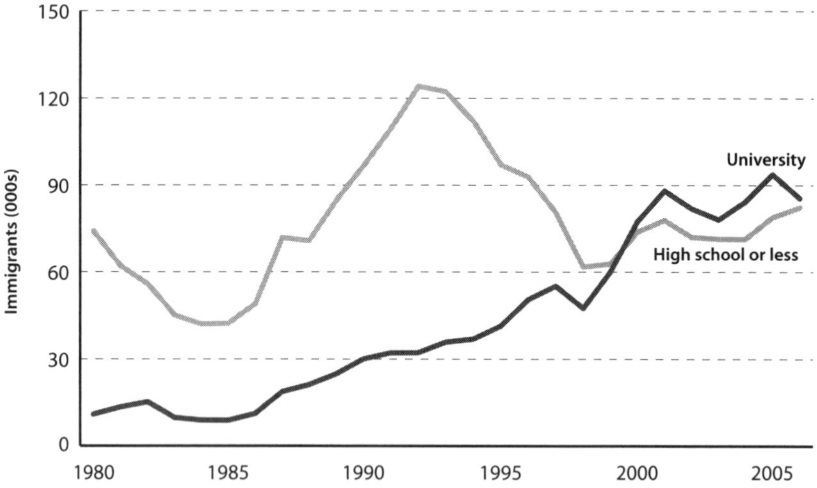

Source: Citizenship and Immigration Canada, 2007.

Figure 5.5: Employment rates of recent immigrants and the Canadian-born, ages 25 to 54 years

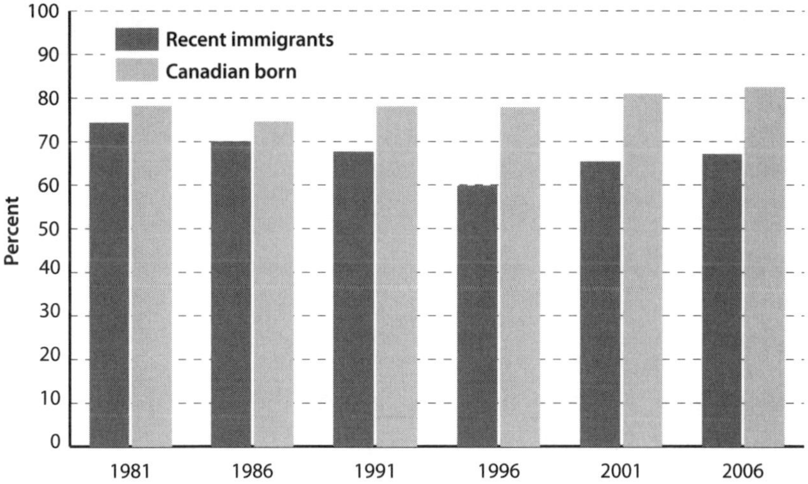

Source: Statistics Canada, Censuses.

Table 5.1: Employment and unemployment rates (%) of recent immigrants and Canadian born aged 25 to 54 (%)

	Men		Women	
	Employment Rate	Unemployment Rate	Employment Rate	Unemployment Rate
Recent immigrants				
2001	74.5	11.4	53.2	15.7
2006	78.6	9.3	56.8	14.3
Canadian born				
2001	85.7	6.3	76.3	5.7
2006	86.3	5.2	78.5	5.0

Source: Statistics Canada, 2008a: 30.

Table 5.2: Employment and unemployment rates (%) of very recent immigrants aged 25 to 54, by place of origin, 2006

	Men		Women	
	Employment Rate	Unemployment Rate	Employment Rate	Unemployment Rate
Europe	84.5	6.5	63.6	10.6
Latin America	78.8	8.7	55.3	13
Africa	65.7	19.8	43.1	21.9
Asia	77.6	9.8	52.2	12.8

Source: Gilmore, 2008b: 34–37.

any downturn in the labor market resulting from the current economic slowdown is likely to affect recent immigrants from the source countries with the poorest performance disproportionately.

In recent years, in spite of the changes in immigration policy introduced by the government, the earnings of recent immigrants have continued to deteriorate relative to those of equivalent Canadian-born workers (figure 5.6). In 2005, recent immigrant men only earned $30,332 if they had a university degree and $24,470 if they did not (table 5.3). Recent immigrant women only earned $18,969 with a degree and $14,233 without. The gap is greatest for those with a university degree where recent immigrants earn less than half that earned by the Canadian born (table 5.4). And the deterioration was largest for women with no degree and men with a university degree. Most troubling of all is the downtrend in the relative performance of recent immigrants, which shows no signs of abating even as the labor market tightened.

Table 5.3: Median earnings, in 2005 constant dollars, of male and female recent immigrant earners aged 25 to 54

	With university degree		With no university degree	
	males	females	males	females
1980	48,541	24,317	36,467	18,548
1990	38,351	25,959	27,301	17,931
2000	35,816	22,511	25,951	16,794
2005	30,332	18,969	24,470	14,233

Source: Statistics Canada, 2008b: 22.

Figure 5.6: Ratio of earnings of immigrants to earnings of the Canadian born, by educational level and sex

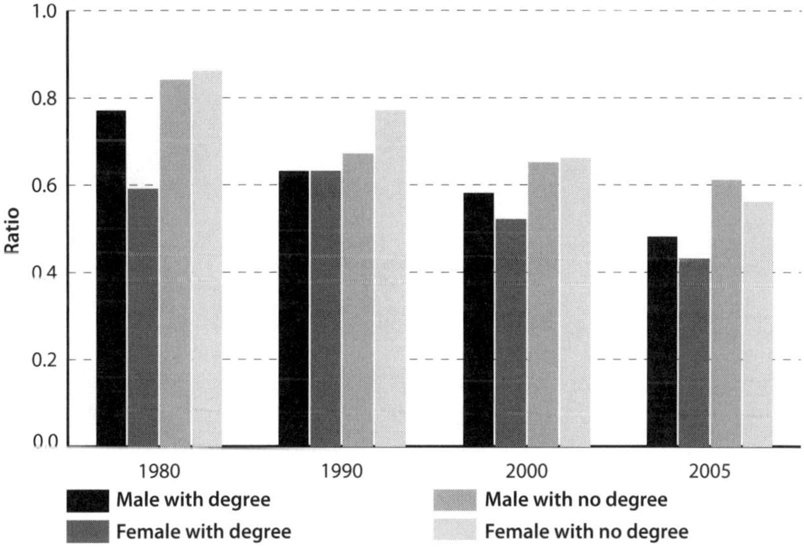

Source: Statistics Canada, 2008b: 22.

Table 5.4: Ratio between earnings of recent immigrants and of Canadian born

	With university degree		With no university degree	
	males	females	males	females
1980	0.77	0.59	0.84	0.86
1990	0.63	0.63	0.67	0.77
2000	0.58	0.52	0.65	0.66
2005	0.48	0.43	0.61	0.56

Source: Statistics Canada, 2008b: 22.

Recent immigrants from the United States, the United Kingdom, and Oceania (mainly Australia and New Zealand) earned the most (figure 5.7). Immigrants from these countries have the advantage of being native speakers of English and benefit from the relatively high quality of their countries' educational systems and the similar industrial structures of their economies. Recent immigrants from Asia, southeastern Europe, Latin America, and the Caribbean had lower earnings than other recent immigrants.

Figure 5.7: Relative earnings of recently immigrated males aged 25 to 44 who worked all year, full time

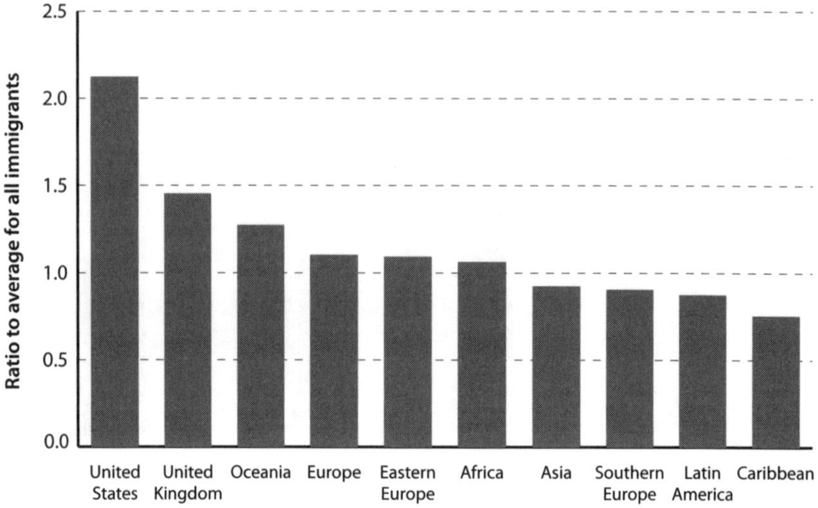

Note: Average for all immigrants equals 1.

Source: Statistics Canada, Census 2001; data for 2005 not available at time of writing.

Citizenship and Immigration Canada has attributed the continuing deterioration to the IT Bust

In an effort to avoid the obvious, but politically unpopular, conclusion that Canada is allowing in more immigrants than can be absorbed by the Canadian labor market, officials from Citizenship and Immigration Canada (CIC) have attributed the continuing deterioration in the relative earnings of recent immigrants to the bursting of the high-tech bubble in 2000 (Picot and Hou, 2008: 24). It cannot be denied that CIC cast caution to the wind when it attempted to fill anticipated labor-market needs during the high-tech boom of the late 1990s by admitting a disproportionate number of computer professionals and engineers. In fact, at the peak a third of the skilled immigrants admitted were computer professionals and engineers. And, sure, there was the bust. But it occurred in early 2000. So why was there still a problem in 2005 after the market had improved and engineering and IT salaries had recovered? And IT professionals and engineers are supposed to have a superior knowledge of the computer and information technology and the related skills that have come to occupy a central place in our modern information economy.

Why were they not able to find alternative employment at higher relative wages? This episode reveals the dangers of allowing CIC and Human Resources and Skills Development Canada (HRSDC) to pick professions in demand given the long lags in processing them for the granting of visas. What will be CIC's next big mistake when it attempts to anticipate occupational demand?

Why do immigrants keep coming?

Given that immigrants do not do as well economically as the Canadian born, one might wonder why they so stubbornly keep coming in such large numbers. The answer is quite simple: they do much better here than in their home countries. The *Longitudinal Survey of Immigrants to Canada* conducted in 2003 reported that new immigrants had a high level of satisfaction with their job two years after landing (84%). And 70% reported that "their experience either met or exceeded their expectations" (Statistics Canada, 2003: 11). And, it is not because the recent immigrants who come to Canada from developing countries earn lower-than-average earnings in their home countries. In fact, they probably earn more than average there even though they will earn less than average in Canada.

Some political explanations for the performance of recent immigrants in labor markets

Some immigrant groups and lobbyists have been quick to place the blame for the disappointing performance of recent immigrants on the usual suspects. Canadians are racists, they claim. And since most of the recent immigrants are visible minorities, their relatively poor employment and earnings prospects are the result of discrimination pure and simple (Flecker, 2007). But this leaves unanswered the simple question: why are Canadians willing to welcome so many immigrants?

Others, such as the Bouchard Taylor Commission (Québec, 2008), contend that the poor performance of recent immigrants is the government's fault, since it does not spend enough money to help immigrants settle. This includes shortfalls in expenditures on such activities as training, subsidized internships and mentoring, language education, and credentials assessment and validation. While there is something to be said for programs to help immigrants integrate, one should not be socially ostracized for observing that the government's past record in designing and delivering such programs has not been a great success.

Analytical studies on labor market performance

An appropriate policy response to the poor outcomes experienced by recent immigrants requires a sound understanding of the causal factors at play. Fortunately, Garnet Picot and his colleagues at Statistics Canada have produced many very high-quality research studies analyzing the available data to try to learn why immigrants are doing so poorly in the labor market. A convenient survey of the studies is provided by Garnett Picot and Arthur Sweetman (2005).[2] They attribute the decline in entry earnings and increasing low-income rates to: the changing characteristics of immigrants, including country of origin, language, and education, which appears to have accounted for about a third of the increase in the earnings gap; the decreasing returns to foreign work experience, which accounts for another third; and the decline in the labor-market outcome of all new labor-force entrants including immigrants. They also discuss a possible reduction in the return on education and quality differences in education. To put it simply, Canadian employers do not value foreign experience and heavily discount the value of foreign education. A lack of fluency in English or French is also a problem (Grondin, 2005).

The importance of educational quality

There is growing evidence that Canadian employers are not just being stupid and that they have reasonable grounds to discount the value of foreign education. The disconnect between education and skills for many immigrants from third-world countries seems to be a definite factor explaining the poorer earnings performance. An obvious source of this discrepancy identified by Schaafsma (2004) is the lower quality of the education in these countries. That this might be the case had earlier been suggested in studies such as that by Schaafsma and Sweetman (2001) that showed that immigrants with Canadian education perform as well as the Canadian born. Moreover, Sweetman (2004) measured educational quality using

2 ◆ A more technical analysis is offered in Aydemir and Skuterud, 2005.

international data and used it to explain labor-market performance. Bonikowska, Green, and Riddell (2006) using the International Adult Literacy Survey, identified a 45-percentage-point difference between the average skill-level test scores of immigrants with no Canadian education and those of the native born. The differences in test scores explain half of the earnings gap for university-educated immigrants. Using the same survey, Coulombe and Tremblay (2005) a report skills-learning gap of 3.0 years for immigrants and 2.1 years even for those whose first language was English or French. That is enough to make a foreign university graduate with a pass degree equivalent to a Canadian high-school graduate.

The latest ranking compiled in 2007 by the Institute of Higher Education at the Shanghai Jiao Tong University (2007) provides an indicator of the quality of the university education in the immigrant-source countries. It is telling that only one university from outside the industrialized world, the State University of Moscow, is on the list of the top 100 universities. In contrast, Canada has four. And there are only 23 universities from the third world among the top 500, whereas Canada has 22. Very few third-world countries have universities in the elite: China (excluding Hong Kong) (12), India (2), Chile (2), Brazil (4), Mexico, Egypt, Turkey. There are none in the Philippines, Pakistan, or Iran, the third, fourth, and sixth top sources (after China and India) for immigrants to Canada in 2006.

It is important to know how many third-world immigrants actually attended any of these elite institutions in their countries or abroad, for that matter, since that is where the real, highly skilled, knowledge workers would have to come from. In contrast, it is known that most Canadian students graduate from the elite Canadian universities since, in effect, almost all the larger Canadian universities are classified as elite. And the same can be said of immigrants who get their university education after landing in Canada, which, by the way, might explain why they tend to do about as well economically as native-born Canadians.

The problem of increasing poverty among immigrants

The poor performance of recent immigrants in the labor market has caused a much larger proportion of recent immigrants than Canadian born to fall below Statistics Canada's Low Income Cut-Off, which is the most widely used indicator of poverty (figure 5.8). The incidence of poverty has been highest for recent immigrants from Africa and Asia (table 5.5) and it explains why poverty has been increasing in the main immigrant-receiving centers of Toronto, Montreal, and Vancouver, where immigrants are becoming increasingly ghettoized (Hou and Picot, 2004). At the same time as poverty has been rising in the immigrant community, it has been falling among the Canadian born. A growing disparity between rich and poor is emerging along ethnic and racial lines. There is a risk that this might undermine the dynamic of intergenerational upward mobility that has made Canadian immigration policy so successful in the past.

Consequences of the poor performance of immigrants for immigration policy

The high and growing level of immigrant poverty calls into question the economic rationale for a high level of immigration. It is to be expected that poor immigrants will take advantage of existing social and welfare programs and perhaps even demand more as their political clout increases.

Figure 5.8: Immigrants living below the Low Income Cut Off, by number of years since immigration, compared to Canadian born

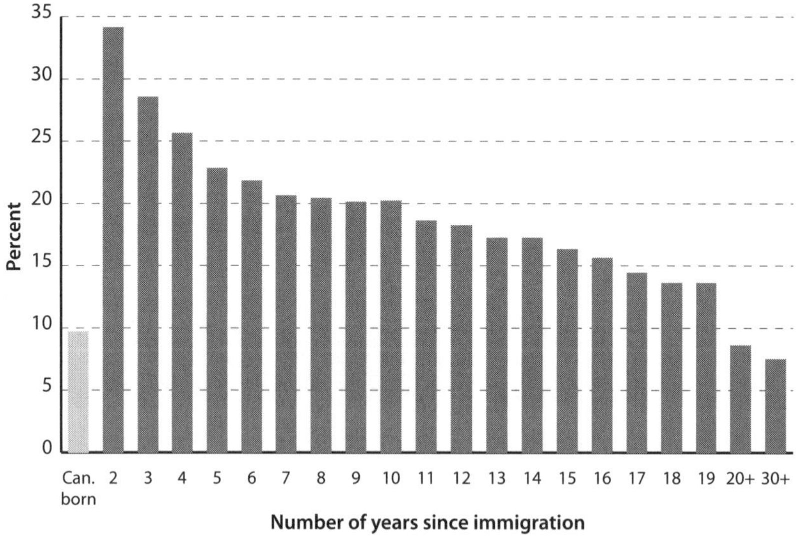

Source: Statistics Canada, Census 2006.

Table 5.5: Low-income rates (%) for immigrant economic families (2000), total and by place of origin

	Total	Period of immigration						
		Before 1961	1961–1970	1971–1980	1981–1990	1991–2001	1991–1995	1996–2001
Immigrant population	19.1	6.8	8.2	10.4	17.2	33.6	25.2	41.2
Place of origin								
United States	10.0	4.2	5.8	7.5	9.7	19.2	13.3	23.2
Europe	10.9	6.9	8.4	8.2	10.5	24.7	14.5	33.7
Africa	28.1	7.1	7.2	10	20.7	42.6	34.8	48.8
Asia	26.9	8.7	8.3	11.3	19.4	36.8	27.8	44.6

Note: The figure for the non-immigrant population is 11.2%.

Source: Statistics Canada, Census, 2001.

In the past, immigrants used to have a lower incidence of reliance on government transfers than the Canadian born, primarily because of their age and ineligibility (or reduced eligibility for certain programs like old age security, C/QPP, and social assistance. However, the 2006 census reported that in 2005 recent non-senior immigrant families with children now receive a higher proportion of their income from government transfer payments than the Canadian born (Statistics Canada, 2008b: 40). If recent adverse trends continue, taxes will eventually have to be raised (or tax cuts have to be smaller than otherwise) to pay for the required increase in spending. This will create disincentives for growth. For new immigrants not to be a fiscal drain, eventually they will need to be capable of earning at least as much as everyone else and certainly to avoid joining the ranks of the poor.

The Conservative government was well aware of the poor performance of recent immigrants and recognized that a continuation of the current immigration policy was only going to make the situation much worse. The *Immigration and Refugee Protection Act* (Bill C-11), passed in a rush after September 11, 2001 by the previous Liberal Government, required the government to process all applications to immigrate to Canada and to admit those who meet the selection criteria set out in the Regulations. This gave the Minister relatively little discretion in selecting immigrants. And, in the mind of some, it conferred a new right to immigrate to Canada on anyone who met the selection criteria, in effect, overriding Canada's right to establish an immigration policy in its own national interest. The result was a backlog of qualified applicants that reached 925,000 early in 2008 and was forecast to grow to 1.5 million by 2012 if nothing were done. As a consequence, the wait time for landing was anticipated to increase from the current six years currently to 10 years. Obviously the immigration system was out of control even on administrative grounds. The government consequently had no choice but to act.

Is Bill C-50 the solution?

The amendments to the *Immigration and Refugee Protection Act* passed as part of Bill C-50, *The Budget Implementation Act, 2008,* have restored to the Minister of Citizenship and Immigration the ability to manage Canada's immigration program. C-50 grants the Minister discretion to decide on which and how many immigrants are to be admitted. It allows the Minister to issue instructions on the processing of applications and requests to ensure that Canada's immigration goals are met. This will enable the Minister to reduce the time it takes for applicants to be landed and will allow a better matching of the skills and experience of the immigrants with the jobs available in Canada. It will thus, at least, stop the growth of backlog and promises to moderately improve the matching between immigrants and jobs.

But C-50 is only a beginning. It is not the complete solution to the problem. Its main shortfall is that it commits the government to admit everyone in the existing backlog (as of February 27, 2008). These are people who have been selected under the same point system that has produced the deterioration in immigrant earnings and the growing problem of immigrant poverty. And, even worse, the way that the backlog has been allowed to mushroom out of control will probably ensure that many of the immigrants most likely to succeed economically in Canada will have already immigrated elsewhere or found successful careers at home, leaving only those without other options or with a special family attachment to Canada waiting patiently to be landed. A more rational approach would have been to tighten the selection criteria and then to reassess those in the backlog. This would guarantee that those admitted to Canada in the future were those most likely to succeed.

250,000 immigrants is too many

The fundamental problem that no one, especially the government in introducing C-50, is yet willing to acknowledge is that the selection system is incapable of choosing as many as 250,000 immigrants every year who are capable of doing well in the Canadian labor market. And this is even after a 16-year expansion that produced an extremely tight labor market, where the unemployment rate dropped below 6%. The situation can only worsen as unemployment climbs, as is now happening with a vengence as the economy is hit by what appears to be the worst recession of the post-war period.

The only way to ensure that the immigrants chosen will do better is to be more selective. The selection system will have to be revamped and the economic performance of immigrants should be much more carefully monitored. A second, and more fundamental, change in immigration policy should be to lower the global target for immigration to no more than 100,000 a year. This would represent a significant cut from current levels. If it, together with a better selection system, produced the desired improvement in the economic success of immigrants, it could be maintained. If not, it should be reviewed.

There are significant benefits for Canada that could be expected from lower immigration. It would promote the integration of immigrants in labor market. It should lead to an increase in immigrants' earnings. It would stop the increase in poverty. And it would prevent the emergence of a large, net fiscal drain. More generally, a tighter labor market would put upward pressure on wages and incomes of Canadians, which, maybe not coincidently, have stagnated in recent years.

How to improve the selection system

Much can be learned from the Australian method for selecting immigrants. This includes: more careful evaluation of occupational and educational credentials; formalized language testing; and fewer points for older workers (Hawthorne, 2008: 39).

The human-capital model used in the Canadian selection process still has merit but it is important to recognize that education is not homogeneous. If Canadian universities chose foreign students the way CIC selected immigrants, half their classes would flunk out. The government's move to focus on international students and foreign workers through the

Canada Experience Program is a move in right direction. It will also be important to make sure that the government does not try to pursue occupational fine-tuning given its past misadventures.

The tools exist to make sure immigration is working

In the past, the main data source for assessing the degree of integration of immigrants was the census. It provides a rich body of data on labor markets and earnings that can be used for analysis. The problem is that the data was only available every five years and, even then, only after a lag of several years. Some data on immigrant earnings was only released in May 2008 and, even then, the detail by source countries was not available.

More timely data on the performance of immigrants is required if immigration flows are to be more closely matched to the needs and absorption capacity of the Canadian economy. Fortunately, the required tools and data do exist. The Immigration Data Base (IMDB) compiled by CIC contains information on all immigrants landing since 1980, including their annual tax information. This can be matched with the Longitudinal Administrative Database (LAD) containing a 20% T1 tax sample. These databases can be used along with the Labor Force Survey (LFS) to monitor annually the performance of immigrants in the labor market. However, to ensure the success of such monitoring, the number of immigrants admitted has to be adjusted with a relatively short lag if their performance falls below acceptable levels.

The tracking of immigrants' performance through these databases should focus on their earnings relative to comparable Canadian workers. This relationship in the past when the immigration program was working and immigrants were able to catch up saw immigrant workers in their first year after landing earning around 80% of the comparable earnings of Canadians. Attention should also be paid to making sure that existing Canadian residents were not displaced by new immigrants, as is supposed to be done with the Temporary Foreign Worker Program.

Conclusions

It is very encouraging that the Government has finally recognized the existence of a problem and has started to do something about it. But the real job will not be done until immigrants admitted to Canada are again being integrated relatively rapidly into the labor market as they were before 1980 when the immigration system still worked in the economic interest of Canadians.

The fundamental conclusion of this paper is that there has been a continued alarming deterioration in the economic performance of new immigrants in recent years as their numbers have remained at high levels and in spite of the apparent increase in their educational levels. Over the last quarter century, the earnings of new immigrant men with a university degree has fallen dramatically to less than half of that of Canadian born and the earning of new immigrant woman with a university degree to almost 40% of that of Canadian born. The unemployment rates of new immigrant men are almost twice as high as Canadian born and those of new immigrant woman even higher. And poverty as measured by Statistics Canada's Low Income Cut-Off has been growing and becoming increasingly concentrated in communities of new immigrants.

It is clear that the recent immigrants coming to Canada from Asia, southeastern Europe, Latin America, and the Caribbean are not doing as well as immigrants from Europe and the United States and are not being successfully integrated into the Canadian labor market. The poor performance of recent immigrants in the labor market can only be addressed through a radical reform of Canadian immigration policy that substantially reduces the number of immigrants and tightens up selection criteria sufficiently to reverse the deterioration.

References

Aydemir, Abdurrahman, and George J. Borjas (2006). *A Comparative Analysis of the Labor Market Impact of International Migration: Canada, Mexico, and the United States*. NBER Working Paper No. 12327 (June). National Bureau of Economic Research. <http://papers.nber.org/papers/w12327>.

Aydemir, Abdurrahman, and Mikal Skuterud (2005). Explaining the Deteriorating Entry Earnings of Canada's Immigrant Cohorts, 1966–2000. *Canadian Journal of Economics* 38, 2: 641–72.

Bill C-11, *An Act Respecting Immigration to Canada and the Granting of Refugee Protection, etc.*, 1st Sess., 37th Parl., 2001, cl. 11(1). Short title: *Immigration and Refugee Protection Act.*

Bill C-50, *An Act to Implement Certain Provisions of the Budget Tabled in Parliament on February 26, 2008 and to Enact Provisions to Preserve the Fiscal Plan Set Out in That Budget,* 2nd Sess., 39th Parl., 2008. Short title: *Budget Implementation Act 2008.*

Bonikowska, Aneta, David A. Green, and W. Craig Riddell (2006). Cognitive Skills and Immigrant Earnings. Paper presented at the Canadian Economics Association Annual Meeting, Montreal (May 26, 2006).

Borjas, George J. (2003). The Labor Demand Curve Is Downward Sloping: Reexamining the Impact of Immigration on the Labor Market. *Quarterly Journal of Economics* 118, 4 (November): 1335–74.

Card, David (2005). *Is the New Immigration Really So Bad?* NBER Working Paper No. 11547 (August). National Bureau of Economic Research.

Citizenship and Immigration Canada (2007). *Facts and Figures 2006: Immigration Overview: Permanent and Temporary Residents.*

Coulombe, Serge, and Jean-François Tremblay (2006). *Migration, Human Capital and Skill Redistribution across Canadian Provinces.* SRI [Skills Research Initiative] Working Paper Series, No. 2006 D-07. Human Resources and Skills Development Canada, Industry Canada and the Social Sciences and Humanities Research Council.

Flecker, Keri (2007). Racism Remains a Problem: Why Are People of Colour Having Trouble Getting Good Jobs? Monitor Issue (October). Canadian Centre for Policy Alternatives. <http://www.policyalternatives.ca/monitorissues/2007/10/monitorissue1784/?pa=BB736455>.

Gilmore, Jason (2008a). *The Canadian Immigrant Labour Market in 2007.* Catalogue no. 72-606-X20008003. Statistics Canada.

Gilmore, Jason (2008b). *The Canadian Immigrant Labour Market in 2006: Analysis by Region or Country of Birth*. Catalogue no. 71-606-X2008002. Statistics Canada.

Grady, Patrick (2006). The Poor Labour Market Performance of Recent Cohorts of Immigrants Has Lowered Productivity Growth. (February 9). <http://www.global-economics.ca/immigrationproductivity.htm>.

Grondin, Chantal (2005). *Knowledge of Official Languages among New Immigrants: How Important Is It in the Labour Market?* Catalogue No. 89-624-XWE. Statistics Canada.

Hawthorne, Lesleyanne (2008). *The Impact of Economic Selection Policy on Labour Market Outcomes for Degree-Qualified Migrants in Canada and Australia*. IRPP Choices 14, 5 (May). <http://www.irpp.org/choices/archive/vol14no5.pdf>.

Hou, Feng, and Garnett Picot (2004). Visible Minority Neighbourhoods in Toronto, Montréal and Vancouver. *Canadian Social Trends* 72: 8–13.

Picot, Garnett, and Feng Hou (2003). *The Rise in Low-Income Rates among Immigrants in Canada*. Catalogue No. 11F0019MIE20052622003198. Statistics Canada. <www.statcan.ca/english/freepub/11-015-XIE/income/rise.htm>.

Picot, Garnett, and Feng Hou (2008). *Immigrant Characteristics, the IT Bust, and Their Effect on Entry Earnings of Immigrants*. Catalogue No. 11F0019MWE2008315. Statistics Canada. <http://www.statcan.gc.ca/pub/11f0019m/11f0019m2008315-eng.pdf>.

Picot, Garnet, Feng Hou and Serge Coulombe (2007). *Chronic Low-Income and Low-Income Dynamics among Recent Immigrants*. Catalogue No. 11F0019MIE2007198. Statistics Canada.

Picot, Garnett, and Arthur Sweetman (2005). *The Deteriorating Economic Welfare of Immigrants and Possible Causes: Update 2005*. Catalogue No. 11F0019MIE2005262. Statistics Canada.

Putnam, Robert D. (2007). *E Pluribus Unum*: Diversity and Community in the 21st Century. The 2006 Johan Skytte Prize Lecture. *Scandinavian Political Studies* 30, 2: 137–74.

Québec, Commission de consultation sur les practiques d'accomodement reliées aux différences culturelles (2008). *Fonder l'avenir : Le temps de la conciliation*. Rapport.

Rao, Someshwar, Jianmin Tang, and Weimin Wang (2003). Canada's Recent Productivity Record and Capital Accumulation. *International Productivity Monitor* 7: 24–38.

Schaafsma, Joseph, and Arthur Sweetman (2001). Immigrant Earnings: Age at Immigration Matters. *Canadian Journal of Economics* 34, 4: 1066–99.

Shanghai Jiao Tong University (2007). *Academic Ranking of World Universities - 2007*. <http://www.arwu.org/rank/2007/ranking2007.htm>.

Statistics Canada (2003). *The Longitudinal Survey of Immigrants to Canada*. Catalogue no. 89-615-XIE.

Statistics Canada (2008a). *Canada's Changing Labour Force, 2006 Census*. Catalogue no. 97-559-X.

Statistics Canada (2008b). *Earnings and Incomes of Canadians over the Past Quarter Century, 2006 Census*. Catalogue no. 97-563-X.

Sweetman, Arthur (2004). *Immigrant Source Country Educational Quality and Canadian Labour Market Outcomes*. Catalogue no.11F00119MIE20004234. Statistics Canada.

Thompson, E., and C. Worswick (2004). *Canadian Research on Immigration and the Labour Market*. Human Resources and Social Development Canada.

Chapter 6

Recent immigration and Canadian living standards

Herbert Grubel

This chapter considers the impact that recent immigration has had on the living standards of Canadians. It does not consider some other issues raised by immigration like criteria for admitting refugees and its influence on Canada's national identity, traditional cultural institutions, and terrorism. These non-economic effects are discussed in other papers contained in this volume and in *Immigration Policy and the Terrorist Threat in Canada and the United States* (Moens and Collacott, 2008), which collects papers presented at a conference in Toronto in 2007.

Individual incomes

The most important determinant of the living standards of Canadians is their individual level of real income. This measure of well-being must not be confused with aggregate national income, which increases whenever immigrants contribute to output.[1] The incomes of resident

1 ◆ Sir Andrew Green notes of *The Economic Impact of Immigration,* a report of the House of Lords' Select Committee on Economic Affairs on Britain's recent immigration policies: "Most pertinently, the Government's key claim that immigration increases Britain's overall gross domestic product (GDP) is dismissed as 'irrelevant and misleading' ... the real issue is whether immigration has boosted

Canadians (persons born in Canada and past immigrants) generally remain unchanged as a result of immigration because immigrants earn incomes equal to their contributions to total output.[2] This conclusion is based on the basic concept that the wages of individuals are determined in the market by their marginal contributions to the nation's output. Immigrants' earnings, therefore, allow them to buy goods and services equal in value to what they produce, leaving unchanged the incomes of resident Canadians.[3]

The economic model leading to these important conclusions is based on two important assumptions, plus some others to be considered below. The first is that immigration does not give rise to economies or diseconomies of scale. The second is that there is no government taxation and spending. The next two sections discuss what happens to the basic conclusions of the simple economic model when these two assumptions are relaxed.

Economies of scale

Economies of scale arise whenever an investment is capital intensive and average costs fall with the size of output until capacity is reached. Public facilities like roads, bridges, railroads, municipal water supply and sewers, schools, hospitals, and universities have these characteristics. When such facilities operate at less than capacity, immigrants increase their use, lower costs for resident Canadians and thus raise their living standards indirectly. In the past when Canada's population was small, this beneficial effect of immigration has been important and has contributed much to the widely held public view that immigration brings positive economic benefits for all Canadians.

---

income per head of population" (Green, 2008). See also Green's contribution to this volume, The challenges of reforming immigration policy in Britain (chapter 12, page 227).

2 ◆ This conclusion has also been reached by the Economic Council of Canada (1991).

3 ◆ However, if the number of immigrants is large, they affect the distribution of income of resident Canadians earned in wages and returns to capital and land. This issue will be discussed below.

The railroads

To provide an illustration of this effect in Canada, consider the continental railroads built in the last half of the nineteenth century. They were built on vacant land and served the populations of relatively small towns at either end of the lines. The high cost of serving the debt of the railroad incurred during the construction and running of the facilities was spread over few users and therefore resulted in high transportation costs. Once the railroads were in place, these costs fell as resident Canadians and immigrants settled on the empty lands along the tracks and increased the number and size of towns served by the railroad. Immigration thus lowered transportation costs and raised living standards for all Canadians.

However, in recent decades this beneficial process has ended as the railroad facilities have been used to capacity and new construction was required to increase them. Unfortunately, the marginal real cost of this new construction is high because much of the land needed has to be bought from other users as tracks are doubled and rail yards expanded. In effect, the lowering of costs due to economies of scale has been replaced by the increase in costs due to diseconomies of scale. To the extent that immigrants have added to the need for the expansion of the railroad facilities, they have indirectly caused transportation costs to be higher and real incomes to be lower for all resident Canadians.

Municipal infrastructure

Infrastructure facilities operated by municipal governments have gone through an historic pattern very similar to that of the railroads. When cities were small, roads, highways, hospitals, schools, universities, water-treatment plants, sewers, and garbage dumps initially showed reductions in average costs as they were spread over more consumers, many of which were immigrants. However, in recent decades, these facilities reached capacity and had to be expanded or added to. The land required for such expansion has alternative economic uses and a high price tag. Often construction involves digging deeply and avoiding existing pipes and wires, which raises costs. As a result, average taxes or user charges levied by governments to pay for a blend of costs of old and new facilities have increased correspondingly. Again, immigration has indirectly resulted in higher living costs of Canadians.

It can be argued that this cost is incurred through all population growth, whether it results from high birth rates, or domestic or international immigration. However, there is an important difference between these sources of population growth. Federal and provincial policies cannot legislate fertility and restrict the free movement of Canadians within the country but the federal government has the authority to determine the number of foreign immigrants. Therefore, the costs imposed through foreign immigration are entirely avoidable through the passage of appropriate legislation.

Private investment and free trade

Many private investments in manufacturing and mining are also subject to economies of scale. In the past, such investments were limited by the size of the local market since trade restrictions and poor transportation facilities prevented sales abroad. Under these conditions, immigrants increased the size of local markets and resulted in lower costs for resident Canadians. However, in recent decades technological advances have lowered transportation costs and international agreements resulted in free trade. As a result, the size of local markets no longer limits the exploitation of scale economies of private investments so that immigration ceases to result in lower prices for resident Canadians consuming the output of these private firms.

Size of cost increases

There are no formal studies that have measured the effect of immigration on living standards of resident Canadians due to increased costs in the operation of infrastructure projects. However, there exists much casual evidence on this matter. Some of it is found in the media serving Montreal, Toronto, and Vancouver, where most of the recent immigrants have settled. In these cities, media frequently discuss the inadequacy of existing infrastructure facilities, in particular roads, bridges, hospitals, schools, and universities, which are often congested, over-crowded or even inaccessible. The media also often present information about the high costs and taxes facing taxpayers as a result of planned attempts to alleviate these problems.

Somewhat more quantitative evidence on the size of the costs imposed by immigrants can be obtained by considering their role played in the growth of the population and the resultant demand for infrastructure in Canada and British Columbia. Table 1 shows that between 2001 and 2008, Canada's population increased by 2.315 million of which 1,380.4 thousand or 60% is due to net external migration (immigration from abroad and emigration by resident Canadians and recent immigrants).

British Columbia's population increased by 359 thousand, 205.3 thousand or 57% of which came from net external migration while net internal migration added 30.2 thousand or 8% to the total population increase. An unknown number of British Columbia's immigrants from the rest of Canada were recent immigrants who had first settled elsewhere in the country.

Housing costs

Putting the figure for British Columbia into perspective, we find that net immigration from abroad resulted in an average annual population increase of 29.3 thousand (205/7). According to government statistics, the average family size of immigrants arriving in 2003 was 1.9 (Citizenship and Immigration Canada, 2005). These figures imply that about 15,000 new dwelling units (apartments or houses) have had to be constructed for them every year, 1,250 every month, and about 280 every week if the immigrants are to enjoy the same housing standards as the rest of Canadians.

This housing construction for immigrants, which comes on top of that needed to serve immigrants to British Coumbia from the rest of Canada, increases the demand for a scarce resource, land, and thus on

Table 1: Sources of population growth, 2001–2008

	Total increase in population, 000s (%)	Natural increase 000s (%)	Net external migration 000s (%)	Net internal migration 000s (%)
Canada Total	2,315 (100%)	781.5 (34%)	1,380.4 (60%)	N.A.
British Columbia	359 (100%)	79.4 (22%)	205.3 (57%)	30.2 (8%)

Note: The components of the increases in population do not equal the total increase due to changes in the number of non-permanent residents, who are counted in the total population.

Source: Statistics Canada, 2008b: 33, 35; calculations by author.

average and through time drives up the prices of land in towns used for the construction of apartment buildings. It also drives up land prices in rural areas as many Canadians are driven to live there by the high prices of housing in towns and in spite of the cost of commuting to jobs in town. At the margin of urban agglomerations, the prices of land are always lower than they are nearer the center, compensating residents for the higher cost of commuting they face.

The higher land prices serve the economic interests of landowners. Also benefiting from the foreign immigration are builders, the suppliers of furnishings, and the workers in these industries.

The increase in the value of existing land and housing caused by the foreign immigrants affects the living standards of Canadians unevenly. Those who have owned their homes for a long time have enjoyed increased wealth and correspondingly higher living standards. On the other hand, younger resident Canadians and all future generations suffer economic hardships and reduced living standards.

The parents of the young who enjoyed the capital gains may provide financial help to their offspring but their ability to do so is limited by the fact that they have to live somewhere and all housing costs in Vancouver have increased dramatically. Many of these parents are likely to need most of their capital gains to finance their retirement.

Congestion, pollution, and need for new infrastructure

The large number of immigrants has other detrimental effects on living standards of resident Canadians. Thus, if only one half of the immigrant families in Vancouver own one car, 5,000 new cars are added to the region's traffic every year. It is no wonder that traffic is congested and improvements in the highway and public-transit systems have been unable to keep up with the growth in demand. This increased traffic, often slowed in jams, also adds to the region's air pollution.

These immigrants similarly increase the demand for government services. Thus, if every family of three immigrants in Vancouver has one child going to school, 10,000 new places have to be created in educational institutions every year and many new teachers have to be employed. The immigrants also add to the demand for medical care, hospital beds, social assistance, fire and police protection, water supplies, sewers, and many other government services in proportion to their numbers.

In a fundamental sense, the inadequacy of infrastructure facilities and the persistence of pollution and crowding are not due to population growth and immigration but to the inadequate rate of construction needed to prevent them. This statement is correct as far as it goes. It neglects the fact that the existing methods for planning and building the infrastructure always lag behind the need for them. It would indeed be highly desirable if these methods could be changed, perhaps through the greater involvement of the private sector and the streamlining of the political approval process, the granting of building permits, and the securing financial resources. The problem is that efforts to speed up infrastructure projects have a long history and have had very little success. If anything, the growth in the public's environmental concern in recent decades has increased the lag between the creation and elimination of the inadequacy of Canada's infrastructure. Until this lag has been eliminated, it follows that immigration, which is determined by deliberate policies of the federal government, aggravates these inadequacies and imposes costs on Canadians.

Income levels of recent immigrants

This section modifies the basic economic model presented in the preceding sections by considering that Canada has a welfare state that redistributes income from high to low income earners mainly through the use of a progressive personal income-tax structure and through the provision of universally available social programs. Because of the progressivity of the personal income-tax system, recent immigrants who have an income below the average income of resident Canadians will pay lower taxes but, because of the universality of social programs, will consume at least as much as the average Canadian, thus imposing a net burden on the latter.

Statistics Canada (2008a) considered census data covering the period from 1980 to 2006 to compare the median incomes of all resident Canadians with the median earnings of all recent immigrant income earners in the core working age (ages 25 to 54) and reported:

> During the past quarter century, the earnings gap ... widened significantly. In 1980, recent immigrant men who had some employment income earned 85 cents for each dollar received by Canadian-born men. By 2005, the ratio had dropped to 63 cents. The corresponding numbers for recent immigrant women were 85 cents and 56 cents, respectively. The gap widened even though the educational attainment of recent immigrant earners rose much faster than that of their Canadian-born counterparts, during this 25-year period.[4] (Statistics Canada, 2008a: 21)

Another way of measuring the income gap involves the comparison of the average incomes of the two groups with the same demographic characteristics. Thus, Statistics Canada reported that immigrants who arrived in 1990 had average earnings that were relative to those of resident Canadians with the same age, gender, and level of educational attainment: 65% one year, 77% five years, and 80% ten years after their arrival. There is evidence that there is no further improvement in this relationship after ten years.

Effects on federal tax revenue

As a result of the lower average incomes of immigrants they pay, on average, fewer taxes than residents because Canada's taxation system is progressive and more resident Canadians have incomes in the top brackets. The facts are that, in recent years, the top 10% of all filers of personal income-tax returns pay about 50% of all taxes, the bottom 50% pay about 5%, and the 6th through 8th decile pay the rest, or 45%.[5]

---

4 ◆ Research is going on to determine the reasons for this relatively poor record of recent immigrants. Of the reasons given in the preliminary study by Picot and Hou (2003), the most promising are that Canadian employers have virtually no reliable information about the real occupational skills of graduates from Asian universities unknown to them and that actual experience in hiring them has often shown that their skills are not sufficiently suitable for conditions in Canada. The 2008 study of Statistics Canada (2008c) suggests that the lower earnings of the immigrants with higher education may be due to their preponderant specialization in information and communications technology, which has experienced a relative downturn in growth since the high-tech bust in 2001/02.

5 ◆ These figures are approximate and vary slightly through time. See Veldhuis et al., 2003 and other editions of *Tax Facts*.

As a result of the low average incomes, recent immigrants also paid less on average than the amount of GST and sales taxes paid by resident Canadians. Since typically these low-income immigrants also have below-average wealth, they also pay below-average taxes on their asset holdings, like financial investments, land, and dwellings.

Effects on federal spending

Immigrants are entitled to the benefits of government spending that consist of three types relevant to the present analysis. The first type involves spending on projects that does not increase as a result of immigration such as defence, diplomacy, culture, and debt-service payments. The largest of these are debt payments, which are excluded from the estimates presented below, that use data on program spending only.

The second type of spending increases with immigration. It involves universal social programs like health care, education, pensions, welfare, and other social services. This spending absorbs over two thirds (69.3%) of total federal program spending (Statistics Canada, 2008c).

The third type of spending, such as settlement assistance, support for multicultural activities, training, and language, aimed specifically at immigrants. Statistics that measure spending aimed at immigrants tend to be hidden in the budgets of federal and provincial departments administering these spending programs. Due to limited resources, this study has not compiled the relevant statistics and has not used them in the calculations below. However, the resultant downward bias in the estimates below is offset to some degree by the assumption that spending on defense and culture do not increase with the size of population and number of immigrants, while spending for these purposes is included in total program spending used in the estimates below.

In sum, in the empirical analysis presented next, it is assumed that immigrants and resident Canadians absorb government services of the same value, which is equal to the per-capita federal spending on programs.

Estimating the size of the fiscal burden

Based on the assumptions spelled out above and others noted in the original study, Grubel (2006) estimated the impact of the welfare state on the average level of taxes paid by the average recent immigrant relative to that of the average Canadian. He also estimated the average value of the government services absorbed by recent immigrants and resident Canadians.

The basic finding of the study is that in the year 2000 the value of government services consumed by the average immigrant who arrived in 1990 exceeded the value of the taxes paid by $6,294. This estimate implies that the cost of transfers in 2000 was $1.36 billion for the 216,396 immigrants who arrived in Canada in 1990. Assuming that the immigrants who arrived in 1990 on average live for another 45 years, the total cost to resident Canadians for that cohort comes to $62.1 billion over their life-times.

In the year 2002, there were 2.9 million immigrants who had arrived in the preceding 12 years. The transfers to that group of immigrants in 2002 were $18.3 billion. The $18.3 billion represents 16% of total federal program spending in the fiscal year 2000/2001, which is more than the federal government spent on health care and twice what it spent on defense.

It is important to note that these costs do not constitute a social investment for Canada that will be repaid to the generation that subsidized them initially. Even future generations of Canadians are unlikely to be repaid for the investments made by their ancestors. The reason is that, while the average income gaps between Canadians and the offspring of the recent immigrants will disappear, the income distributions of both groups are likely to be very similar. As a result, the high taxes paid by the offspring of the high-income recent immigrants go to pay for the services absorbed by the offspring of the recent immigrants with lower incomes. This conclusion is perfectly consistent with highly touted stories about the extraordinary economic success of some of the offspring of previously poor immigrants.

In other words, the complete story has to consider the total income distribution of the offspring of recent immigrants and the best guess about that distribution is that it will be equal to that of other Canadians. Given that basic distribution of income in the country, the extra taxes paid by those with higher incomes pay for the extra social services absorbed by those with lower incomes.

In conclusion of this section, it should be noted that the calculations presented here are based on a number of important assumptions, some spelled out and some implicit. Only further work can establish the extent to which the results were influenced by unrealistic assumptions.[6] Four years after publication of the study, no such studies have been published.

Labor shortages and productivity

Some advocates for more immigration base their case on the need for workers to fill vacant jobs for which resident Canadians do not qualify or which they do not want.[7] Such labor shortages can be resolved by either increasing the supply of labor through immigration or by letting wages rise until demand equals supply. These alternative approaches to solving labor shortages are understood easily by considering the normally sloped demand-and supply-curves for labor. A shortage means that at the market wage demand exceeds supply. The shortage can be eliminated by an outward shift of the supply curve—immigration—or an increase in the market wage to where demand equals supply.[8]

---

6 ◆ After the original publication of these figures in 2005, they were discussed widely in the media but there were no serious challenges to these results by government agencies or organized and often government-subsidized groups defending immigrants' interests. These organizations have on staff substantial numbers of trained economists, who might have been expected to criticize and find fault with my estimates. While the absence of such efforts is not a proof of the accuracy of my calculations, one may conclude at least that the estimates do not contain glaring errors.

7 ◆ A vocal advocate is the Conference Board of Canada (2008) but many employers share the views of this organization.

8 ◆ See figure 5.2 (page 80), which shows a downward-sloping demand curve for a homogeneous category of "labor" and an upward-sloping supply curve, with the initial disequilibrium wage creating an excess demand for labor. The downward shift of the supply curve caused by immigration increases the area under the demand curve, which represents output and the profits accruing to the firms whose behavior gives rise to the demand curve. The graph also shows clearly that the outward shift of the supply curve reduces the wages earned by all workers. While this simple model makes much intuitive sense—the more cheese is imported into Canada, the lower the price of cheese produced and income earned by Canadian cheese manufactureres—as is the case with much economic analysis, this simple model can be made more realistic by changing some assumptions and the basic conclusions can be modified. See Grady for some of this analysis, which in the end does not invalidate the fundamental propositions of the basic model.

These two approaches to the elimination of labor shortages have much different effects on resident Canadian workers. Filling vacant jobs with immigrants raises the profits of employers (that is why they lobby for immigrant workers even if their unions insist that they be paid the same wages as other Canadians), but leaves wages low and increases income inequality and poverty in Canada. Given the concern of the Canadian public that there be a more equal distribution of income, immigration thus indirectly is responsible for more income redistribution policies, including higher tax rates and more government spending.

The second approach to the elimination of labor shortages leads to higher wages and profits that are lower than they are when immigrants fill the vacant jobs. The higher wages reduce income inequalities and increase incentives for resident Canadians to leave lower-paid employment or postpone or leave retirement. The latter decisions result in lower claims for public pensions and other social benefits and higher tax payments. Resident Canadians benefit correspondingly.

When employers are induced to pay higher wages to fill job vacancies, there are two beneficial developments that increase labor productivity so that the employers can pay the higher wages without reductions in profits. First, the higher wages induce workers to acquire new skills needed to fill higher-paying jobs. While such training takes time, the expectation of growing demand for these high-paying jobs allows resident Canadians to get the training in time to fill the vacancies. Second, the high wages and the anticipation of even higher wages in the future encourage employers to make capital investments in labor-saving technology and the producers of the needed capital to direct it towards labor-saving investments.[9]

The latter process of private firms adapting to higher wages is very important and it may be useful to consider some examples from the real world to illustrate how they have done so in the past. Agriculture in

---

9 ◆ It may well be that the wages brought on by Canada's mass immigration is responsible for some of the difference between productivity in Canada and in the United States, which has widened in recent years when immigration as a percent of the labor force has been much higher in Canada than in the United States. For more on this issue, see chapter 5 (page 75) and Grady's discussion there of Borjas, 2003. George J. Borjas from Harvard has done much theoretical and empirical work in this field.

California, for example, for decades had relied on migrant workers to fill job vacancies. When the flow of migrants was reduced by government policy and wages rose, none of the forecast catastrophic consequences took place. Farmers introduced machines to pick tomatoes and they developed new varieties suitable for this process. The productivity and wages of workers in this industry rose while profits of employers remained unchanged.

Another example is found in Japan, where government does not allow mass immigration to meet labor shortages. This policy forced employers and machine makers to develop the advanced industrial robots known best for their employment in the automobile industry, first used in Japan and since introduced in the rest of the world. Japanese employers increasingly use robots in service industries like retailing and health care.

Overall labor-market conditions

Under normal cyclical conditions in Canada, the labor market is in equilibrium and there are no overall labor shortages. Changes in technology and demand for different products and services always lead to a shift of labor from one industry to another, giving rise to temporary shortages and surpluses found in different regions and industries. Overall and persistent labor shortages, however, are caused by excessively easy monetary and fiscal policies that created aggregate demand in excess of aggregate supply.

The problems caused by these expansionary monetary and fiscal policies cannot be solved by immigration. Immigrants earn income that they spend on private goods, services, and housing that require yet more labor to produce. They also add to the demand for public services like schools, universities, roads, buses, water, sewage, and waste services. Meeting these demands adds to the demand for labor in the construction and staffing of the facilities and it is quite possible that, in the end, immigrants do not eliminate but increase existing labor shortages.

Such increases in labor shortages arise also when immigrants come from the rest of Canada to places like British Columbia but, as was argued above, given the free movement of people in Canada, such internal migration and problems cannot be prevented and have to be dealt with as best as possible. On the other hand, the federal government has the power to limit foreign immigration and avoid these dynamic labor shortages.

Externalities

Economic activity can impose costs or benefits on others that are not reflected in their wages and are not recorded in national income statistics. These effects are called "externalities." They affect the living standards of resident Canadians in ways that are not reflected in the very basic market model presented at the very beginning of this study. Pollution of the air, rivers, and oceans, for example, is increased through immigration by more than it would if population and economic growth were fed only by domestic increases in population. The greater population causes increased pollution as the number of vehicles grows and more factories are built. Some of this pollution is alleged to bring global climate changes that may well lead to costly measures to combat it, reducing the living standards of resident Canadians indirectly. It is worth noting that, from a global perspective that concerns so many environmentalists, Canadian immigration from developing countries adds to the problems faced by the world as a whole since such immigrants have much higher incomes and produce much more pollution in Canada and therefore in the world than they would have in their native countries.

On the other hand, it is believed that immigrants also produce important positive externalities through their activities as scientists, inventors, entrepreneurs, writers, and artists. In fact, the number of immigrants who have excelled in these endeavors is quite large. Accounts of their contribution to scientific knowledge, commercial success, the creation of employment opportunities, the sale of books and works of art are part of the Canadian story. However, there is much room for questioning the size of these externalities because immigrants in most of these activities tend to be compensated for the value of their contributions. In the case of entrepreneurship, patentable knowledge and the output of artists and writers, the producers receive income from the sale of their output and benefit also from government subsidies. In other words, they receive incomes equal to their contribution to output and thus leave the incomes of other Canadians unchanged, as is implied by the basic model presented at the beginning of this paper. Immigrants' contributions to pure scientific knowledge are somewhat different. The social benefits from this work cannot be appropriated by the researchers. However, these scientists tend to be subsidized by the government of

Canada, which rationally sets the subsidies at levels so that the marginal social benefits are equal to the marginal costs.[10] In sum, the proposition that the success of immigrants as entrepreneurs, researchers, and artists brings great benefits to other Canadians is invalid and cannot be used in support of policies for immigration.

The viability of social program financing

One frequently made argument in favor of immigration is that it is needed to save Canada's social programs from insolvency. The taxes paid by these immigrants are expected to make up deficits that will develop in the administration of Canada's pay-as-you-go social programs. These deficits will develop as the number of Canadians active in the labor force and paying taxes falls relative to the number in retirement and receiving payments through the Canada Pension Plan and needing publicly financed medical care.

Guillimette and Robson (2006)[11] used forecasts of future fertility and death rates made by Statistics Canada to estimate the number of immigrants that would be needed to eliminate the expected deficits. They did so using the concept of the dependency ratio, which is defined as the number of Canadians of retirement age (older than 65) over the number of workers in the labor force (between the ages of 18 and 64), which is a proxy for the level of taxation on active workers needed to pay for those in retirement. In 2006, this dependence ratio was .20, which means that there were 20 retired Canadians for every 100 taxpaying workers. At this ratio, tax revenues have been roughly equal to payments and, if the ratio were to be maintained, there would be no more deficits in the future.

---

10 ◆ In fact, the benefits of scientific discoveries tend to be available freely to all peoples of the world and it makes no difference where they are produced. Therefore, Canadians do not have to subsidize this production of knowledge to benefit from it though, as a responsible member of the global community, their government contributes its fair share of the global spending on the production of pure knowledge.

11 ◆ See also Immigration's Impact on the Growth and Age Structure of the Canadian Workforce (chapter 7, page 121) and The Immigration Option to Population Aging in Canada (chapter 8, page 147).

Guillimette and Robson found that in the absence of immigration, the dependency ratio would rise sharply from .20 in 2006 to .46 in 2050, with some fluctuations in the intervening years. They then analyzed what number of immigrants would be needed to prevent such increases in the dependency ratio, assuming that immigrants have the same age profile in the future as they have had in recent years, which has made them on average somewhat younger than Canadians. Their crucial finding is that the rate of immigration would have to rise sharply after 2006 from the present 0.7% of the population to 4.8% in 2012 and remain there for about a decade. Thereafter, the levels could fall to a low of 2.0% of the population because of the large number of children born to Canada's baby boomers that will be in the labor force at that time. After 2038, the level would rise again sharply to about 4.3% of the population.

The implications of these rates of immigration for the absolute numbers of immigrants are staggering. There would have to be more than 7 million immigrants in the year 2050 alone. Canada's total population that year would be 165.4 million, or more than five times the current level, with virtually all of the increase made up of immigrants. The authors also considered the implications of restricting immigrants to persons aged between 20 and 24. They found that this strategy would only slightly lower the number of immigrants needed to maintain the current dependency ratio and the corresponding absolute level of the population and annual immigrants.

The estimates produced by Guillimette and Robson show clearly that immigration cannot realistically be used to solve Canada's problem of the unfunded liabilities of its social programs without bringing about impossibly large problems of finding employment for the huge numbers required and preventing a sky-rocketing increase in all of the impacts of immigration on the living standards of resident Canadians noted above. In addition, Canada would face growing problems in finding such large numbers of immigrants willing to come to Canada, especially since many of the developing countries of the world that have supplied recent immigrants are experiencing rapid economic development that is accompanied by excellent career-development opportunities there. Falling fertility rates in these countries will further reduce the stock of recruits for immigration to Canada.

Policy implications

The main findings of the preceding analysis are easy to summarize. Under the provisions of Canada's present welfare state, mass immigration causes the living standards of resident Canadians to be diminished significantly and, through the creation of congestion, pollution, and pressure on existing infrastructure, immigrants impose further costs on them. The analysis showed that there are no positive benefits, like the reaping of scale economies, the filling of job vacancies, and relief from the fiscal burden of unfunded liabilities of social programs, which mass immigration can provide to compensate Canadians for these costs.

Before turning to the discussion of possible policies to reduce or eliminate these costs, it is worth repeating an important point made in the text above. In principle, the costs analyzed can be eliminated by ending the welfare state or disqualifying immigrants from access to it; by making sure that infrastructure projects are always put into place so that no shortages exist; and that pollution and other negative externalities are eliminated by proper regulation. The following policy recommendations are based on the assumption that these changes will not take place in the foreseeable future for reasons beyond the scope of this study. Under this assumption, there are two classes of policies to reduce or eliminate the costs of mass immigration.

Change the characteristics of immigrants admitted

First is the class of policies that changes the characteristics of immigrants so that their average incomes and the distribution of incomes around the average are the same as those of resident Canadians. If this policy goal is attained, the costs of the welfare state imposed on other Canadians will disappear, though the problems associated with pollution and inadequate infrastructure remain.

The process that Canada uses to select immigrants has been designed to ensure the economic success of immigrants. The results cited above show that it has not been successful. Several analysts (see chapter 1, page 5) suggest reforms to remedy this shortcoming. Among these is the elimination of the family class of immigrants, which by definition does not use the criterion of economic success in granting admission to foreigners. Another policy change would put greater weight on properly established language proficiency and reduce the weight given to formal education. Yet another proposal is to rely more heavily on the judgments of private employers by issuing immigration visas to applicants who hold a valid contract for employment in Canada, with the interests of the welfare state and of low-skilled citizens protected by government-stipulated minimum wages offered in these contracts.

These and other marginal changes in the immigrant-selection process have been proposed in the past but, for political reasons, the government has chosen to ignore them. This paper recommends that the government in the future put the welfare of Canadians first and their political self-interest second and adopt the proposed changes.

Reduce the rate of immigration

The second approach to the reduction or elimination of these costs involves reducing the rate of immigration. The smaller it is, the lower the costs. The costs will be zero if immigration is zero. But since there is substantial annual emigration from Canada, I propose that immigration be allowed to match the level of emigration so that there will be a net zero effect of migration on the size of Canada's population. In practice, this policy would have meant in 2007 that, since about 45,000 people emigrated from Canada, 45,000 rather than 250,000 immigrants would have been admitted (http://www40.statcan.gc.ca/l01/cst01/demo33a-eng.htm).

Under this policy, Canada would remain a country that welcomes immigrants, albeit in much smaller numbers than presently. Emigration allows Canadians the freedom to maximize their welfare by moving abroad. The costs of pollution, lagging infrastructure expansion, and other externalities due to mass immigration would be eliminated. However, to the extent that domestic population growth continues or some regions receive many internal migrants, the costs of lags in the construction of infrastructure and of the passage of regulation to control pollution and so on, would remain.

The proposed policy has the added advantage that the resultant rate of population growth would reflect fully the decisions of Canadians about the number of children they wish to have. These decisions may be presumed to be determined rationally in the light of personal, practical, and moral considerations as well as concerns over the environment, congestion, and taxation. A good case can be made that the government has no right to interfere with the outcome of these decisions by changing the rate of population growth through its immigration policies from what the people have decided it to be.[12]

The annual inflow of immigrants equal in number to those emigrating from Canada still gives rise to the possibility that they impose costs on Canadians through the operation of the welfare state, if they have average incomes below those of other Canadians and the distribution of income around the average is different. To eliminate this problem, reforms of the immigrant selection process also need to be undertaken, as discussed above. However, even if this goal cannot be attained, the significant reduction in the annual inflow ensures that the costs are lowered considerably.

It should be noted that the proposed policy recommendations are based on economic considerations alone. Several papers in this volume suggest that mass immigration reduces the welfare of other Canadians also through its negative influence on Canadian culture, national security, and other non-economic issues. The existence of these social costs should also be taken into account in any reforms of the present immigration system.

In conclusion, it is important to note that the proposals for policy changes involve many complex issues of implementation, timing, and the sanctity of past commitments. All of these issues can and will be resolved in due time. What has to come first is a commitment by government to adopt the proposed policies in principle.

References

Aydemir, Abdurrahman, and George J. Borjas (2006). A Comparative Analysis of Labor Market Impact of International Migration: Canada, Mexico and the United States. NBER Working Paper No. 12327 (June). National Bureau of Economic Research. <http://papers.nber.org/papers/w12327>.

12 ◆ This point is also made convincingly by Krikorian (2008: ch. 6).

Borjas, George J. (2003). The Labor Demand Curve Is Downward Sloping: Reexamining the Impact of Immigration on the Labor Market. *Quarterly Journal of Economics* 118, 4 (November): 1335–74.

Citizenship and Immigration Canada (2005). Family versus Individual Immigration: A New Perspective. *The Monitor* (Winter). <http://www.collectionscanada.gc.ca/webarchives/20071123005954/http://www.cic.gc.ca/english/resources/statistics/monitor/issue08/06-feature.asp>.

Conference Board of Canada (2008,). Immigration Reforms Put Canada on the Right Track. News release 09-36 (October 24). <http://www.conferenceboard.ca/press/2008/immigration.asp>.

Economic Council of Canada (1991). *Economic and Social Impacts of Immigration.* Minister of Supply and Services Canada.

Green, Andrew (2008). Devastating Demolition of the Case for Immigration. *Daily Mail* (March 31). <http://www.dailymail.co.uk/news/article-1004185/Devastating-demolition-case-mass-immigration.html>.

Grubel, Herbert, and Anthony D. Scott (1966). The International Flow of Human Capital. *American Economic Review* 61, 21: 268–74.

Guillimette, Yvan, and William Robson (2006). *No Elixir of Youth: Immigration Cannot Keep Canada Young.* Backgrounder 96 (September). C.D. Howe Institute.

Krikorian, Mark (2008). *The New Case against Immigration.* Sentinel.

Moens, Alexander, and Martin Collacott, eds. (2008). *Immigration Policy and the Terrorist Threat in Canada and the United States.* Fraser Institute. <http://www.fraserinstitute.org/researchandpublications/publications/5587.aspx>.

Picot, Garnett, and Feng Hou (2003). *The Rise in Low-Income Rates among Immigrants in Canada.* Catalogue No. 11F0019MIE20052622003198. Statistics Canada. <www.statcan.ca/english/freepub/11-015-XIE/income/rise.htm>.

Statistics Canada (2008a). *Earnings and Incomes of Canadians over the Past Quarter Century, Census Year 2006.* Catalogue no. 97-563-X. <http://www.statcan.ca/bsolc/english/bsolc?catno=97-563-X>.

Statistics Canada (2008b). *Report on the Demographic Situation in Canada, 2005 and 2006.* Catalogue no. 91-209-X, ISSN 1718-7788 (July). 2008 <http://www.statcan.ca/english/freepub/91-209-XIE/91-209-XIE2004000.pdf>.

Statistics Canada (2008c). *Consolidated Government Revenue and Expenditures.* <http://www40.statcan.ca/l01/cst01/govt48b.htm>.

Veldhuis, Niels, Joel Emes, and Michael Walker (2003). *Tax Facts 13.* Fraser Institute

Demographic issues

Chapter 7

Immigration's impact on the growth and age structure of the Canadian workforce

Robin Banerjee and William Robson

Declining fertility and rising life expectancy are exerting powerful pressure on the growth of Canada's population and on its age structure.[1] Projections based on current fertility rates and immigration levels, with moderately rising life expectancy, show growth rates of the population of traditional working age (18–64) going from an average of 1.5% annually between 1972 and 2007 to 0.3 percent between 2008 and 2058, and the ratio of the population age 65 and over to the working-age population rising from 20.5% in 2007 to more than 44% in 2050. There are many reasons to worry that a slower-growing and older population may make living standards rise more slowly in the future than they did in the past (Guillemette, 2003). The combination of slower growth in the tax base and increases in age-related expenditures will put significant pressures on public finances (Robson, 2007).

Can immigration help Canada address this challenge? On its face, immigration looks like a useful tool. Canada is a major recipient of immigrants. From 1972 to 1986, Canada admitted immigrants equal to some

1 ◆ We gratefully acknowledge helpful suggestions from Yvan Guillemette.

0.54% of the resident population on average per year and, from 1987 to 2006, immigrants equal to 0.74% of the population. After allowing for outflows, average net immigration during these two periods was 0.42% and 0.66% of the resident population, respectively. As a result, immigration has been a major and growing contributor to the growth of the workforce (figure 7.1). Since the age profile of immigrants differs from that of the resident population, immigration will affect the age profile of the population as well. While the age profile of immigrants has changed over the years, immigrants tend on average to be younger than people already resident in Canada (figure 7.2). So, future changes in the number of immigrants can influence both the growth rate of the working-age population and the size of that population relative to the population that is past working age.

In the pages that follow, we quantify those effects and draw some conclusions about the relative merits of changes in immigration flows as ways to address these challenges. Our key conclusions are that the increases in immigration necessary to offset or even significantly reduce the effects of past declines in birth rates on the growth and age structure of Canada's workforce are unrealistic.

Figure 7.1: Contributions of immigration and natural increase to growth in Canada's working-age population (1972–2006)

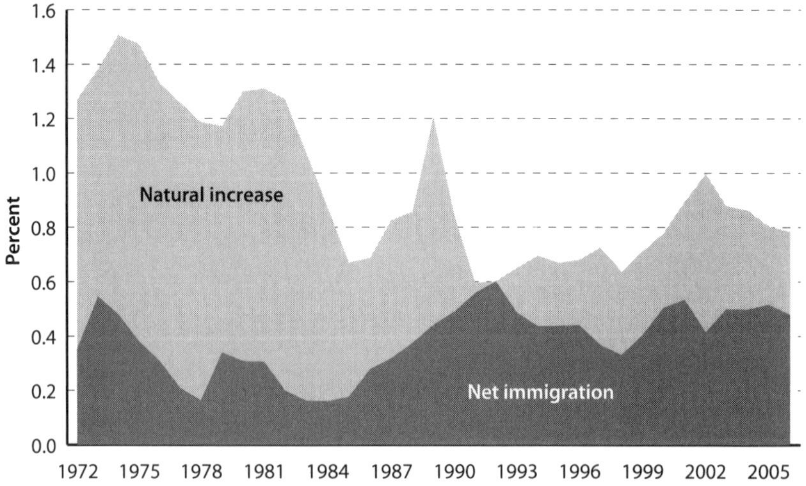

Source: Statistics Canada; authors' calculations.

Figure 7.2: Age distribution of immigrants and current Canadian population (2007)

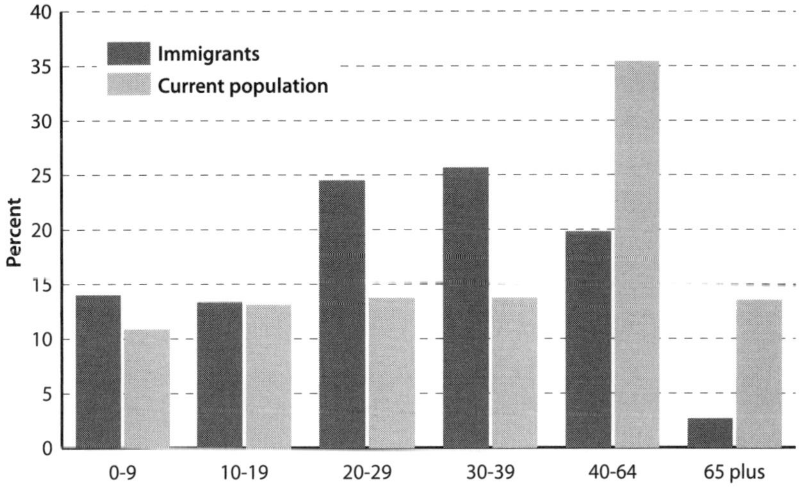

Source: Statistics Canada.

Higher immigration can meet specific labor-market shortages and can to some degree mitigate the imminent slowing and eventual reversal in the growth of Canada's labor force. Even accompanied by measures to attract relatively more young people, however, only improbably dramatic increases in immigration—near-term net inflows more than 2.5 times those of the recent past, for example—can offset the effect of a lack of natural population increase on workforce growth in the decades ahead. Immigration's limited power to alter Canada's macroeconomic future emerges even more strikingly from our investigations of its potential impact on the coming shift in the ratio of older to working-age Canadians. Even very large increases in immigration and implausibly extreme age filters can only slow the coming increase in Canada's old-age dependency (OAD) ratios.

We contrast immigration's limited effects on workforce growth and age structure with those of two other measures that could be used to offset slower population growth and aging: postponing the age at which we generally expect people to stop participating in the workforce from 65 to 70 and raising the fertility rate to its replacement level of 2.1 children per woman. While the uncertainties and political difficulties of pursuing these options are severe, our simulations do reveal them to be more powerful tools to address Canada's coming demographic challenges.

Notwithstanding our judgment that immigration to Canada has major benefits to both immigrants themselves and those already in the country, then, our simulations suggest that immigration alone is not a particularly promising tool to address the challenges posed by a slower-growing and aging population. Canadians should not let the hope that immigration will solve their problems distract them from pursuing other demographic and economic measures to enhance living standards in a future of slower growth in the potential workforce and a relatively larger population of seniors.

What others have said

Accounts in the popular press on the demographic challenges facing most developed nations, as well as comments by advocates, sometimes suggest that increasing immigration might be something of an elixir of youth for countries faced with demographic strains. In general, however, demographic research on the effects of immigration at levels that appear economically and politically feasible has tended to yield more sober findings.

A study by the RAND Corporation (Grant et al., 2004), for example, looked at the demographic consequences of low fertility in Europe and reached conclusions broadly similar to ours on the question of whether immigration could compensate for the demographic challenges faced by EU nations. Schertmann (1992) shows that a constant inflow of immigrants, even relatively young ones, does not necessarily rejuvenate low-fertility populations, and may in the long term actually contribute to population aging. Specific studies on Canada (United Nations, 2004; Denton and Spencer, 2004; Guillemette and Robson, 2006) have found that the dynamic of aging among the resident population is so strong that immigration's ability to affect it is remarkably small.

Because most Canadians view immigration positively, however, and because immigration looks like a policy lever that is relatively easy to use, its potential impact on demographic structure is a prominent theme in public discourse. In late 2005, then-federal Minister of Citizenship and Immigration Joe Volpe proposed a sizeable increase in immigration—to approximately 1% of the population annually—with purported benefits to

Canada's demographic structure front and center in its rationale (Canadian Press, 2005, Sept. 24). More recently, Citizenship and Immigration Canada's 2007 annual report on immigration refers to "the demographic reality of aging and shrinking populations" as a motive for all developed countries to seek immigrants more aggressively and says, "[i]n a few short years, given our aging population, Canadians who leave school for the workplace will only offset the number of retirements. Immigration will therefore be a key source of labour force growth in the future" (CIC, 2007: 6).

Strategies and scenarios

So the potential of immigration to improve Canada's demographic outlook continues to excite popular imagination and some policy makers as well. Our hope, therefore, is that further numerical investigations of these impacts can help the understanding of how much, and how little, Canadians can truly hope for on this front.

Two strategies

Policymakers seeking to influence the growth rate of Canada's population or its age structure through immigration can work on one or both of two fronts: the volume of immigration or the age structure of immigrants. For the growth of the workforce, volume matters for the obvious reason that immigration adds to numbers. Beyond its effects on overall numbers, moreover, changes in volume can affect the growth rate of the workforce to the extent that immigrants tend, more than the resident population, to be already of working age or about to "age into" the workforce. As figure 7.2 showed, immigrants do tend to be younger than the resident population. So, in the short run, higher levels of immigration will boost the growth of the workforce through both these channels. Policies that affect the age-profile of immigrants could amplify this effect.

As for Canada's demographic structure, immigration would have no effect if immigrants had the same age profile as the resident population. Since they do not, increasing the number of immigrants will result in a lower average age of the population and a smaller increase in the old-age dependency ratio. Policy changes that accentuated the relative youth of immigrants would amplify this effect.

In fact, the numbers and age-structure of immigrants tend to vary together. As Beach et al. (2006) have documented, factors such as the state of the economy, the emphasis on different immigration streams in Canadian immigration policy, and the weights attached to different factors in the point system Canada uses to evaluate economic migrants affect both volumes of immigration and the average age of migrants. Since economic-class immigrants are younger on average than non-economic-class immigrants, to provide one example, a booming economy historically attracted more immigrants and lowered their average age. After the mid-1990s, to provide another, revisions to the point system gave more weight to experience and years of schooling, which raised immigrants' average age. In the simulations that follow, we treat the two variables separately, but the links between them matter for possible policy responses.

Four scenarios

We now proceed to simulations of the effect of various immigration strategies on the future old-age dependency ratio. We use a model maintained at the C.D. Howe Institute to project Canada's future population on the basis of several assumptions about fertility, mortality, and migration (table 7.1 summarizes some key assumptions and results in our Baseline scenario):[2]

- each province's total fertility rate remains at its 2005 level through the projection period;
- life expectancy at birth by sex rises at rates akin to those in Statistics Canada's "medium" assumption for improvement in life expectancy;
- a constant share of the population of each age and sex emigrates every year.[3]

---

2 ◆ The model is based on the ILO-POP model developed by the International Labour Organization. We simulate gross immigration in our model, which we refer to throughout the paper as immigration. We refer to net immigration as the difference between gross immigration and net emigration (gross emigration minus returning emigrants).

3 ◆ Younger immigrants to Canada appear likelier to emigrate again (Aydemir and Robinson, 2006). Scenarios that feature a younger age profile of immigrants may therefore understate the level of gross immigration required to alleviate population aging.

Table 7.1: Assumptions and results of the Baseline scenario

	1997	2007	2017	2027	2037	2047	2057
Assumptions							
Life expectancy at birth (years)							
Male	75.7	78.0	79.0	80.0	81.0	82.0	82.5
Female	81.3	82.7	83.7	84.7	85.7	86.7	87.5
Total fertility rate	1.55	1.54	1.54	1.54	1.54	1.54	1.54
Net international migration (as % of resident population)	0.54	0.66	0.65	0.65	0.66	0.66	0.66
Results							
Total population (millions)	29.9	33.0	36.1	39.2	41.6	43.5	45.2
Old-age dependency ratio (%) = age 65+ / ages 18–64	19.2	20.5	25.7	35.3	40.8	43.0	46.3

Note: Values for 1997 are actual; for 2007 are inputs into model from latest available data; and for 2017–2057 are projections.

Sources: Statistics Canada; authors' calculations.

We model four immigration scenarios:

1 ◆ a Baseline scenario in which the annual flow of immigrants remains at the same percentage of the already resident population as in 2007 (0.7%) with the same age distribution observed on average between 2002 and 2006;

2 ◆ a More scenario in which immigration rises to 1% of total population annually with an age structure identical to the 2002–2006 average;

3 ◆ a Younger scenario in which the immigration rate continues at its 2007 level but with the younger age structure shown in figure 7.3 (see note to figure 7.3);

4 ◆ a More and Younger scenario in which immigration rises to 1% of total population and has the younger age structure illustrated in figure 7.3.

Figure 7.3: Age distribution of immigrants, actual and hypothetical younger (2007)

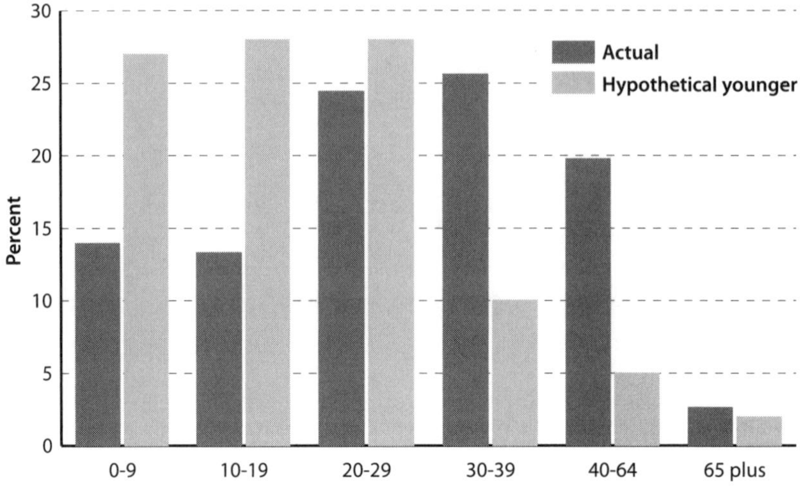

Source: Statistics Canada; authors' calculations.

Note to figure 7.3: Selecting younger immigrants

The age profile of immigrants in the Younger scenario contrasted with recent actual experience in figure 7.3 is illustrative rather than the product of any specific proposed change in immigration policy. It depicts the result of a hypothetical screen that tilts immigration policy dramatically in the direction of parents aged 20 to 29 with young children. To make the screen more concrete, one could imagine a much stronger focus on refugees, which are on average the youngest admission class, and on the economic class, combined with a much more restrictive policy toward family-class immigrants, which are on average older, combined with a revised point system that gave much higher weight to ages in this range. (In the Independent and Skilled Worker categories, the point system currently gives a maximum of 10 points to people aged 21 to 49, with 2 points deducted per year either side of that range, and zero for people 16 and under or 54 and older.) To maintain a modest degree of realism, the Younger scenario does not completely eliminate older immigrants; it might therefore represent an extreme of what is feasible but it is emphatically not something we would recommend.

Figure 7.4: Growth in Canada's working-age population (1972–2058)

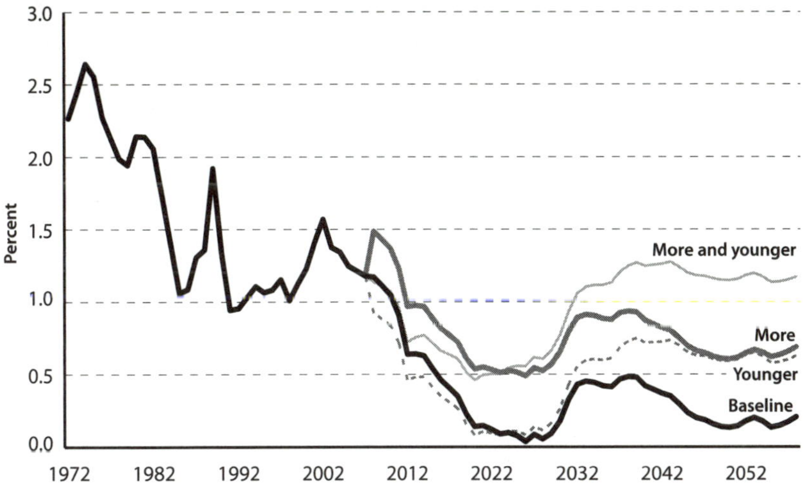

Source: Statistics Canada; authors' calculations.

Figure 7.4 shows the actual growth of the workforce since 1972, along with projections through the year 2058 in the four scenarios. The Baseline scenario shows a continuation of the declining trend in workforce growth evident during the past 40 years, with the exit of the "Baby Boomers" from the workforce causing growth virtually to cease in the 2020s. After a return to modest positive growth in the 2030s, our baseline projection shows labor-force growth settling near 0.2%, with net immigration and natural increase at current fertility rates marginally exceeding exits from the labor force. Although population growth rates are not the primary focus of the simulations, we note that in the baseline projection, Canada's total population rises from about 33 million today to more than 45 million in 2058.[4]

The other three scenarios in figure 7.4 show that immigration can affect the growth of the labor force. The More scenario produces a growth rate consistently higher than the baseline, though still averaging below all but the weakest years of actual experience. In this scenario, total population would exceed 55 million by 2058.[5] The Younger scenario initially

4 ◆ Statistics Canada's population projection under a "medium growth, recent migration trends" scenario is 42.6 million by 2056 (Statistics Canada, 2005).

5 ◆ Statscan projects 51 million in 2056 with 1% immigration (Statistics Canada, 2005).

dips below the Baseline because a large number of those under 18 are admitted under this scenario. But, as the first wave of those youngsters matures and enters the workforce, the workforce growth rate stabilizes at slightly over 0.6% annually (slightly lower than in the More scenario). Population in this scenario differs little from the baseline, ending up at just over 48 million. Even the More and Younger scenario cannot avoid a dip to growth around 0.5% annually in the next two decades, before working-age population growth stabilizes later at growth rates closer to those of recent history. The total population in this scenario would finish the projection period at about 59 million.

Figure 7.5 shows the actual evolution of the OAD ratio since 1971, along with projections through the year 2058 in the four scenarios. The OAD ratio has been rising since 1971, but it will start rising more steeply around 2012 as increasing numbers of baby boomers begin passing age 65. In the Baseline scenario, with immigration rising from just under 235,000 in 2008 to over 320,000 in 2058, and having an age structure similar to that of the recent past, the OAD ratio rises by approximately 0.76 percentage points per year, on average, until 2030. Although it rises more slowly after that, when the rapidly falling post-boom birthrate shrinks the number of people passing age 65, it does keep rising. So the total increase over the projection period is from about 21% today to almost 47% by 2058.[6]

In the More scenario (annual immigration at 1% of the population, with an age structure like that of the recent past) the rate of population aging is slower than in the baseline. The OAD ratio rises to almost 42% by 2058. In the Younger scenario (aggressive targeting of younger immigrants with no change in overall numbers), the old-age dependency ratio differs little from that in the Baseline scenario in the early years, while those under 18 are still maturing to working age. When they begin to enter the workforce in large numbers, after about 2030, the OAD ratio ceases to rise, remaining around 38% through to 2058.

Finally, the More and Younger scenario shows the combined effect of both changes from the Baseline scenario. This scenario would see the

6 ◆ This baseline projection is very close to United Nations projections, which place Canada's old-age dependency ratio at 0.45 in 2050 (United Nations, 2002).

Figure 7.5: Evolution of the old-age dependency ratio (1972–2058)

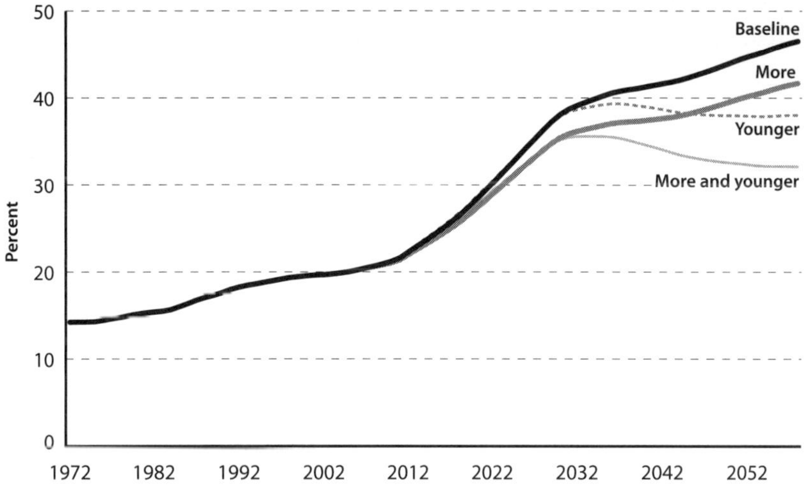

Source: Statistics Canada; authors' calculations.

old-age dependency ratio going from 21% today to over 35% by the mid-2030s. At that point, it would begin falling again, ending the projection period at just over 32%. So, in a numerical sense, a very aggressive policy of selecting younger immigrants in much larger numbers could prevent the old-age dependency ratio rising above a peak of about 35% about 25 years from now. Before considering the moral and other problems of this scenario, however,[7] we note that the old-age dependency ratio would still rise much faster between 2006 and 2030 than at any time over the past 35 years.

Target-based policies

These scenarios do not exhaust the range of conceivable immigration-policy responses to slower workforce growth and population aging. Another

7 ◆ A broader definition of the dependency ratio that covers both youth and seniors illustrates one problem. In the very aggressive scenario, the total dependency ratio (0–17 and 65+ relative to age 18–64) rises from 53% in 2008 to over 72% in 2035. In the More scenario, this ratio stays below 70% through 2050. A higher proportion of young comes with its own fiscal costs (e.g., for school funding).

way of thinking about these challenges is to come at them from the other end, picking a demographic target and asking what immigration policy could achieve it.

Targeting labor-force growth

What policies, for example, would maintain growth in the Canadian workforce at the 1.3% rate that prevailed from 2003 to 2007? Again, we can think of two main methods for achieving this result: changing the number of immigrants—which we call the Workforce Target More scenario—and changing both numbers and age distribution—the Workforce Target Younger scenario. (A change in age distribution only, without a change in numbers, cannot achieve the target, so we do not consider this option.) The numbers of immigrants needed under these two scenarios, with a comparison to the Baseline scenario, are illustrated in figure 7.6.

An immediate and large increase in the immigration rate would be required to achieve the target workforce growth rate. In both scenarios, immigration rates double in the next half decade and peak at more than 2.5 times a few years after that. The pronounced dip in immigration in the 2030s in the Workforce Target More scenario and its even more pronounced counterpart in the Workforce Target Younger scenario occur when people who immigrated as children begin entering the workforce, reducing the total number of immigrants required to keep workforce growth at 1.3%. (The higher initial jump under the Workforce Target Younger scenario is because it brings in more of those under 18; as they mature into the working-age population, the total numbers required under this scenario fall below those in the Workforce Target More scenario.) Once this maturing-in effect peters out, required immigration levels stabilize at about double current rates. The total population of Canada in these scenarios would be almost 70 million by 2058.

Targeting the old-age dependency ratio

In the same spirit, we can ask what rate of immigration would stop the OAD ratio rising above the 2008 figure, which we estimate at 20.7%. Figure 7.7 plots the level of immigration required to stabilize the old-age dependency ratio at 20.7% starting in 2009 in two parallel scenarios: one

Figure 7.6: Immigration rate required to maintain 1.3% growth in working-age population (1972–2058)

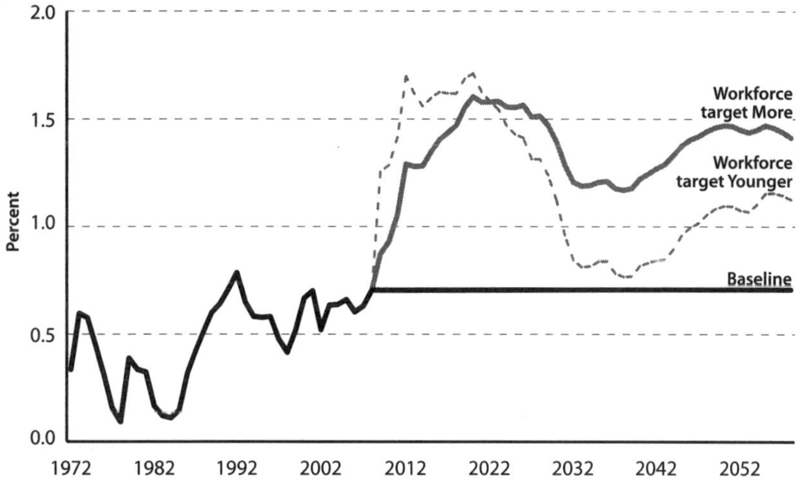

Source: Statistics Canada; authors' calculations.

Figure 7.7: Immigration rate required to stabilize old-age dependency ratio (1972–2058)

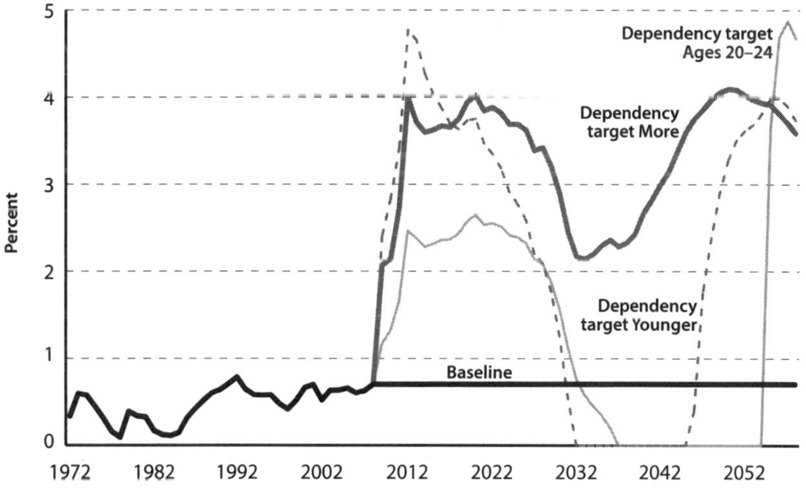

Source: Statistics Canada; authors' calculations.

in which only the numbers of immigrants change, the Dependency Target More scenario; and one in which both numbers and age distribution change, the Dependency Target Younger scenario.[8] (As in the previous scenario, a change in age distribution alone cannot achieve the target.)

Under the Dependency Target More scenario, the required increase is immediate and colossal: immigration would spike rapidly to 2%, then to 4% of the population, in the first five years. The dynamics of reproduction and aging among the newly arrived immigrants reduces the required inflow to just over 2% of the population by 2035; then it rises again, surpassing 4% of the population by 2050. By the end of the period, Canada's population would be an eye-popping 235 million.

Under the Dependency Target Younger scenario (using the younger age profile of immigrants shown in figure 7.3), the time profile of immigration required to cap the old-age dependency ratio initially resembles that in the Dependency Target More scenario, but the delay in immigrants under 18 reaching working age lifts the early peak and deepens the later valley. Immigration spikes even higher initially, drops to zero by 2032, then rockets upward again after 2045. By the end of the period, Canada's population would be 139 million. The scale and volatility of immigration in this scenario is scarcely more realistic than in the Dependency Target More scenario.

---

8 ◆ We assume that every year, the government estimates what the OAD ratio would be in the upcoming year's population with no immigration, then sets the immigration level to achieve the target OAD ratio of 20.7%. Effectively, the government solves the following formula for M:

$$.207 = \alpha \frac{C}{C + M} + \beta \frac{M}{C + M}$$

where α is the OAD ratio in the current population, β is the OAD ratio in the immigrant populwation, C is the size of the current population, and M is the desired immigrant population. If desired immigration is negative, immigration is zero for that year. This formula can be simplified in the extreme age filter case to .207 = elderly/(current workers + desired immigration).

Stopping the OAD ratio from rising above 20.7% has the disadvantage of producing wild swings in the required level of immigration but it has the advantage of being a transparent methodology reproducible by other researchers. These scenarios fix the OAD ratio at almost exactly 20.7% except during a few years in some scenarios when required immigration goes to zero.

These huge numbers are not merely the result of an insufficiently stringent age filter on immigration. A ludicrously extreme scenario demonstrates the hopelessness of stabilizing the dependency ratio even with an inconceivably stringent age filter on immigration. Suppose, for example, that some such extreme filter ensured that *all* new immigrants were equally distributed between the ages of 20 and 24, for an average age of 22. This scenario is also illustrated in figure 7.7 as Dependency Target Ages 20–24. Because the old-age dependency ratio divides the population at the date of people's sixty-fifth birthdays, such a filter would ensure that every single immigrant lowers the old-age dependency ratio on arrival and for at least 40 years afterwards. Even so, immigration would have to spike over 2% initially and then remain at this high level for another 20 years; between 2012 and 2030, Canada would admit an average of 1.8 million immigrants 20 to 24 years old annually, compared to about 24,000 in that age range now.

Discussion

So far, we have made only a few concessions to realism, such as the less than ludicrously extreme age filter in the Younger scenarios. Noting all the caveats about, and possible consequences of, implementing immigration policies such as those just illustrated would be a multi-volume effort. We note in this section a few of the issues such attempts would raise: first, some caveats about large changes in immigration numbers; second, concerning impacts on the domestic population; and third, concerning where such flows of immigrants would come from.

Caveats

We noted earlier that the distinction we implicitly draw between policies that affect the total numbers of immigrants and their age distribution in our simulations is blurred in practice. Immigration policy clearly has other priorities, moreover; a change in the points system that aggressively sought to bring younger immigrants in and keep older ones out, for example, would cut against the goal of attracting immigrants with higher levels of education and work experience. Beach et al. (2006) have documented some other interesting interactions: for example, Ontario has tended to attract the youngest immigrants in the past, while the Atlantic provinces have tended to attract older ones, raising the question as to whether national goals might have unintended regional side effects.

Another key caveat in any discussion focused on the growth rate of, and relative size of, the workforce is that immigrants, at least initially, have lower employment rates than contemporaries born in Canada. An analysis of different population groups from the 2007 Labour Force Survey (Gilmore, 2008) (figure 7.8) shows that convergence with Canadian-born employment rates takes time in two senses: it is a function of the age of immigrants and of the amount of time they have been in Canada. Notwithstanding the fact that immigrants 55 years and older who entered the country more than five years ago have employment rates higher than their Canadian-born contemporaries, this effect is relatively small in economic terms (since employment rates among those 55 years and older are much lower to begin with) and would presumably only come about after many years when the employment rates of younger and more recent immigrants were below those of Canadian-born contemporaries. In a nutshell, our simulations overstate the immediate impacts of higher and younger immigration on the population actually employed.

Judging the scale of the proposed flows—Canada's absorptive capacity

That Canada can take in large numbers of immigrants is abundantly clear. The share of Canada's population born outside the country puts it fifth among 27 OECD countries (OECD, 2007). That such high numbers coincide with strong popular support for immigration testifies to the success of this strategy. That said, changes in the volume or age structure of immigration on the scale contemplated in these simulations, or even milder versions of them, raise some important questions.

Expressing immigration as a percentage of the resident population is misleading, for example, when immigration has the potential to change the population's age structure. If Canada adopted a much more aggressive policy of enlarging its supply of young people through immigration, resident young people would notice the impact, particularly through intensified competition in the job market. The volumes of immigration in our simulations are huge, not just compared to past experience, but compared to the resident population in the relevant age range. For example,

Figure 7.8: Employment rates by age group, immigrants compared to those born in Canada (2007)

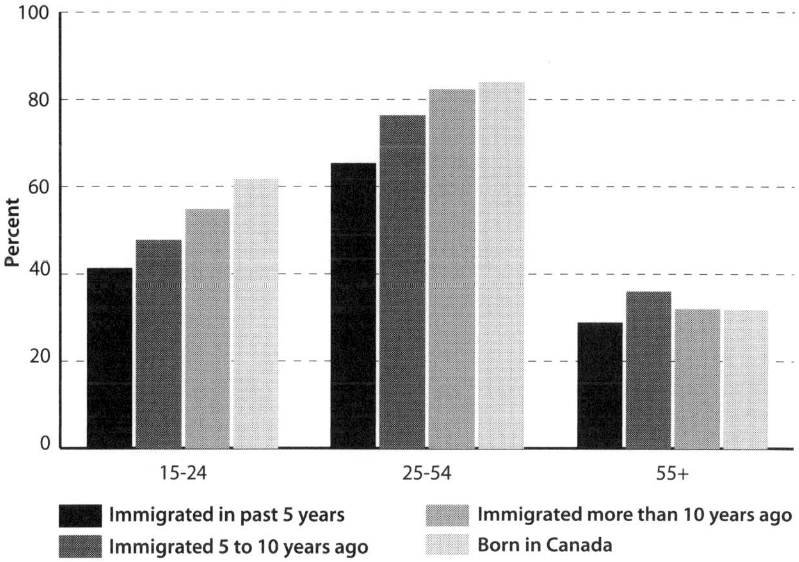

Source: Gilmore. 2008.

the population of those aged 20 to 24 years is now almost 2.3 million. So in the admittedly extreme Dependency Target Younger scenario, the *annual* inflow would be equal to more than 10% of the population of contemporaries born in Canada, as opposed to less than 1% in the Baseline (table 7.2). The impact of such an accelerated inflow on wages for that age group would surely be devastating for the already resident population.

Judging the scale of the proposed flows—source

Another perspective on the monumental scale of these imaginary flows is to consider where they would come from. As international competition for skilled labor increases, the host country's attractiveness has to be viewed increasingly against that of competing destinations (Beach et al., 2006). There are many young people in the world but most of them do not actually cross national borders in a given year, and a brief glance shows how large Canada's proposed draw would be relative to actual recent flows.

No comprehensive data on worldwide international migrants by age exist. However, partial data for 18 major countries suggest that

Table 7.2: Average yearly flow of young migrants required from 2009 to 2029 to stabilize the OAD ratio

	000s	% of 2007 base population in Canada	% of migrants to major counties
Ages 20 to 24			
Baseline	19.7	0.9	2.7
With current age structure	176.4	7.8	23.7
With younger age structure	238.7	10.5	32.1
With only immigrants 20 to 24	1,041.6	45.9	140.2
Ages 25 to 39			
Baseline	80.5	1.2	4.3
With current age structure	721.3	10.5	39.0
With younger age structure	409.2	6.0	22.1

Note: Major countries are Australia, Austria, Belgium, Canada, Denmark, Finland, Germany, Greece, Ireland, Italy, Netherlands, Norway, Portugal, Spain, Sweden, Switzerland, the United Kingdom, and the United States.
Sources: Statistics Canada; Migration Policy Institute; EuroStat; authors' calculations.

in recent years an average of some 730,000 people in the 20-to-24 age range have moved into those countries.[9] So, as a first approximation, in the Dependency Target More scenario, Canada would be trying to divert almost a quarter of all the people in this age range who would currently select one of those other countries as their destination (table 7.2). The 18 countries for which we have age data capture only a portion of the total flows but for Canada to "sell" itself as a destination for a much larger share of young immigrants would clearly require a major effort.

Two alternatives: later retirement and higher fertility

For a final perspective on immigration as a boost to the workforce and a way of maintaining the youthfulness of Canada's population structure, we compare it to two other demographic solutions. One is the familiar

9 ◆ See <www.migrationinformation.org/GlobalData/countrydata/country.cfm>; <epp.eurostat.ec.europa.eu> (retrieved May 2008). Data on migration flows are extremely spotty. As this is an illustrative exercise, we took the values from the latest year available for each country.

suggestion of pushing back the normal retirement age. Advances in longevity and shifts toward later entry into the workforce and less physically demanding occupations mean that today the lifetime equivalent of working until age 65 in 1970 is working until at least age 70. Yet, for a variety of reasons, not least the incentives in many private and public pension plans, people are retiring earlier than they did in 1970.[10] A later average or standard retirement age would provide a medium-term boost to workforce growth. To put some numbers behind this simple point, we use the Baseline projection and move the point at which the population is assumed to become inactive from 65 to 70, by raising that age by three months every year between 2009 and 2028.

A second, admittedly much more speculative, change would be a rise in the fertility rate. Because pro-natal policies are uncertain in their impact, not to mention politically controversial, we use a simple benchmark: a rise in the total number of births expected over a typical woman's lifetime from the current national value of 1.54 to 2.1, which is approximately the replacement rate, over the next 10 years.[11]

The impact of these changes on growth in the working-age population, which by the end of the shift in retirement age would be defined as 18 to 69, appear in figure 7.9. The figure also contrasts those growth rates with growth of the working-age population in the Baseline and in the More and Younger scenarios. The later retirement age would raise the growth rate of the working age population relative to the baseline for a couple of decades. By 2030, however, the lengthening of normal working life is complete and the average growth rates no longer differ appreciably from the Baseline.

Rising fertility naturally takes time to affect the growth rate of the working-age population, since the additional newborns under this

10 ◆ For examples of the early-retirement incentives built into pension plans, see Schirle, 2008.

11 ◆ The replacement rate is the number of children which a couple would need to have to exactly replace themselves in the population, i.e. 2. The actual rate is slightly higher to take into account the probability that some female children do not live long enough to bear children of their own. In advanced countries where mortality among youngsters is low, the replacement rate is slightly less than 2.1 children per woman.

Figure 7.9: Projected growth in Canada's working-age population with gradual rise in retirement age or fertility rate (1972–2058)

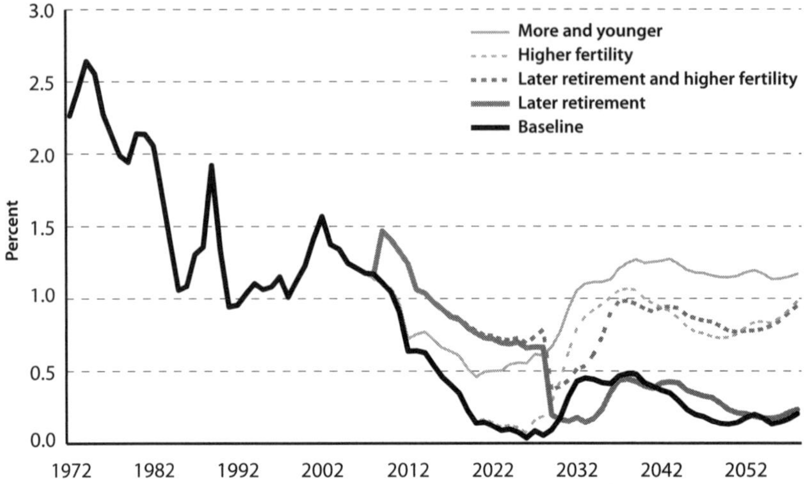

Source: Statistics Canada; authors' calculations.

scenario take 18 years to reach working age. Once they do begin to enter the potential workforce, however, their impact is considerable: since this scenario involves substantial natural increase in the population, a 0.7% average immigration rate translates into a growth rate for the working-age population comparable to current rates after the late 2020s.

The later retirement and higher fertility rate scenarios are interesting to look at together. In this implementation of these changes, the impact of the latter accelerates just as the impact of the former is dissipating, meaning that together (the Later Retirement and Higher Fertility scenario), they would have an immediate and sustained impact on Canada's potential workforce.

Finally, we consider the impact of these changes on the OAD ratio. Figure 7.10 compares the evolution of the OAD ratio under the redefinition involved in the later retirement scenario with the evolution of the ratio assuming higher fertility, and again contrasts them to their counterparts in the Baseline and More and Younger Scenarios. Not surprisingly, later retirement reduces the level of the OAD ratio relative to the Baseline in the near term, and both delays and mutes its eventual rise. The impact of higher fertility is, as noted already, delayed by the period it takes for

Figure 7.10: Projected old-age dependency ratio with gradual rise in retirement age or fertility rate (1972–2058)

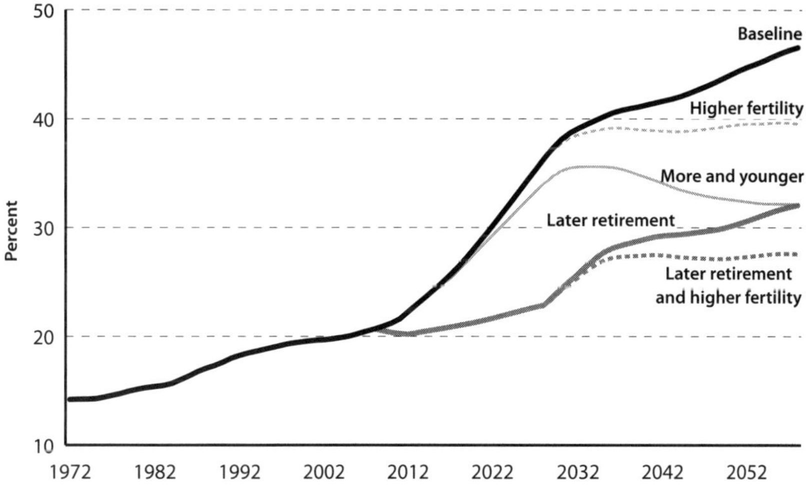

Source: Statistics Canada; authors' calculations.

the newborns to reach working age but is then pronounced, capping the OAD ratio at about 40% after 2020. With the combined effect of the two changes, the influence of the higher fertility rate would kick in shortly after the initial impact of later retirement on the growth of the OAD ratio had ceased, resulting in an OAD ratio consistently lower even than in the More and Younger Scenario throughout the projection period.

These results show how powerful a modest and gradual change in the normal work and retirement pattern is in changing the dependency ratio, by comparison with significant changes in both the volume and age-structure of immigration. An increase in the fertility rate is a far less certain, and far more controversial, object of policy. Over time, however, it too would have tremendous power to change the age structure of Canada's population, on a par with some of the more extreme immigration scenarios.

Conclusion

The message of these simulations is that we should not overstate the contribution immigration can make to workforce growth and keeping Canada young. Workforce growth is the easier of the two demographic variables to address with immigration. Even so, immigration rates equal to 1% of the already resident population would not prevent workforce growth in Canada dipping to historic lows in the 2020s, and the immigration that would be needed—even with major efforts to attract a larger share of younger people—to maintain workforce growth at its recent rate would be well outside the realm of economic or political feasibility.

Aging is more difficult yet. Increasing immigration to 1% of population a year without varying its age distribution would slow the rise in the OAD ratio only marginally. And raising immigration to this level while trying to select only very young immigrants with children, so as to lower dramatically the average age of immigrants, would still not prevent a historic rise in the ratio. Only extreme and unpalatable policies, such as rapidly increasing immigration from less than 1% of the population to well over 3% for decades, could come close to stabilizing the OAD ratio.

If Canada is prepared to undertake major policy reforms to mitigate the impact of a slower-growing and aging population on its workforce and age structure, other tools have—at least in a numeric sense—at least as much promise as immigration. Delaying the normal age of retirement can help both workforce growth and the OAD ratio in the near term, and higher fertility would help both of them in the next generation and beyond.

While Canadians have many economic, cultural, and humanitarian reasons to welcome more immigrants, immigration on its own cannot decisively change the paths of workforce growth and rising old-age dependency that the past fertility patterns of the resident population have set. Even if Canadians do choose to raise immigration rates in the future, and even if they choose to target younger immigrants for demographic reasons, such measures need complementing with other policies to delay retirement and raise fertility if Canada truly wishes to transform its demographic future.

References

Aydemir, Abdurrahman, and Chris Robinson (2006). *Return and Onward Migration among Working Age Men*. Analytical Studies Branch Working Paper Series No. 273. Statistics Canada.

Beach, Charles, Alan G. Green, and Christopher Worswick (2006). Impacts of the Point System and Immigration Policy Levers on Skill Characteristics of Canadian Immigrants. Queen's [University] Economic Department Working Paper No. 1115.

Canadian Press (2005, September 24). Liberals Preparing to Unveil Immigration Plan. *CTV Toronto.* <http://toronto.ctv.ca/servlet/an/local/CTVNews/20050923/canada_immigration_050923?hub=TorontoNewHome>.

Citizenship and Immigration Canada [CIC] (2007). *Annual Report to Parliament on Immigration.* Minister of Public Works and Government Services.

Denton, Frank T., and Byron G. Spencer (2004). *Population Aging and the Macroeconomy: Explorations in the Use of Immigration as an Instrument of Control.* QSEP Research Report No. 398. McMaster University.

Gilmore, Jason (2008). *The Canadian Immigrant Labour Market in 2007.* Statistics Canada.

Grant, Jonathan, et al. (2004). *Low Fertility and Population Aging: Causes, Consequences, and Policy Options.* RAND Corporation.

Guillemette, Yvan (2003). *Slowing Down with Age: The Ominous Implications of Workforce Aging for Canadian Living Standards.* C.D. Howe Institute Commentary 182. C.D. Howe Institute.

Guillemette, Yvan, and William Robson (2006). *No Elixir of Youth: Immigration Cannot Keep Canada Young.* C.D. Howe Institute Backgrounder No. 96.

Organisation for Economic Co-operation and Develpment [OECD] (2005a). *Trends in International Migration—Annual Report 2004 Edition*. OECD.

Organisation for Economic Co-operation and Develpment [OECD] (2005b). *Ageing and Employment Policies—Canada—Vieillissement et politiques de l'emploi*. OECD.

Organisation for Economic Co-operation and Develpment [OECD] (2006). *International Migration Outlook—Annual Report 2006 Edition*. OECD.

Organisation for Economic Co-operation and Develpment [OECD] (2007). *International Migration Outlook—Annual Report 2007 Edition*. OECD.

Robson, William B.P. (2007). *Time and Money: The Challenge of Demographic Change and Government Finances*. C.D. Howe Institute Backgrounder 109. C.D. Howe Institute.

Schirle, Tammy (2008). *Greener Pastures: Understanding the Impact of Retirement Incentives in Defined Benefit Pension Plans*. C.D. Howe Institute Commentary 262. C.D. Howe Institute.

Schmertmann, Carl P. (1992). Immigrants' Ages and the Structure of Stationary Populations with Below-Replacement Fertility. *Demography* 29, 4: 595–612.

Statistics Canada (2005). *Population Projections for Canada, the Provinces and Territories*.

United Nations (2002). *World Population Prospects 1950–2050* (2002 revisions). United Nations.

Chapter 8

The immigration option to population aging in Canada

Marcel Mérette

As is the case for many major industrialized countries, population aging is an inevitable and central feature of Canada in this first half of the twenty-first century. Population aging is explained by a combination of demographic factors such as rising life expectancy, declining fertility rates and migration. The demographic shift in Canada will be significant. According to United Nations (UN) demographic projections (UN Population Division, 2005), the proportion of the Canadian population aged 65 and over is projected to more than double over a 50-year period, from 12.5% in 2000 to 26% in 2050.

Population aging of the magnitude projected for Canada is likely to have sizeable implications for intergenerational equity (public debt and pensions), government budgets (health care and public pension spending), trade and international capital flows, and the regional and sectoral reallocation of resources. In this paper, I focus on the implication of population aging for the workforce, namely, the rising average age of the Canadian workforce and the relative scarcity of workers.

◆ I would like to thank Herbert Grubel for valuable advice, Yuan Liu for helpful assistance, and the participants at the Canadian Immigration Policy Conference for relevant suggestions. All errors are mine.

One of the major challenges associated with workforce aging is the reduction in the growth of the labor force. A slowdown in the workforce growth rate may increase the elderly dependency ratios (population 65+ / population 15–64), which in turn results in a reduction in living standards. One method available for preventing such a rise in this ratio is increasing the number of immigrant workers. It is important to note that these immigrant workers will have to be highly skilled and educated if developments in the world economy force Canada to shift into more knowledge-intensive production activities.[1]

This chapter analyzes issues raised by the prospective increase in elderly dependence and need for more workers and the opportunity to deal with the resultant problems through immigration policies. The analysis starts in the next section with an elaboration of the demographic facts about aging populations in Canada and potential labor shortages. The following section presents the results of simulations I have made to quantify the impact of increasing the flow of immigrants on the workforce and on the performance of the economy. Then I use general equilibrium arguments to discuss the potential economic consequences of using alternatives to increasing immigration for the solution of Canada's problems of aging and pending worker shortages.

Demographic and labor-force facts in Canada

Natural population growth has been declining in Canada since 1991. Figure 8.1 shows that the natural population increase was around 200,000 in 1976, was under 100,000 in 2006 and is predicted to turn negative in 2026. After 2026, immigration is projected to be the only contributing

1 ◆ Storesletten (2000) demonstrates that selective immigration policies that involve increasing the inflow of highly skilled and medium-skilled immigrant workers would remove the need for fiscal reform in the United States. Fehr, Jokisch, and Kotlikoff (2004) also examine the effects of increasing the number of skilled immigrants in the United States, Europe, and Japan with a CGE model. They find that doubling the number of highly skilled immigrants would mitigate significantly future tax increases expected with population aging in the US, Europe, and Japan.

Figure 8.1: Population growth in Canada (1976–2045)

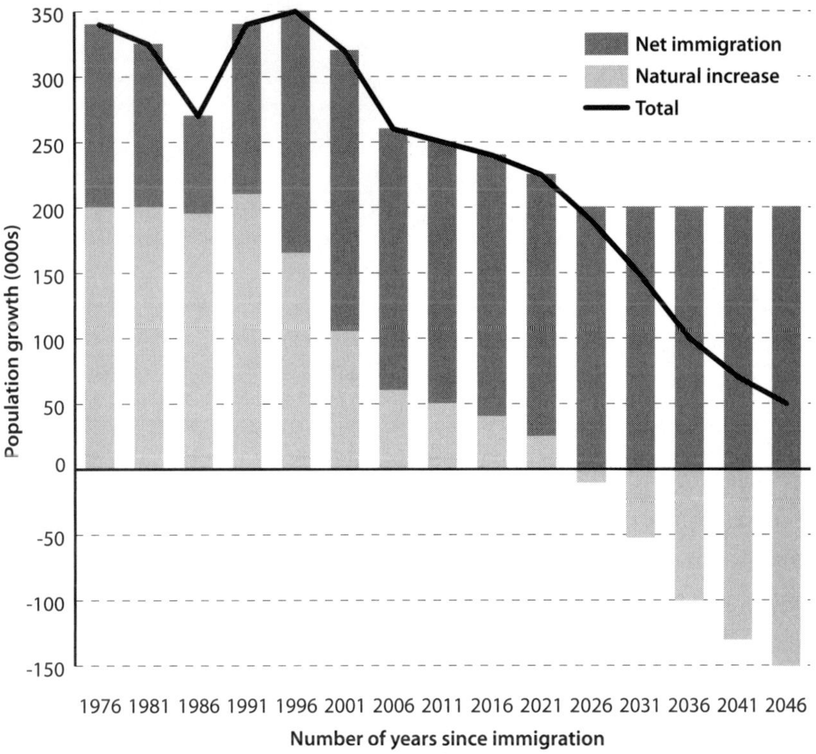

Source: Léonard and Rainville, 2006.

factor to Canada's population growth. The figures shown are based on the assumption that 200,000 new immigrants arrive in Canada annually.

The projected demographic changes in Canada hide the fact that the changes will affect regions of the country differently. For example, the Atlantic region and, in particular, the province of Newfoundland currently has one of the lowest fertility rates in the world, while the rates in the provinces of Manitoba and Saskatchewan are much higher. In addition, regional differences will be accentuated by the fact that the vast majority of immigrants choose the provinces of Ontario and British Columbia as their regional location, although these two provinces represent just a little more than 50% of the Canadian population.

The regional impact of the differing fertility and immigration rates is summarized in table 8.1, which shows the changes in projected regional elderly dependency ratios between 2000 and 2045. As can be seen, the

Table 8.1: Projected regional elderly dependency ratio (population 65+ / population 15–64)

	2000	2030	2045
Canada	18.4	36.5	40.4
Atlantic	18.9	48.9	61.2
Quebec	18.6	40.6	44.8
Ontario	18.4	32.9	37.0
Prairies	21.8	35.6	35.5
Alberta	15.6	32.3	37.0
British Columbia	19.4	40.2	44.6

Source: Léonard and Rainville, 2006.

Atlantic region and Quebec will exhibit the largest increases in their elderly dependency ratios, while the Prairies and Ontario will have the smallest increases. The increases in Alberta and British Columbia fall in between the two extremes.

Turning to labor force growth, figure 8.2 shows that the growth rate of the population 15 years and older in Canada has been declining since 2000 and will continue to decline over the next decades, assuming a continuation of net immigration of 200,000 annually. Consequently, total labor-force growth rate is expected to reach zero by 2030. The size of new cohorts of workers in the next few years will thus be much smaller than what we usually observe in the Canadian labor market. The workers will also be older on average.

The effects of a rise in the proportion of older workers due to population aging depend on retirement decisions. If the average age of retirement remains unchanged, retirement rates will rise as older cohorts reach retirement age. This in turn will reduce aggregate labor supply, result in excess demand, and increase the cost of labor. In addition, there may also be shortages of workers with special skills. However, if the present trend towards early retirement continues, the impact of population aging on the labor market and the economy will be aggravated. If, on the other hand, older workers decide to retire later the effects of aging on labor markets would be significantly reduced. I will return to this last argument in the section on alternatives to immigration.

Figure 8.2: Growth in the Canadian labor force (1976–2030)

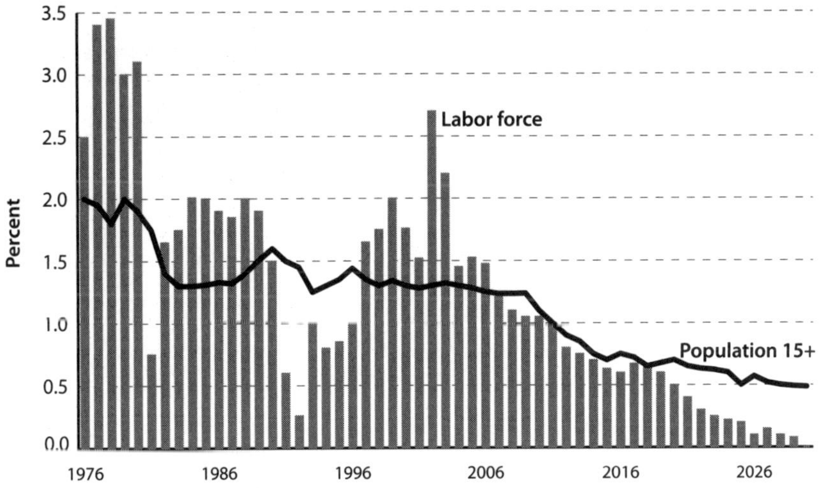

Source: Léonard and Rainville, 2006.

The effects that recent trends in retirement and labor-force participation of older workers have on the labor market have been examined by Statistics Canada (2007), the results of which are summarized in figure 8.3. As can be seen, the average age of retirement has declined steadily in Canada over the period from 1976 to 1998 for both men and women, from around 65 for men and 64 for women during the second half of the 1970s to 61.5 years for men and 60 for women in the late 1990s.[2] However, since 1998, this trend in retirement seems to have halted. In fact, from the bottom level observed in 1998, the average retirement age has tended to increase somewhat, ranging between 62 and 62.5 in 2003 to 2005 for men and around 61 for women.

To assess likely future trends, it is useful to consider the determinants of the average age of retirement. It turns out that the age of retirement is sensitive to institutions and to current economic conditions. For instance, the decline in the effective retirement age during the late 1970s and 1980s is correlated with reforms to the Canadian Income Security programs. The Spousal Allowance (SA) program was introduced in 1975 and designed to bridge certain individuals who are not yet eligible to

---

2 ◆ We shall see later in this chapter that a one-year change in the average age of retirement has a significant impact on the economy.

Figure 8.3: Average age of retirement, by sex (1976–2005)

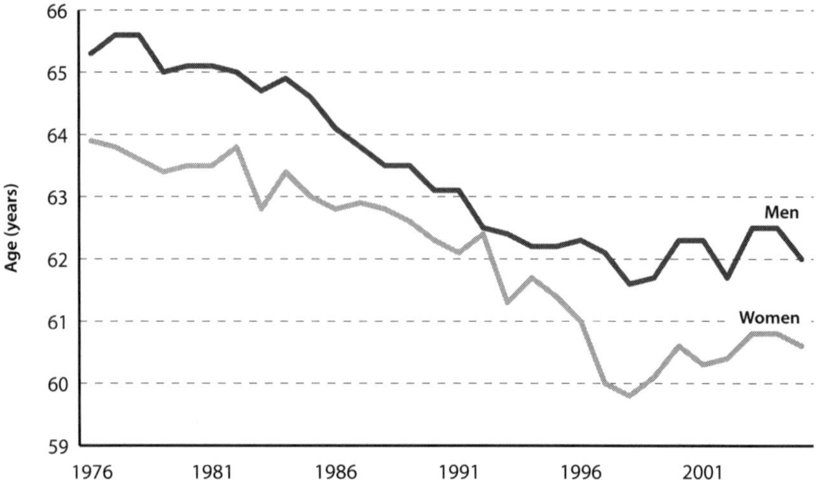

Source: Statistics Canada, 2007.

receive the Old Age Security (OAS) and Guaranteed Income Supplement. The SA is paid to 60-to-64-year-old spouses of OAS recipients, widows, and widowers. According to Baker (2002), the introduction of the SA has reduced the labor-force participation of older men in eligible couples by 6 to 7 percentage points. Another institutional factor that likely played a role in lowering the average age of retirement is the introduction of the early retirement provision in the QPP in 1984 and in the CPP in 1987.3 However, the influence of these factors is not settled. Baker and Benjamin (1999) have found that, while these reforms led to an increase in pension benefits, they had little immediate effect on labor market behavior because men who initially took advantage of early retirement provisions had limited labor-market attachment in any case.

3 ◆ The Canada and Quebec Pension Plans (CPP/QPP) provide earnings-based pensions funded through payroll taxes paid by both employers and employees. The normal uptake age for the CPP/QPP is 65. Since 1984 in Quebec and 1987 in the rest of Canada, individuals may apply for early benefits starting at age 60, subject to an actuarial reduction of 0.5% for the number of months until the individual's 65th birthday (6% per year). Conversely, individuals who delay receiving CPP/QPP benefits after age 65 are entitled to a 0.5% per month actuarial increase.

The drop in the effective retirement age during the first half of the 1980s is in part be explained by the 1981–1982 recession. Rising unemployment during that period provided incentives for older unemployed workers to exit the labor market. Canada was hit by another major recession in 1990 to 1991, followed by a slow recovery. During the first half of the 1990s, the Canadian unemployment rate averaged more than 10%, compared to 7.5% in 1989, which helped lower the overall participation rate and possibly led to involuntary retirement. Finally, according to Kieran (2001) and Fortin and Fortin (2004) the significant drop in the retirement age that occurred during the middle and second half of the 1990s is due to restructuring and downsizing in the public sector, which encouraged many public servants to take early retirement packages and leave the labor market.

The near-retirement rate

The coming pressure of population aging on the labor force can be approximated by the near-retirement-rate (NRR) indicator, which measures the percentage of workers who are within 10 years of the median retirement age. The NRR is influenced by two factors, the median age of retirement and the age distribution of the workforce. An increase in the median retirement age reduces the NRR, while a rise in the proportion of workers within 10 years of the median retirement age raises the NRR.

As shown in figure 8.4, the NRR has increased continuously over the past 18 years. From 11.4% in 1987, the NRR reached 22.1% in 2005. Between 1987 and 1998, the rise in the NRR is due to both a reduction in the median retirement age and an increase in the proportion of older workers. After 1998, the median retirement age has stabilized or risen somewhat, thus contributing to a reduction in the NRR. However, despite this, workforce aging has remained a dominating factor, leading to a continued increase in the NRR. Over the next decades, it is evident that the rising proportion of older workers will continue to exert upward pressures on the NRR. What is less certain, however, is how retirement behaviors will evolve in the future. A gradual increase in the median retirement age, for example, might reduce labor-market pressures by softening the rise in the NRR.

Finally, a look at the retirement pattern by province suggests that regional differences in demographics and retirement behavior also generate important labor-market pressure differences at the provincial level.

Figure 8.4: The near retirement rate (1987–2005)

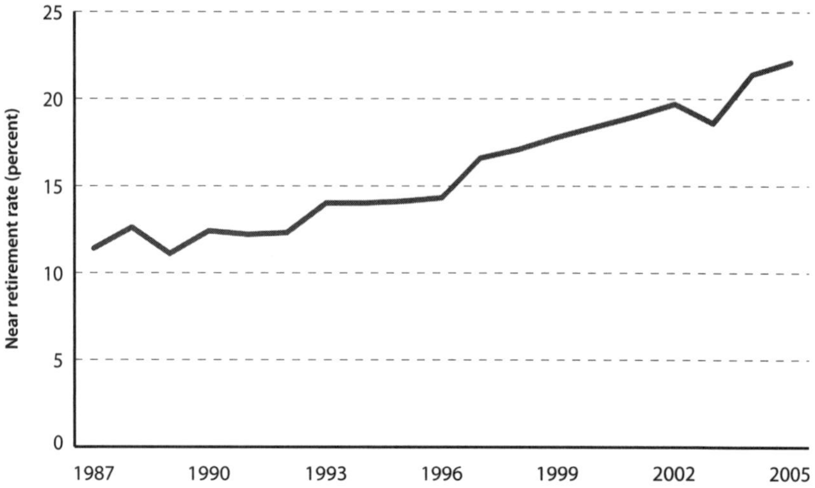

Note: The near retirement rate is defined as the percentage of the workforce within 10 years of the median retirement age.
Source: Statistics Canada, 2007.

According to table 8.2, between 1987 and 2002 the Atlantic provinces (Newfoundland & Labrador, Prince Edward Island, Nova Scotia, New Burnswick), Quebec, and British Columbia have led the reduction in the retirement trend in Canada while, in Saskatchewan and Alberta, the median retirement age has risen. Ontario and Manitoba are in between.

Labor-force participation by older workers

It is important to stress that historic data discussed above concerning the NRR and the median and average age of retirement may change in the future as workers retire later. This trend is beginning to show up in figure 8.5. As can be seen, in the earlier years between 1976 and 1998, the participation rate of men from 55 to 59 fell from 84.2% in 1976 to 70.6% in 1998, while the participation rate of men from 60 to 64 fell even more, from 66.5% to 44.6%. Since 1998, however, the participation rate of men from 55 to 59 and 60 to 64 has increased, reaching 76.2% and 54%, respectively, in 2005. Notice as well that the participation rate of women aged 55 to 59 has increased continuously during the past 30 years, while the participation rate of women aged 60 to 64 has remained virtually flat

Table 8.2: Median retirement age and percent of workforce near retirement, by province

	Near-retirement rate (percent)*			Median retirement age (years)	
	1987	2002	Diff.	1987	2002
Canada	11.4	19.8	8.4	64.3	60.6
Newfoundland & Labrador	9.6	21.6	12.0	63.3	59.6
Prince Edward Island	10.0	24.9	14.9	65.7	59.4
Nova Scotia	10.2	21.6	11.4	63.7	59.8
New Brunswick	9.2	20.9	11.7	64.6	59.6
Quebec	10.4	21.6	11.2	64.0	59.8
Ontario	10.8	19.6	8.8	64.7	60.8
Manitoba	11.5	20.3	8.8	64.6	61.2
Saskatchewan	15.3	13.8	−1.5	64.1	65.1
Alberta	11.4	15.0	3.6	63.1	63.4
British Columbia	11.3	23.6	12.3	64.3	60.3

Note: The near retirement rate is defined as the percent of the workforce within 10 years of the median retirement age.
Source: Statistics Canada, 2007.

Figure 8.5: Labor force participation rate of older workers, by sex (1976–2005)

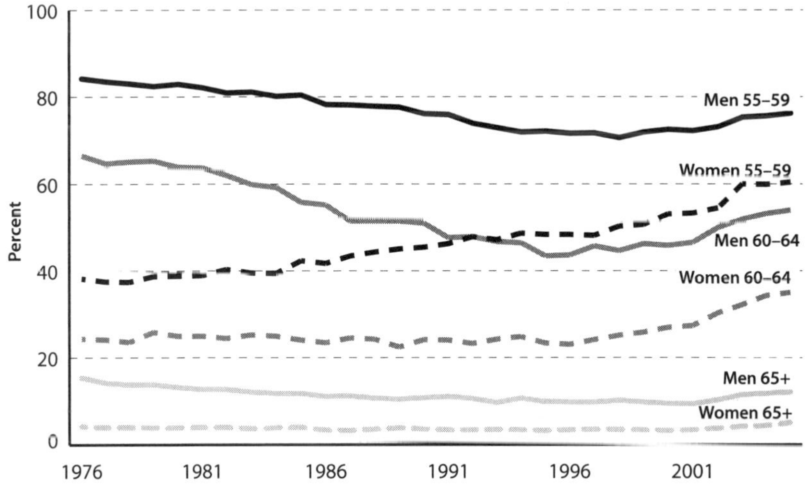

Source: Statistics Canada, 2007.

between 1976 and 1998 and increased since. Therefore, the participation-rate numbers not only suggest that early retirement trends halted in 1998 but also that the participation rate of older workers has increased since. As I explain later, this may be great news for the economy of Canada.

Temporary retirement and later return to the workforce

The preceding conclusion needs to be modified by the fact that a significant proportion of retirees eventually return to the labor market. Thirty percent of older workers who ended a full-time job voluntarily between 1993 and 1997 began a new job within 24 months (Pyper and Giles, 2002). A large longitudinal sample from 1995 to 2002, found that 18% of retirees eventually, and for some time, returned to the labor market (Léonard and Rainville, 2006).

These results suggest that older individuals remain a potential source of labor even after they have retired from their job for a time. This phenomenon might become stronger if employers adjust their human resources strategy and allow a greater share of older individuals in their workforce. This change in strategy will be encouraged because retirees tend to be healthier and better educated than they were in the past and have more experience than new employees. Market forces should override implicit barriers to the adoption of these strategies, such as agism (Lagacé and Tougas, 2006).

An economic analysis of population aging

The economic implication of population aging is not limited to the labor force. Savings and investment, trade and international capital flows, and fiscal policy are likely to be significantly affected as well. Moreover, both the macroeconomic and fiscal effects will influence wages, the returns to physical and human capital, consumer and producer prices, the terms of trade and real-world interest rates.

The complexity and dynamics of demographic, fiscal, and economic influences associated with population aging can be studied though the use of large-scale economic models using appropriate theoretical models. Especially, dynamic life-cycle (overlapping-generations) computable general equilibrium (CGE) models can be used for this task because they allow modeling the behavior of agents over their lifetimes.[4] In this section, I report and discuss the results from various simulation experiments for Canada using this modelling framework.

Impact of population aging on the productive capacity of the Canadian economy

In theory, population aging affects productive capacity through several key channels. The first channel is the change in effective units of labor, which combines the impact of population aging on the labor force participation and the quality of the workforce. The second channel works through aging of the "baby boom" generation as it retires. This retirement reduces the relative size of the active population, the total labor-force participation, and thus lowers real per-capita GDP relative to a situation with no population aging. Third, during the period preceding retirement of the "baby boom" generation, labor productivity may rise due to an increase in the proportion of experienced workers. Fourth, more recent cohorts of workers are better educated and thus raise the proportion of skilled workers. According to the standard overlapping generations CGE model (with no change in labor supply behavior) developed by Fougère et al. (2005a, 2004), total effective labor supply, which combines both quantity and quality of labor, is expected to fall sharply over the next several decades (table 8.3). This decline takes place in spite of a projected increase in the quality of labor.

Real GDP in the future will be reduced by lower national savings and investment caused by aging. This result is based on the life-cycle theory of savings, which implies that households during their working life, save and accumulate wealth, which they spend and use up during retirement. Accordingly, the rise in the proportion of older people reduces aggregate net private savings and hence the country's stock of physical capital eventually declines.[5]

---

4 ◆ See, for example, Ferh et al., 2005; Börsch-Supan et al., 2001; Équipe INGENUE, 2001; Hviding and Mérette, 1998.

5 ◆ This is an argument from a closed economy model. But as population aging is a common feature of all industrialized countries, the closed economy framework is a

Table 8.3: Simulated economic impact of population aging in Canada (percent deviations from initial steady state of no population aging)

	2006	2014	2018	2026	2034	2038	2042	2050
Real GDP per capita	0.5	0.8	0.7	−0.3	−2.5	−4.0	−5.9	−10.5
Effective labor supply	1.9	2.3	0.6	−5.9	−15.8	−21.3	−26.8	−41.1
Physical capital	4.0	9.3	10.3	8.4	1.8	−3.2	−9.2	−24.3
Capital-labor ratio	2.1	6.9	9.6	15.3	20.9	23.0	24.1	20.1
Real wage rate	0.8	2.7	3.7	5.8	8.2	9.3	10.2	10.2
Rate of interest	−0.1	−0.3	−0.7	−1.0	−1.5	−1.7	−1.8	−1.8

Source: Fougère et al.,2005a.

It is important to observe here that population aging also has positive economic implications. The negative labor-supply shock leads to increased labor-market pressures and to an increase in real wages, which induces employers to use more labor-saving capital and technology. The decrease in the size of the labor force will facilitate this process as it leads to an increase in the supply of capital per worker and a reduction in the price of physical capital. I will return to the rise in the real wage rate in discussing alternatives to immigration as policy measures in the context of aging.

Table 8.4 shows the results of our estimates using the theories outlined above in a dynamic computable general equilibrium model. The first line shows the decline in per-capita incomes for all of Canada, while the following lines show those of the country's different regions. As can be seen, the Atlantic provinces and Quebec will experience the largest reductions in per-capita incomes, followed by Manitoba, Saskatchewan, and British Columbia. Ontario and Alberta are estimated to enjoy higher per-capita incomes, at least during the first few decades.

The results for the different regions are explained by differences in the variables discussed above. The populations of the Atlantic region and Quebec are aging most rapidly and have the strongest trend toward

good approximation for Canada with respect to aging issues. Mérette and Georges (2009) demonstrate that, in a multicountry framework, however, globalization through international trade may generate a significant increase in Canada's terms of trade, which would sustain real consumption per capita.

Table 8.4: Simulated impact of population aging on regional real GDP per capita (percent deviations from initial steady state of no population aging)

	2006	2014	2018	2026	2034	2038	2042	2050
Canada	0.5	0.8	0.7	−0.3	−2.5	−4.0	−5.9	−10.5
Atlantic provinces	0.1	−0.5	−1.4	−4.8	−11.2	−15.4	−19.9	−28.5
Quebec	−0.3	−1.9	−3.1	−6.9	−12.3	−15.2	−18.0	−22.8
Ontario	0.6	1.2	1.0	−0.1	−1.5	−2.1	−2.8	−5.5
Prairies	−0.3	−1.1	−1.7	−2.3	−2.4	−2.7	−3.7	−8.0
Alberta	1.3	2.5	2.7	2.8	0.8	−1.4	−4.5	−12.0
British Columbia	−0.4	−0.8	0.1	0.1	−0.5	−2.2	−5.0	−13.6

Source: Fougère et al., 2005a.

earlier retirement. The provinces of Alberta and Ontario are expected to enjoy an increase in effective units of labor due to both an increase in the number and quality (experience) of their workforce, until 2018 for Ontario and 2026 for Alberta.

Other factors explaining the different experiences of provinces are as follows. Ontario receives the greatest share of immigrants, a significant proportion of which is highly skilled and contributes to the projected rise in per-capita income. Alberta's population has a higher fertility rate than other provinces and its workforce retires later than that of the rest of Canada. However, as the "baby boom" generation eventually retires, in the long run real per-capita GDP falls more significantly than in Ontario. The Prairies experience a more moderate decline in real per-capita GDP than the rest of Canada because, like Alberta, in these provinces fertility rates and effective retirement ages are relatively higher.

Large immigration flows also affect Ontario and British Columbia by making their populations age less rapidly and keeping real per-capita GDP virtually unaffected by population aging until 2034. Over the long run, the magnitude of the impact is similar to that experienced by Alberta due to its higher fertility rate.

Figure 8.6 shows the long run impact of population aging in Canada on regional income disparity. As can be seen, disparity will increase substantially over the next decades. The gap in real GDP per capita increases substantially for the Atlantic region and Quebec especially, while it fluctuates within a tighter margin in the rest of Canada.

Figure 8.6: Gap in provincial and regional real GDP per capita relative to Canadian GDP (percent difference 2002–2050)

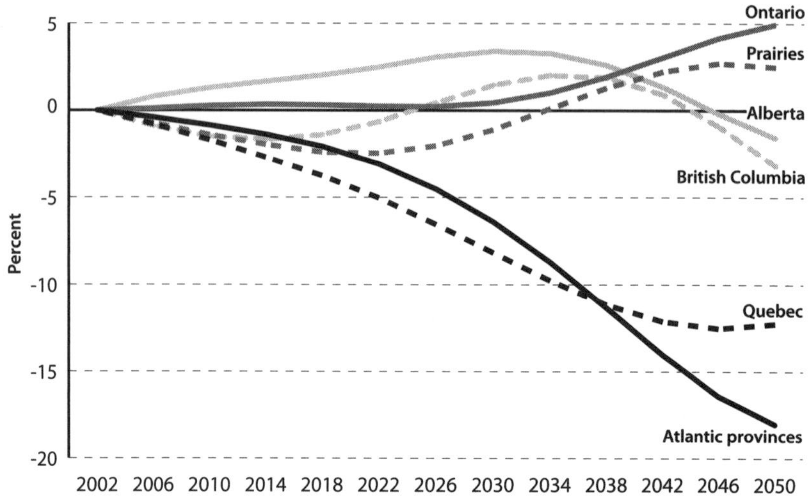

Note: All real GDPs per capita are normalized to 1 in 2002 and the regional GDP gap is measured as the percent change in regional GDP relative to the national level.
Source: Fougère et al., 2004.

Can we moderate the impact of aging by selecting more immigrants?[6]

Since 2000, recent immigrants equal about 0.75% of the population per year and, since the early 1990s, the immigrants were more highly educated than before. To explore the economic effects of selecting more immigrants, I analyze the effect of increasing immigration from 0.75% to 1% of the population, beginning in 2002, under two alternative assumptions about their skill-levels. In the first simulation, the skill-composition of the additional flow of new immigrants is proportionally the same as the first 0.75%, which in the period from 1997 to 2000 consisted of highly skilled (24%), medium-skilled (13%), low-skilled (28%), and individuals without labor force attachment (35%) (as in Fougère et al., 2005b). In the second simulation, the additional flow of new immigrants is composed of highly skilled immigrants only. The impact on real GDP per capita is presented in figure 8.7.

6 ◆ The analysis here is mostly taken from Fougère et al., 2004, 2005b, 2007.

Figure 8.7: Impact of population aging on real GDP per capita according to alternative immigration policies (% shock-minus-control impact, 2002–2050)

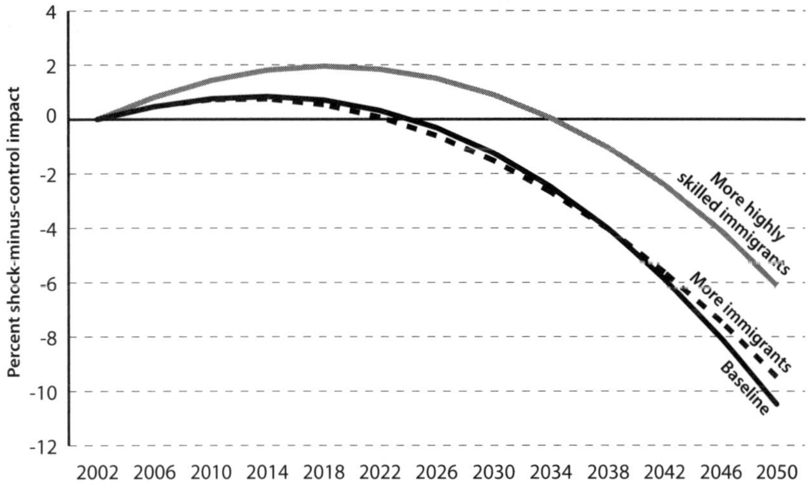

Source: Fougère et al., 2005b.

The solid line in figure 8.7 shows the annual percentage decline in real per-capita income under the assumption that the present rate of immigration is maintained in the future. The broken line shows the effects of increasing the immigration rate from 0.75% to 1.0% while maintaining the recent mix of skills. As can be seen, this line differs only very little from the solid line, suggesting that increasing the immigration rate has negligible effects on per-capita income and only in later years will show a small positive effect. The effect of a rise in labor supply on productive capacity is more than offset by a reduction in the capital-to-labor ratio and a fall in labor productivity. On the other hand, the third line in the graph shows that attracting more highly skilled immigrants generates substantial benefits relative to the other two scenarios. This favorable development is due to the fact that the highly skilled immigrants have strong labor-market attachment and raise the quality and productivity of the labor force.

However, raising the number of immigrants with high skill levels has a drawback shown in table 8.5. The increased supply of highly skilled immigrants lowers the difference in earnings between those with low and high skills. As a result of such a development, fewer Canadians would invest in human capital and acquire the high skills that bring high

Table 8.5: Impact of selecting more high-skilled immigrants on skill premium relative to the baseline scenario

Skill premium for ...	1998	2010	2022	2030	2042	2050
high over medium skill	−0.8	−2.8	−4.6	−5.6	−7.1	−8.0
high over low skill	−0.8	−3.1	−5.1	−6.3	−8.0	−9.1
medium over low skill	−0.1	−0.3	−0.5	−0.7	−0.9	−1.0

Source: Fougère et al., 2005b.

incomes and other satisfaction. This effect is not included in the simulations that produced the figures in figure 8.7.

It is worth noting that Fougère et al. (2004) show that the distribution of recent immigrants according to the provincial share of the population in the total population would generate significant economic benefits to regions like the Atlantic provinces, the Prairies, and Quebec in the long run relative to the base scenario. Moreover, it would also significantly contribute to a reduction in regional differences in real wage levels and growth.

Bruno et al. (2007) extend this model by taking into consideration the reduction in the premium that high skills earn over lower skills brought about by the larger inflow of skilled immigrants. This reduction would induce fewer Canadians to invest in higher education, which would lower productive capacity in the long run. This effect could be eliminated if firms developed at the same time a greater preference for the hiring of highly skilled workers. Under this scenario, the immigration policy would increase labor quality, boost labor productivity, and raise the productive capacity of the Canadian economy.

Without any change in firms' demand for highly skilled workers, larger flows of young, highly skilled immigrants have a positive effect on labor productivity through a rise in labor quality in the short run. However, in the longer run they lower real GDP per capita because they reduce incentives for young Canadians to invest in human capital. Politically, the larger inflow of highly skilled immigrants reduces earnings inequality; however it does so by making highly skilled workers worse off rather than by raising income for lower skilled workers.[7]

7 ◆ Please note that the above studies do not take into consideration the cost of integration of new immigrants either.

Alternatives to immigration

What would happen if older workers retire later?

This section simulates the implications of assuming that the effects of Canada's aging population on the labor market are offset by policies that induce workers to stay in the work force longer. Such a change in the behavior of workers can be achieved by eliminating early retirement incentives in Canada's public pension system, eliminating retirement ages mandated by provincial governments, income tax incentives, and others.[8]

Before considering effective policies to increase the retirement age, however, it is useful to estimate the marginal effect on Canada's productive capacity resulting from an increase in the average age of retirement from its present 61.2 to 62.2 and then to 65, the latter increase taking effect gradually over the period ending in 2014. The first policy of increasing the average retirement age by one year has the same marginal effect as an increase in the rate of immigration from 0.75% to 1% of the population, in which the additional flow of new immigrants is composed of highly skilled immigrants only (Fougère et al., 2005a). Increasing the average age of retirement to 65, however, would basically triple the economic benefits and would be equivalent to a 9% rise in the labor supply in 2030 relative to the baseline.

Under these simulations, real per-capita GDP would rise 8.4% in 2030 and nearly 10% by 2050 (table 8.6). The substantial increase in labor supply would also lead to a 1.2% reduction in real wages before tax by 2050 but a 3.3% increase after tax. Finally, a universal average retirement age of 65 would allow the governments to reduce the CPP contribution rate by 25% and the QPP rate by 38%. The QPP contribution-rate reduction would be larger since the policy would raise the effective retirement age from the relatively low level of 59.7 to 65. Simulation analysis indicates that the economic and financial costs of early retirement in terms of unused productive capacity and reduced taxation base are significant. Correspondingly, the benefits of working longer are potentially large.

---

8 ◆ Côté (2005) presents a number of policy recommendations to encourage older workers to work longer.

Table 8.6: Simulated impact of an increase in the effective retirement age (percent difference relative to baseline)

	2006	2010	2022	2030	2042	2050
Real GDP per capita						
Working one extra year	1.6	1.9	2.4	2.7	3.0	3.2
Working until age 65	2.7	5.0	7.5	8.4	9.3	9.9
Labour supply						
Working one extra year	2.0	2.1	2.4	2.4	2.3	2.1
Working until age 65	4.5	7.7	8.9	9.0	8.4	7.5
Real wages before tax						
Working one extra year	−0.3	−0.3	−0.1	−0.1	0.0	0.3
Working until age 65	−1.5	−2.1	−1.1	−1.1	−1.1	−0.4
Real wages after tax						
Working one extra year	−0.2	0.2	0.6	0.6	1.0	1.2
Working until age 65	−1.3	−1.3	1.0	1.4	2.2	3.3
Federal effective labor income-tax rate						
Working one extra year	0.0	0.0	−1.6	−1.6	−1.6	−2.3
Working until age 65	0.0	−0.8	−5.6	−6.4	−8.8	−10.3
Canada Pension Plan contribution rate						
Working one extra year	−8.3	−7.9	−7.8	−7.9	−7.8	−7.7
Working until age 65	−15.0	−24.6	−25.5	−25.8	−25.1	−25.1
Quebec Pension Plan contribution rate						
Working one extra year	−7.8	−7.2	−7.0	−6.2	−6.2	−6.0
Working until age 65	−24.1	−39.5	−39.3	−38.8	−38.4	−38.4

Source: Fougère et al., 2005a.

Behavioral changes of young and new cohorts

Population aging will have positive effects on wages and returns to education. This may encourage young adults to invest in human capital and older workers to offer a larger participation to the labor market. Fougère et al. (2009) entered these theoretical considerations into a simulation model to estimate their effect on productive capacity. This model is similar to the one discussed by Mérette (2002). Its key features are that representative individuals maximize lifetime consumption of all goods and leisure, subject to their lifetime income and time constraint, while earnings depend on an individual's level of human capital. All of these determinants of productive capacity are endogenous to the model rather than assumed.

The results of simulations from this model are reported in figure 8.8 for GDP per capita from 1982 to 2050. The solid line in figure 8.8 shows what happened to income per capita during the 1970s and 1980s, when the "baby boom" generation entered the labor market, assuming that the age of retirement and education levels were not affected by these demographic changes. As can be seen, real GDP per capita increased sharply during the 1980s, 1990s, and 2000s. Later, as the "baby boom" generation gradually retires, the model forecasts that productive capacity stabilizes and begins to fall by 2014.

The dotted line in figure 8.8 shows the trend of income per capita under the assumption that the education and retirement decisions are made by individuals able to forecast correctly the changes in wages and returns to education stemming from the forecast demographic changes.

Figure 8.8: Impact of population aging on real GDP per capita according to endogenous and exogenous time allocation decision scenarios (1982–2050)

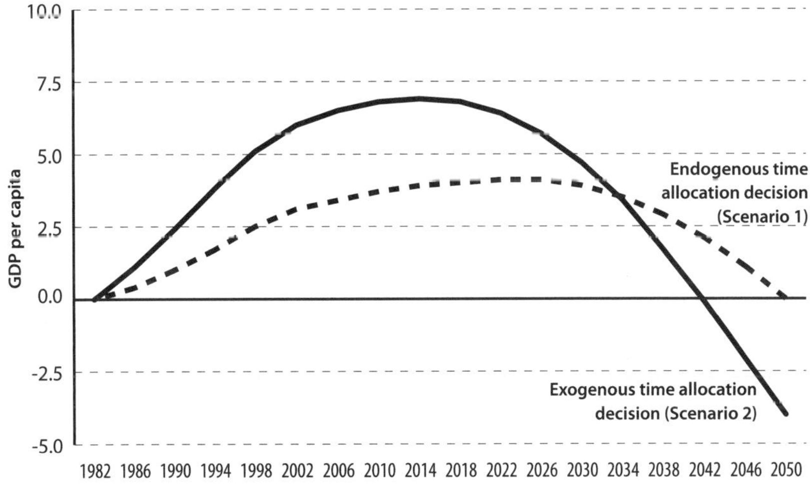

Source: Fougère et al., 2009.

As the graph shows, initially the time used in obtaining more education reduces labor supply of young adults and results in lower per-capita income relative to the base line. However, in the longer run and after 2035, this higher education more than offsets the effects of aging on per-capita income and raises it above that shown for the baseline.

Summary and conclusion

Over the next several decades, Canada will experience an accelerating process of population aging. This chapter has investigated what effects this aging will have on Canadian labor markets and per-capita real incomes and dealt with the widely held view that immigration can offer relief for the expected negative consequences of population aging.

Simple forecasts of aging based on demographic trends can overestimate its effects on labor markets and per-capita incomes because it neglects the fact that higher labor force participation rates and higher retirement ages can to a considerable degree offset the negative economic effects of aging alone. In addition, higher levels of education for new entrants to the labor market and the adoption of more labor-saving technology and investment can similarly reduce the economic impact of aging. It is encouraging that in Canada labor-force participation rates and the mean retirement age have already begun to increase.

The ability to reduce the economic impact of aging through increases in the rate of immigration was examined with the help of sophisticated, dynamic models that use computer simulations to track feedbacks and incentives driven by exogenous demographic changes. The results of these simulations show that increases in immigration rates have a marginal impact on economic developments, even if the additional immigrants all have very high levels of education.

We need to consider alternative policies for dealing with the problems raised by the aging of Canada's population. One of these involves getting new immigrants to settle throughout Canada, rather than having the present pattern that sees most of the new immigrants settle in Toronto, Vancouver, and Montreal. The second alternative, superior to higher rates of immigration, involves policies that increase the average age of retirement and raise the average level of education of Canadian workers.

References

Baker, M. (2002). The Retirement Behavior of Married Couples: Evidence from the Spouse's Allowance. *Journal of Human Resources* 37: 1–34.

Baker, M., and D. Benjamin (1999). Early Retirement Provisions and the Labor Force Behavior of Older Men: Evidence from Canada. *Journal of Labor Economics* 17: 724–56.

Börsch-Supan, A., L. Alexander, and J. Winter (2001). *Aging and International Capital Flows*. NBER Working Paper No. 8553. National Bureau of Economic Research.

Côté, S. (2005). Population Aging and Labour Market Reforms in OECD Countries. Policy Research Initiative Working Paper (July).

Équipe INGENUE (2001). *Macroeconomic Consequences of Pension Reforms in Europe: An Investigation with the INGENUE World Model*. CEPII Working Paper No. 01-17. <http://ideas.repec.org/p/cpm/cepmap/0116.html>.

Fehr, J., and L. Kotlikoff (2004), *The Role of Immigration in Dealing with Developed World's Demographic Transition*, NBER Working Paper No. W10512. National Bureau of Economic Research.

Fortin, M., and P. Fortin (2004). The Changing Participation Rate of Canadians: New Evidence from a Panel of Demographic Groups. Presentation at the CEA's 38th Annual Meetings, Toronto.

Fougère, M., S. Harvey, J. Mercenier, and M. Mérette (2005a). Population Ageing and the Effective Rate of Retirement in Canada. Working Paper 2005, A-03. HRSDC-IC-SSHRC Skills Research Initiative.

Fougère, M., S. Harvey, J. Mercenier, and M. Mérette (2005b). Population Ageing, High-Skilled Immigrants and Productivity. Working Paper 2005 A-07. HRSDC-IC-SSHRC Skills Research Initiative.

Fougère, M., S. Harvey, J. Mercenier, and M. Mérette (2009). Population Ageing, Time Allocation and Human Capital: A General Equilibrium Analysis for Canada. *Economic Modelling* 26, 1 (January): 30–39.

Fougère, M., S. Harvey, M. Mérette, and F. Poitras (2004). Ageing Population and Immigration in Canada: An Analysis with a Regional CGE Overlapping Generations Model. *Canadian Journal of Regional Science* 27, 2 (Summer): 209–36.

Fougère, M., J. Mercenier, and M. Mérette (2007). Population Ageing in Canada: A Sectoral and Occupational Analysis with a CGE Overlapping Generations Model. *Economic Modelling* 24 (July): 690–711.

Hviding, K., and M. Mérette (1998). Macroeconomic Effects of Pension Reforms in the Context of Ageing Populations: Overlapping Generations Model Simulations for Seven OECD Countries. OECD Working Paper No. 201 (June). OECD.

Kieran, P. (2001). Early Retirement Trends. *Perspective on Labour and Income.* Cat. No. 75-001 (Winter). Statistics Canada.

Lagacé, M., and F. Tougas (2006). Les répercussions de la privation relative personnelle sur l'estime de soi. Une étude du rôle du désengagement psychologique auprès de travailleurs de la santé de plus de 45 ans. *Les Cahiers Internationaux de Psychologie Sociale* 69: 59–69.

Léonard, A., and B. Rainville (2006). Retraite anticipée et retour sur le marché du travail. Mimeo. Human Resources and Social Development Canada.

Mérette, M. (2002). The Bright Side: A Positive View on the Economics of Aging. *Choices IRPP* 8, 1.

Mérette, M., and P. Georges (2009). Demographic Changes and the Gains from Globalisation: A Multi-Country Overlapping Generations CGE Model. Department of Economics Working Papers No. 0903, University of Ottawa.

Pyper, W., and P. Giles (2002). À l'approche de la retraite. *Perspective on Labour and Income* 14, 4 (Winter). Cat. No. 75-001. Statistics Canada.

Statistics Canada (2007). *Labour Force Survey.* Cat. 71-001-XIE.

Storesletten, K. (2000). Sustaining Fiscal Policy through Immigration. *Journal of Political Economy* 108, 2: 300–23.

United Nations Population Division (2005). *World Population Prospects: The 2004 Revision.* <http://esa.un.org.unpp>.

Social issues

Chapter 9

The creation of a global suburb and its impact on Canadian national unity

Stephen Gallagher

Recently the *National Post* ran a contest to describe Canada "in six words or less." The winner of this "motto contest" was "Canada—A Home for the World" (*National Post*, 2007, December 7). After more than 60 years of mass immigration dating from the end of the Second World War, this motto is revealing of the new Canada. This is Canada perceived as a country with little underlying coherence in the sense of sustaining a primary national identity aside from being a desirable place to settle. In other words, what this new motto provides is a more palatable description of "a nation of immigrants."

Since 1945, Canada has received approximately 10 million immigrants of diverse origins (CIC-REB, 2007: 5). I believe that this on-going mass immigration is causing Canada to evolve into a diasporatic society. Canada is becoming a home away from home for a range of peoples whose identities are rooted not in Canada but in countries and regions of origin. In other words, Canada is evolving into a global suburb: a comfortable, secure, and tolerant bedroom community where business and activities can be conducted that do not necessarily involve regions of origin. Of course, there is no guarantee that in the long run the new residents of this suburb will get along with each other or with more rooted residents. Furthermore, there is no guarantee that all will be equally prosperous or that going forward the whole will be easily governed. A policy of mass immigration constitutes first and foremost a commitment to social, economic, and demographic change and the challenges faced by Canada as a diasporatic society are impossible to predict.

Canada's identity has not always been so firmly connected to the idea of a "nation of immigrants." The emerging identity of Canada as a diasporatic country and the profession of a "creed" that supports such an evolution is partly due to the high level of diversity that has been achieved. An important part of this new Canadian creed is the protection and promotion of openness, tolerance, and diversity that is used to justify policies of mass immigration, multiculturalism, and the defense of human rights viewed broadly.[1] Taken together, these articles of belief mean that immigrant acceptance has become an element of what it means to be Canadian.

The objective of this chapter is to provide an understanding of how Canada came to have and sustain such permissive and non-controversial migration policies and practices. I note that Canada is not alone in maintaining a mass immigration policy but it stands alone in the world as a country where mass migration is so fully accepted as a policy norm. To begin with, I provide some background on Canada's immigration policies in the early post-war period when policy makers had a relatively free hand to set target levels and source countries. Later, immigration and multiculturalism policy played a role in the 1960s and 1970s as Canada sought to redefine itself in an effort to insure national unity. I also provide an explanation for why, regardless of the wide-ranging impact of mass immigration on all aspects of Canadian life, the policy is now hardly debated and faces little opposition. I note the role of the electoral system, the electoral calculations of political parties, the absence of anti-immigrant parties, and the play of interest groups, which can be understood broadly as the workings of "client politics" (Freeman, 1995: 886). Finally, I examine

1 ◆ Other elements of the creed, which are also relatively new, include a perception of Canada as a more just, fair, and peaceful country than the United States, which is operationalized programmatically in such policies as Medicare, gun control, and support for peacekeeping and the United Nations.

some implications of mass immigration for national unity and identity in Quebec and the rest of Canada (ROC). Overall, these features of the Canadian system can be contrasted with trends elsewhere in the developed world where issues related to migration are core areas of contestation.

Canada and global migration patterns

Canada is not unique in having a contemporary policy of mass immigration although in comparison with other immigrant-hosting, developed countries Canada's flow rate is higher. On a per-capita basis in 2007, Canada is estimated to have a net migration approximately four times that of the European Union, double that of the United States, and a third greater than Australia and New Zealand (CIA, 2007). In addition, Canada's annual flow of around 250,000 permanent residents is very diverse in terms of origins and ethnicity, unlike the United States where the Latin American influx makes up more than half of the total (Camarota, 2007: 10).[2] Australia accepted 131,000 new "settlers" in 2006, of which immigrants from the United Kingdom and New Zealand were about 30% of the total (Australia, Dep't of Immigration and Citizenship, 2008).

As a result of the unique size and pattern of immigration to Canada, the country is undergoing a societal and demographic evolution that is much more rapid and profound than is taking place in the other major immigrant-welcoming countries. For example, while only 10% of Americans are foreign born, in Canada nearly 20% are. While many of the United States' largest cities have sizable non-rooted populations—in Miami 36.5% and in Los Angeles 34.7% are foreign born—in Canada two of its largest cities, Toronto and Vancouver, have even larger shares of foreign-born populations. In 2006, 45.7% of the population of Toronto and 39.6% of Vancouver were born outside Canada (Chui, Tran and Maheux, 2007: 18)

2 ◆ In recent years, Canada has also seen a major net growth in its population of temporary residents, which includes temporary workers and foreign students. From 1996 to 2006 the stock grew from 272,986 to 487,699 (CIC-REB, 2007: 65) but for 2007/8 the net growth is estimated to be 50,000 (Statistics Canada, 2008: 38) and there is every expectation that this net growth will continue as provincial governments such as Alberta aggressively seek out new temporary foreign workers.

and, according to Statistics Canada, it is very likely that by 2017 metropolitan Toronto will have a majority "visible minority" population. It is likely that by this date the same will be true of metropolitan Vancouver (Bélanger and Malenfant, 2005: vi).

Overall, population and social planning in the absence of a willingness to assimilate is difficult. Immigration policy should take into consideration market concerns and a desire for a free flow of labor but also other considerations including the acceptance of Canadian values. While immigration can act in support of market needs, it is important to remember that the vast majority of new Canadians are coming from countries that do not have free markets or liberal governments as we would understand them.

Mass immigration, which is a driver of fundamental social, political, and economic change, is a major public-policy issue in other developed countries. Japan has, for the most part, blocked migratory flows but as a result has exposed itself to much criticism, especially with respect to closing its doors to asylum seekers (Tsuda and Cornelius, 2004: 467–68). In the United States, in late 2007 a major bipartisan immigration reform package was voted down amid much controversy and "comprehensive" immigration reform will be a top priority in the future. European countries have had until recently few effective migratory controls and have come to realize that illegal immigration, asylum migration, and family reunification policies have led to a large but often unwelcome build-up of non-European populations. Efforts are now under way to design common policies for the European Union (EU) to address these problems.[3] The policies proposed include the provision that the labor-market needs of western Europe are to be met primarily with migration within the EU from eastern European countries. Furthermore, family reunification for non-European immigrants is becoming more difficult and is increasingly subject to significant mandatory and stringent integration criteria (Joppke, 2007). The EU is also well advanced in its development of a Common European Asylum System (CEAS).

---

3 ◆ The main policy elements of these initiatives are found in the Hague Program (European Union, European Council, 2004) and the recently concluded European Pact on Immigration and Asylum (European Union, Council of the European Union, 2008).

Canada and the missing debate on mass immigration

Although Canada's policy of mass immigration raises many important issues there is a strange absence of national political or public debate on the subject. Debate should normally be expected to arise on such issues as the number of immigrants allowed into Canada annually, their real impact on Canada's society and economy, and the identity and meaning of Canada in a situation of growing diversity and potentially lessening social cohesion. In fact, however, these questions have not been the subject of major public discussion and little effort has been made to consider what Canada will look like 20, 50, or 100 years in the future.

For example, as Canada enters what is predicted to be the deepest recession since the depression, debate in Parliament on 2009 immigration target levels illustrates the superficiality of policy debate. When Jason Kenney, the new Conservative Immigration Minister, suggested in a newspaper interview that the government might reconsider immigration target levels if the provincial governments were seeking reductions (Greenaway, 2009, February 11), Maurizio Bevilacqua, the Liberal Immigration Critic, accused the Minister of having an agenda to "turn his back on immigrants and shut Canada's doors" (*Hansard*, February 11, 2009, 674). The next day the Minister entertained a question from a Conservative backbencher deploring cuts to immigration put in place by the Trudeau government during the recession in the 1980s. The backbench MP also drew attention to a statement made the day before by Liberal Senator Pierrette Ringuette supposedly calling for a "halt" to immigration programs for foreign workers. Kenney responded that the "Liberal caucus member [was] giving voice to nativist sentiments, pitting immigrants against Canadians" (*Hansard*, February 12, 2009, 755). The following week in a news release the Minister pledged to maintain immigration levels of up to 265,000 new permanent residents in 2009 and suggested that he was "particularly concerned by short-sighted, divisive rhetoric that pits immigrants against Canadians in our economy" (Canada, Citizenship and Immigration, 2009).

If Parliament were to seriously review the issues it would conclude that mass immigration has profound implications for Canada's society, culture, politics, and work force. Especially important is the impact of this mass immigration on the size of Canada's population, which appears to grow without any official objectives related to growth and composition

(Ley and Hiebert, 2001: 121). Given the absence of such a "population policy" and the lack of parliamentary scrutiny it is not surprising that new census reports are often greeted by the media with amazement and with little realization of the relationship between mass immigration and demographic change (Hamilton, 2008, April 3).

In spite of the lack of an official population policy, the Canadian public supports mass immigration. In a recent Gallup poll Canadians responded to the question "would you like to see the level of immigration in this country increased, decreased, or remain the same?" as follows: 20% thought it should be decreased and 22% felt that it should be increased (the rest did not know). In contrast, the same Gallup polls in the United States and the United Kingdom found that about 60% of the respondents felt that immigration should be decreased and about 5 % that it should be increased (Jedwab, 2006).

Furthermore, in the three most recent national elections in Canada immigration was not a central issue in spite of the fact that in the 2005 election the governing Liberal Party reiterated its commitment to raise Canada's immigration intake, from the recent annual rate of 0.7% of the nation's population to 1.0%. At this rate, more than 300,000 immigrants would enter Canada annually; if applied to France or the United Kingdom, it would mean 600,000 immigrants annually. For the United States, this rate implies the inflow of approximately three million immigrants annually, which is more than twice the recent number. In these countries, an election promise for a further increase in immigration rates as was proposed by the Liberals in the 2005 election campaign would be political suicide. In the 2005 election, this promise for an immigration increase was not challenged by the main opposition party, the Conservatives, who won the election and formed a minority government.

Overall, in Canada outside Quebec mass immigration is celebrated without much evidence of the fundamental intellectual engagement on immigration issues that has been taking place in the rest of the developed world.[4] In these countries, the key question is whether national majorities

4 ◆ An exception can be found in the work of the Fraser Institute, which has become a source of publications outlining the facts about migration-related issues. See <http://www.fraserinstitute.org/researchandpublications/researchtopics/immigration.htm>.

are willing to accept the social and identity change accompanying it. Of course, some such change is continuous and inevitable and migratory pressure on borders cannot be easily contained. But countries have different thresholds of tolerance to both the rate of change and the presence of foreigners in their midst. François Mitterrand famously said in an interview given in 1989 that France had reached its threshold (seuil de tolérance) in the 1970s when the number of immigrants was just over four million (Institut National de l'Audiovisuel, 1989, December 10). Therefore, depending on the country and situation, national majorities can resist a change of identity, can naturally evolve to accommodate change, or can simply acquiesce to migratory forces that result in minoritization. Canada appears to be a case of acquiescence because there is little debate, let alone opposition, to the ongoing fundamental social, cultural, and demographic change that is a function of high rates of immigration.

Why is there no opposition to mass immigration in Canada?

The absence of political leadership

First, there is no political leadership in Canada on migration-related issues for reasons of electoral expediency. The Liberal party has in recent years strongly supported policies of mass immigration and holds the ridings in Canada's largest cities where new Canadians are concentrated. The Conservative party has to follow the Liberal lead if it wishes to win these ridings and therefore also supports a policy of mass immigration (Martin, 2008, February 19). The public debate of immigration issues in Canada is also stymied by the fact that the Liberal party often plays the race card whenever immigration policies are discussed (Ivison, 2007, Feb. 23). In the process, Conservatives are painted as intolerant, racist, and extremist (Wattie, 2005, May 5).

This strategy is effective because, aside from hurting the Conservative party in communities of new Canadians, it also affects the support for the Conservatives in their strongholds outside urban areas where there are relatively few immigrants. This is because, as noted above, acceptance of immigration has become an article of faith and almost a litmus test of being Canadian, except perhaps in francophone Quebec. The political dynamics around immigration issues may be illustrated by the fact that when the Immigration Minister Diane Finley in 2008 announced a policy change to rationalize the immigration application process that had become seriously backlogged, Maurizio Bevilacqua, the Liberal Immigration Critic, suggested that the Conservatives were "shutting the door on immigration." Accusations like this are made even though, if anything, the Conservatives have raised immigration levels since taking office and, as noted above, appear willing to sustain this level regardless of the current economic downturn (Ivison, 2008, March 13).

The Canadian electoral system

Secondly, Canada's electoral system with its single-member constituencies works against the rise of third parties or issue-oriented parties that might oppose mass immigration. This is because of the need to secure substantial and broad support to be successful in this type of electoral system. The importance of urban voters in the electoral competition is clear to everyone and given the size and political importance of new Canadian communities and their concentration in Canada's largest cities, it is not surprising that reform of immigration policy has not been a priority of Canada's national parties (Black and Hicks, 2008: 245–49). Those who are cosmopolitan in outlook recognize this relationship and oppose reform of Canada's electoral system because, for example, a proportional representation electoral system could lead to the rise of ethnic, religious, or anti-immigration parties (Cardozo, 2004, November 16).

The implications of the ongoing fundamental demographic change are potentially enormous, however, and Canada seems destined to reach the point where these implications cannot be disregarded. Therefore, my concern is that Canada's "broad-based parties"—adept as they are at smoothing out the sharp edges—are facilitating a headlong rush into the unknown. If that unknown turns out to be strongly negative we will lament our previous unwillingness to debate the issues. If it is positive, then the worst that can be said is that there were opportunity costs in not reaching the new age of harmony and prosperity sooner.

Canadian media and human rights commissions

A third reason there has not been a wide public debate and backlash over the issues raised by mass immigration is that generally the Canadian media views immigration positively. For example, the *National Post* responded to a Statistics Canada report that showed significant immigration-driven demographic change with an editorial entitled Statistics Canada Counts Our Blessings (*National Post,* 2007, December 5). There simply is no equivalent in the Canadian media to the popular tabloid-style newspapers in Australia and the United Kingdom that regularly discuss the failures of immigration policies and especially the influx of so called "bogus asylum seekers" (Colville, 2006).

In short, it seems that every other country vigorously debates these issues because over time the forces of demographic change have such significant implications. However, in Canada there is such a chill surrounding these issues that market demand for information dubious of the benefits of immigration is stunted, as those who might meet the demand conclude that it is too much trouble or there is too much risk in trying. Consider, for example, the effect of the actions of Canada's various human rights commissions upon free speech. If critics of Canada's immigration policy are artificially silenced or silence themselves, the policy-making process is, in effect, short-circuited and incomplete. In other words, just because only a few people are saying there is an immigration problem does not mean there is no problem.

Academic complacency and cosmopolitan bias

A fourth reason for the existing state of the public debate over mass immigration is the relative absence of any concern voiced by academics. There has been some academic work critical of government policies on the issues of national security and Canada's refugee system but these problems are not generally connected to mass immigration. Instead, academic work on immigration has focused primarily on the integration of immigrants, social justice, and the battle against intolerance. These studies put little value on social coherence because of a general bias in favor of cosmopolitan values and a tendency to consider migration controls and even nationalism as being of questionable legitimacy.

It is beyond the scope of this work to survey the huge volume of academic research on immigration and integration in Canada but I would like to identify one basic reality. It is becoming difficult to study such concepts as social cohesion and integration when Canada's largest cities are increasingly dominated by large and distinct immigrant communities. To take an example, in their 2002 *Ethnic Diversity Study*, Jeffrey Reitz and Rupa Banerjee found that "[r]egarding life satisfaction and trust in others ... experiences of discrimination and vulnerability account for part of the lower levels for visible minorities among earlier immigrants and the second generation" (Reitz and Banerjee, 2005: 22). In this study, immigrants and especially visible minorities are being polled about their views on Canadian identity, belonging, and integration. For the most part, these opinions are based on conditions they observe in Canada's largest cities and especially Toronto and Vancouver. But, given the diversity of race, culture, and origins in these cities noted above, is it possible to conclude that discrimination and trust problems found among them are due to interaction with Canadians, rather than other groups of immigrants?

This proposition is supported by a study of "ethnic segregation" in Toronto by Mohammad Qadeer who notes that in 2001 what is euphemistically referred to as "English (Anglos)" only form a majority in a quarter of metropolitan Toronto's "census tracts"' (Qadeer, 2003: 13). In interviews of Laotian immigrants in Toronto, John C. Harles found that they had a concern about multiculturalism being too pervasive. The Lao were uncertain about what was the real Canadian identity that would allow for assimilation, which they would welcome (Harles, 1997: 733–34). Given immigration levels and demographic trends and without incentives to disperse migrants from urban areas,[5] the impact of mass immigration on efforts to promote integration and a sense of belonging can only become more salient.

The federal government appears to be aware of the difficulties of creating social solidarity in a country consisting of large enclaves of recent immigrants from many different parts of the world. It therefore has begun to adopt a different approach. According to Anna Vorobyova, Canada's multicultural policy is now structured to promote integration in the sense of "inclusion" or "active participation" of the members of various diverse groups into a standard North American culture (Vorobyova, 2006: 138). However, it remains to be seen whether such federal policies will be

5 ◆ According to Roderic Beaujot, the current trend is towards greater migrant concentration in urban areas (Beaujot, 2003: 9–10).

successful, in spite of the fact that they involve the spending of large sums of money. In 2006/07, Citizenship and Immigration spent $622 million on citizenship and integration and Heritage Canada spent $595 million on the promotion of "linguistic duality and social inclusion" and multicultural policy (Canada, Canadian Heritage, 2008: 82).

Information about costs of immigration not readily available

A fifth reason for the absence of any widespread public discussion of immigration issues in Canada is that the basic facts about the costs and trade-offs are not well known, partly because governments have not made much effort to publicize relevant information. In the absence of this information, public debate tends to degenerate into name calling, which in turn discourages political and public discourse.

Conditions in Canada are much different from those existing in the United States and the United Kingdom where there is a vast literature on the costs and benefits of immigration that is used in policy debates. When the US Senate passed the Comprehensive Immigration Reform Act in 2006, the Congressional Budget Office produced a cost estimate (United States, Congressional Budget Office, 2006). In the United Kingdom, a special committee of the House of Lords recently undertook an extensive public investigation of the costs and benefits of immigration and produced an authoritative report (United Kingdom, House of Lords, Select Committee on Economic Affairs, 2008). In the case of refugee policy, the UK government has recently published detailed cost figures (United Kingdom, National Audit Office, 2008) and such information is used by politicians in public debates (*BBC News*, 2005, January 28).

In Canada, research on the cost and benefits of the immigration system are pretty much left up to academics and think tanks (e.g., Grubel, 2005), which can provide at best an incomplete picture. For example, there currently exists no detailed public accounting of the cost of the extended Canadian refugee system, which would include spending by the Immigration and Refugee Board (IRB), Citizenship and Immigration Canada (CIC), and the Canadian Border Services Agency (CBSA). Other elements to consider would be legal aid, court costs, and the wide range of services provided to asylum seekers by the provinces including education, health, accommodation, and income support.

A basic reason for the absence of empirical information on the cost of immigration and refugee policies is that in Canada elites have generally decided that the issues need to be depoliticized.[6] The problem with this elitist view is that it is justifiable only if immigration is relatively small and has minimal costs and effects on society. These conditions do not hold in Canada and the absence of data on the cost of immigration prevents rational public discussion and plays into the hands of immigration advocates who rely on emotional appeals. According to James Freeman, conditions of limited factual information favor the efforts of those who seek to maintain a permissive migratory environment (Freeman, 1995: 884).

Influence of professional advocates, activists, and interest groups

A sixth element limiting the discussion of immigration issues in Canada is the role played by professional advocates including immigration lawyers and rights activists who benefit directly from the flow of immigrants. In addition, interest groups and service organizations of immigrants already in Canada have a stake in promoting immigration. Professionals and interest groups become especially active whenever there are challenges to existing immigration policies. Thus, in the mid-1990s in preparation for immigration reform legislation, the federal immigration minister of the day, Lucienne Robillard, commissioned a report by an advisory group, held hearings on it, and in 1999 tabled a white paper entitled *Building on a Strong Foundation for the 21st Century: New Directions for Immigration and Refugee Policy and Legislation*. The white paper was the foundation for parliamentary hearings and new legislation, which was eventually passed in 2001 as the *Immigration and Refugee Protection Act* (IRPA).

During these years, an extensive range of organizations with vested interests submitted their views to the minister and to the parliamentary committee reviewing the legislation. These organizations included the various ethnic group representatives, including the Hispano-Canadian Congress and the Chinese-Canadian Association, all of which opposed strengthening the immigrant language requirement. There were also refugee, antiracism, and human-rights advocacy groups like the Canadian

---

6 ◆ James Freeman refers to this as an "antipopulist norm" (Freeman, 1995: 885).

Council for Refugees that opposed a more efficient refugee determination system. Finally, there were business interest groups and members of the Canadian Bar Association that sought to smooth the immigration pathways and secure increased protection for their clients. There were very few submissions that questioned the need for a policy of mass immigration.

No populist or political backlash after 60 years of mass immigration

Finally, in contrast with Europe and elsewhere, Canada has never had a populist backlash to mass immigration nor in recent times has there been a high profile political or business leader who questioned the need for mass immigration. It should be noted that although populist anti-immigration parties and leaders have not had much electoral success in Europe, they have nevertheless had important influences on national immigration policies (Schain, 2006). In the past, the absence of opposition to mass immigration in Canada meant policy elites in Ottawa had a free hand. Currently, however, a relative absence of opposition coupled with the range of interests supporting a permissive migration policy means policy elites are now constrained. This is because in Canada the advocacy forces are all on one side, creating a "client politics" situation. Hence, the lack of contrasting opinions on immigration hinders effective policy making because politicians have a lessened capability to balance competing national interests.

During the early post-War period, senior officials in government were preoccupied with economic issues and initiated a policy of mass immigration from Europe that proceeded without much public attention (Hawkins, 1988: Part 2). By the early 1960s, the public and politicians in Canada had begun to focus on concerns about national unity, which were driven by the rise of separatist movements in Quebec. To address this problem, the government advanced a policy of official bilingualism and biculturalism and also introduced the concept of multiculturalism for strategic purposes (Hawkins, 1988: 390–92). This is the origin of the new Canadian creed identified above. The historian Michael Bliss suggests that the rise of multiculturalism as a defining vision of Canada along with a Charter of Rights, support for asymmetrical federalism, and a studied caution in international affairs in deference to an increasingly diverse social base came at the expense of an earlier vision of a path for Canada. In the earlier vision, Canada would evolve to greatness because of its "northern destiny," its British heritage, good government, and international policies that differed from those of the United States (see also Berger, 1966). Bliss concludes that from this "more traditionalist perspective, Canada's evolution may appear to be moving increasingly toward decline into global irrelevance and social and political incoherence" (Bliss, 2006: 5).

By the late 1960s, mass immigration from Europe had built up significant immigrant enclaves and the process of assimilation was beginning to slow. There also arose at this time the emergence of globalized communication and travel networks that allowed for the progressively easier maintenance of connections with countries and regions of origin. Soon dual citizenship, endogenous marriages, and circular migration would begin to reinforce the emerging diasporic features of Canadian society.

While the assimilation of immigrants was slowing, the ongoing dissipation of rooted Canadian culture and its replacement with the more superficial new Canadian identity and creed, including an acceptance of diversity, was progressing. At this point, there developed an opening for the powerful assimilationist force of American mass culture. This was the case even though resistance to American culture had long factored prominently in English Canada's identity (Lipset, 1990). For new Canadian populations, however, who were receiving so much of their cultural awareness through the mass media, the pull of American culture was overwhelming. Ironically, the element of American culture that is not being transmitted is the United States's powerful attachment to its history and national symbols out of which is stirring the current unease with mass immigration and internationalism in that country (Huntington, 2004). Over time, the "thick" British North American connected identity began to dissipate among rooted Canadians and was not inculcated in new migrant communities so that in the contemporary period essentially American norms and cultural yardsticks dominate English Canadian culture. Of course, the veneer of the new Canadian identity and creed exists but, as I note below, elements of this formulation tied to national bilingualism for example, are increasingly disconnected from the reality on the ground in much of contemporary Canada.

Overall, one impact of the national rebranding initiative of the 1960s that eventually led to the patriation of the Constitution in 1982 was that mass immigration continued unnoticed. In addition, changes to regulations and the passage of the Immigration Act in 1976 allowed a realignment of immigrant source countries, which introduced new diasporas into Canada. By the election of the Mulroney government in 1984, the full workings of the contemporary politics of immigration can be seen. In this period the Progressive Conservative party joined other national political parties in actively courting voters in new Canadian communities (Veugelers, 2000). Also, immigration had developed into an industry populated by a range of facilitators that included immigration lawyers and consultants. Furthermore, many of the cultural associations, service organizations, and advocacy groups such as the Canadian Ethnocultural Council (founded 1980), the Ontario Council of Agencies Serving Immigrants (founded 1978), and the Canadian Council for Refugees (founded 1978) had become active. Finally, by the end of the 1980s Canada was receiving a substantial flow of asylum seekers, which led to the creation of the Immigration and Refugee Board in 1989.

Implications of mass immigration for national unity

The preceding analysis implies that Canada is becoming a diasporatic country. I believe that this trend is not sustainable and that the existence of Canada as a unified nation is threatened. The traditional vision of Canada based on its British heritage and French fact is being replaced by a vision of Canada as a multicultural society that has "national minorities" such as Francophones and aboriginal peoples, who may make special claims on the nation. But, as the centrifugal implications of this formulation are increasingly recognized, Canada may be forced to fundamentally re-examine the merits of mass immigration.

This is especially the case because Francophone Quebecers have recently woken up to the implications of mass immigration. Driven by populist concerns that appear to be in conflict with official multiculturalism, the Quebec government was forced to hold public hearings under the auspices of the Bouchard-Taylor Commission to consider what citizens should be obligated to do in order to afford immigrants "reasonable accommodation" of their special cultural and religious needs (Bouchard and Taylor, 2008). These hearings and the accompanying publicity significantly raised public awareness of issues related to migration but did not accomplish the additional objective of allaying concerns about the integration of immigrants. This led some immigrant organizations to criticize the government for establishing the commission in the first place.

One result of these developments has been that Quebec's political parties, most notably the Parti Québécois (PQ) and Action démocratique du Québec (ADQ), are considering lowering immigration targets in response to studies that show, for example, that immigration is the main factor in the decline of the use of French on the island of Montreal (Termote, 2008, January 30). In contrast with the rest of Canada, Quebeckers are aware of similar European concerns and appear willing to use European policy prescriptions, which are viewed as fully justified and legitimate. Mario Dumont, then leader of the ADQ, the official opposition in Quebec at the time, visited France in early 2008 and met France's Minister of Immigration, Brice Hortefeux. They discussed questions of immigration, integration, and national identity, which are concerns in both Quebec and France. In a contemporary speech, President Nicholas Sarkozy suggested that the impact of immigration on identity was "le sujet le plus important de la société française" (Ridet, 2008, March 13). On returning to Canada, Dumont proposed that Quebec reduce immigration because of difficulties in integrating immigrants (White, 2008, March 13).

The Parti Québécois has also been active in responding to immigration's perceived challenge to Quebec's identity. In October 2007, Pauline Marois (Quebec, 2007) introduced legislation to strengthen Quebec's identity by requiring that immigrants show evidence of their capacity to integrate and that they should be required to sign "integration contracts," which are immigration prerequisites now widely employed in Europe. An editorial in the *National Post* described this as an example of "ugly nativism" (*National Post*, 2007, October 23), which suggests an ignorance of legitimate global concerns as well as complacency concerning failed multicultural and immigration policies. The reaction of the *National Post* was echoed by Quebec's Liberal Premier Jean Charest, who suggested that the policy proposals of the opposition parties were "driven by fear and intolerance" (Charest, 2007, October 30). Nevertheless, widespread criticism of existing integration policies appears to have had some effect. The Charest government went on to propose a robust range of measures to address the perceived erosion of the French language in Quebec, which is a function of mass immigration (Dutrisac, 2008, February 3).

An implication of this debate is that, although the sovereignty movement in Quebec has traditionally been associated with the political left, mass immigration threatens to make it also an agenda of the right because federal laws and especially the Canadian Charter of Rights and Freedoms may limit the ability of Quebeckers to protect their culture. In fact, this argument was made by representatives of the town of Herouxville in testimony to the Bouchard-Taylor Commission (Hamilton, 2007, October 25).[7] Overall, if it turns out that federal laws and the Charter cannot be interpreted with enough flexibility to permit Quebeckers to protect their language and culture, there may evolve a profound realignment of political forces in Quebec pitting the Francophone majority against Anglophones and Allophones (Robitaille, 2008, May 22). Needless to say, this would not be in the interest of national unity.

In the rest of Canada, a further effect of mass immigration is that it threatens the existence and relevance of national bilingualism, which is an important lynchpin of national unity. According to a Statistics Canada study, currently 5.2 million people have a mother tongue other than English or French; by 2017, this figure is predicted to rise to "between 6,872,000 and 9,044,000" (Beaujot, 2003: 19). Since there are only about one million French-speaking Canadians outside Quebec, they will soon be outnumbered by major groups of immigrants speaking other languages. In the legislated framework of bilingualism and multiculturalism, these developments could well lead to a demand for the public provision of services in these languages in the tradition of those provided in French. A first step in this direction and perhaps a harbinger of future policy developments tied to the changing demography of the rest of Canada is the Edmonton public school system's offering of a comprehensive bilingual program in Mandarin Chinese (Harding, 2007, May 20).

---

7 ◆ The Bouchard-Taylor Commission was originally set up in large part to deal with the controversies arising from the efforts of the inhabitants of Herouxville to require that immigrants modify their behavior to make it consistent with Quebec's cultural traditions.

Conclusion

At some point, at current rates of immigration Canada will cease to be anything approximating a nation and be best described as a prosperous and secure global suburb. In this global suburb, little effort need be made to assimilate newcomers, as the real identity of groups of inhabitants is associated with their ethnic background and country of origin. Assimilation would be very difficult in any case because of the tendency of different enclaves of immigrants to retain intensive contacts with their native countries and cultures, made possible through the low cost of communication and travel.

Of course, the definition of "nation" presents a challenge here. Although space constraints limit a full exploration of this, I subscribe to the analysis of Samuel Huntington (2004), who argues that a nation is a function of the identity of its majority population and in the United States this identity is rooted in an original founding Anglo-Protestant culture and a value system described as the American Creed. Huntington argues that this framework is not compatible with multiculturalism. Thus, there are profound implications to immigration-driven demographic change if there is an unwillingness or incapacity to assimilate new arrivals. If Huntington is correct and European countries and Japan have relatively clear majority-defined national identities, then this leaves Canada and Australia at the cutting edge of immigration-driven social experimentation. Of course, Australia has not fully relinquished what in the United States is described as a "national origins" immigration policy and, furthermore, because of geography and character, Australia is de facto more assimilationist than Canada. In other words, more than any other country Canada has bought into the cosmopolitan logic that there can exist a "civic nationalism" in the absence of any ethnic or cultural majority, shared roots, or social coherence.

In this emerging global suburb that is Canada, the integration of peoples replaces assimilation. Successful integration is associated with economic success, which is achieved through linguistic competence and the acceptance of Canadian rules and regulations. This evolution also requires Canadians to set aside traditional national values and standards and, in fact, Canada appears to be leading the way towards a questioning of traditional understandings of nation on the way to the development of a global culture and citizenship. As former Prime Minister Paul Martin said, "Canada has become a 'post-modern' country" (Canada, 2004).

While discarding nationalism and embracing a cosmopolitan vision may result in a more peaceful and secure world, I have several concerns about this development for Canada. First, as Robert Putnam (2007) found in his study of the United States, a lack of social coherence, which can be the result of years of mass immigration, gives rise to some serious social pathologies like reduced trust and confidence in human interactions (social cohesion). Writing about the United States, Otis Graham (2004: ch. 7) suggests that the "pause" that followed the "great" (first) wave of mass immigration that ended in the early 1920s of the last century, was needed to restore social cohesion and prepare the way for America's phenomenal success in the era after the Second World War.

Secondly, although the government of Canada promotes cosmopolitan values, there appear to be few if any enthusiastic followers. In many countries, including France, Netherlands, the United Kingdom, and the United States, there exist contentious debates over the need for cuts to immigration, the effectiveness of migration controls, and a strengthening of integration policies. This should give Canadian decision makers pause, promote a cautious approach, and stimulate a thorough review of the issues related to migration and citizenship.

Finally, Canada's national unity may be endangered by unmanaged immigration. There is an emerging sense among Francophone Quebecers that the protection of their national identity may not be compatible with high levels of immigration. At one level, there is a concern that new Quebecers tend to assimilate into English communities. This may not be objectively true and the accommodation debate may hide some deeper concern about cultural survival. Regardless, should a consensus arise among rooted Quebecers that the French language and culture are threatened by mass immigration and that the federal government is not responsive to their concerns, then the separatist movement will gain strength and national unity will be threatened.

In conclusion, I believe it is imperative that the government of Canada comprehensively analyzes, debates, and develops plans to address the many implications of mass immigration, which is so quickly and profoundly changing Canada. Canada should debate the range of issues related to citizenship, integration, asylum, and enforcement and then develop a population policy. But, to accomplish this, Canada must first find a way to transcend the superficiality of progressive advocacy and set aside partisan politics in order to reach conclusions on Canada's national interest with respect to immigration.

References

Australia, Department of Immigration and Citizenship (2008). *Fact Sheet 2—Key Facts in Immigration.* <http://www.immi.gov.au/media/fact-sheets/02key.htm>, as of March 14, 2008.

BBC News (2005, January 28). Howard Attacks Cost of Asylum. <http://news.bbc.co.uk/2/hi/uk_news/politics/4214085.stm>, as of April 5, 2008.

Beaujot, Roderic (2003). Effect of Immigration on the Canadian Population: Replacement Migration? Discussion Paper No. 03-03. Population Studies Centre, University of Western Ontario.

Bélanger A., and É. Caron Malenfant (2005). *Population Projections of Visible Minority Groups, Canada, Provinces and Regions 2001–2017.* Catalogue no. 91-541-XIE. Statistics Canada, Demography Division.

Berger, Carl (1966). The True North Strong and Free. In Peter Russell, ed., *Nationalism in Canada* (McGraw-Hill): 3–26.

Bill C-11, *An Act Respecting Immigration to Canada and the Granting of Refugee Protection, etc.*, 1st Sess., 37th Parl., 2001, cl. 11(1). Short title: *Immigration and Refugee Protection Act.*

Black, Jerome H., and Bruce M. Hicks (2008). Electoral Politics and Immigration in Canada: How Does Immigration Matter? *International Migration & Integration* 9 (August): 241–67

Bliss, Michael (2006). A Working Non-nation? *Literary Review of Canada* 24 (March): 3–5

Bouchard, Gérard, and Charles Taylor (2008). *Building the Future: A Time for Reconciliation. Abridged Report of the Consultation Commission on Accommodation Practices Related to Cultural Differences.* Gov't of Quebec.

Camarota, Steven A. (2007). *Immigrants in the United States, 2007: A Profile of America's Foreign-Born Population.* Backgrounder (November). Center for Migration Studies.

Canada (2004) Address by Prime Minister Paul Martin on the occasion of his visit to Washington, D.C. (April 29).

Canada, Canadian Heritage (2008). *2008–2009 Estimates, Part III Report on Plans and Priorities.*

Canada, Citizenship and Immigration Canada (1998). *Building on a Strong Foundation for the 21st Century: New Directions for Immigration and Refugee Policy and Legislation.* Minister of Public Works and Government Services Canada.

Canada, Citizenship and Immigration (2008). Government of Canada Announces New Funding for Research on Immigration and Diversity. News Release (January 7).

Canada, Citizenship and Immigration (2009). Canada Welcomes a Record High Number of Newcomers in 2008. News Release (February 20).

Canada, Citizenship and Immigration Canada, Research and Evaluation Branch [CIC-REB] (2007). *Facts and Figures: Immigration Overview Permanent Residents and Temporary Residents 2006.*

Charest, Jean (2007, October 30). Quebecers Must Remain Open. *Montreal Gazette*: A21.

Chow, Lenn, Des Verma, Martin Collacott, and Steve Kaufmann (2004, March 31). Ethno-politics Threaten Canadian Democracy. *National Post*: A18.

Chui, Tina, Kelly Tran, and Hélène Maheux (2007). *Immigration in Canada: A Portrait of the Foreign-Born, Census Year 2006*. Social and Aboriginal Statistics Division, Statistics Canada.

CIA (2007). Field Listing: Net Migration Rate 2007. *World Fact Book.* <https://www.cia.gov/library/publications/the-world-factbook/fields/2112.html>, as of March 25, 2008.

Colville, Rupert (2006). Words and Images. *Refugees* 142, 1: 14–19. UNHCR.

Dutrisac, Robert (2008, February 3). Francisation des immigrants — Le gouvernement préfère la persuasion à la coercition. *Le Devoir:* A8.

European Union, Council of the European Union (2008). *European Pact on Immigration and Asylum*. 13440/08 ASIM 72 (Brussels, September 24).

European Union, European Council (2004). *Presidency Conclusions.* European Council Meeting, Brussels (December 8). Annex 1.

Freeman, Gary (1995). Modes of Immigration Politics in Liberal Democratic States. *International Migration Review* 29, 4: 881–902.

Gallagher, Stephen (2003). *Canada's Dysfunctional Refugee Determination System: Canadian Asylum Policy from a Comparative Perspective.* Public Policy Sources 78 (December). Fraser Institute.

Graham, Otis L. (2004). *Unguarded Gates: A History of America's Immigration Crisis.* Rowman & Littlefield.

Greenaway, Norma (2009, February 11). Tories Consider Immigration Cuts; Minister Says Government Has Not Ruled Out Changes to Ensure Those Who Do Move Here Won't Face Unemployment. *Vancouver Sun*: B2.

Grubel, Herbert (2005). *Immigration and the Welfare State in Canada: Growing Conflicts, Constructive Solutions*. PPS 84. Fraser Institute.

Hamilton, Graeme (2007, October 25). Commissioner Challenges Code Authors. *The National Post:* A4.

Hamilton, Graeme (2008, April 3). Visible Minorities the New Majority. *National Post*: A1.

Harding, Katherine (2006, May 20). Bold Strokes on Language. *Globe and Mail*: A1.

Harles, John C. (1997). Integration before Assimilation: Immigration, Multiculturalism and the Canadian Polity. *Canadian Journal of Political Science* 30, 4: 711–36.

Hawkins, Freda (1988). *Canada and Immigration: Public Policy and Public Concern*. 2nd edition. McGill-Queens University Press.

Huntington, Samuel P. (2004). *Who Are We? The Challenges to America's National Identity*. Simon & Schuster.

Institut National de l'Audiovisuel (1989, December 10). *Miterrand : le seuil de tolérance*. Video. YouTube. <http://www.youtube.com/watch?v=9j69nsxbj6c>, as of April 7, 2008.

Ivison, John (2007, February 23). Liberals Playing Immigration Card. *National Post*: A5.

Ivison, John (2008, March 13). Ottawa Moves to Slash Immigrant Backlog. *National Post*: A1.

Jedwab, Jack (2002). *Immigration and the Vitality of Canada's Official Language Communities: Policy, Demography and Identity*. Office of the Commissioner of Official Languages.

Jedwab, Jack (2006). *Canadians Remain World Leaders in Openness to Immigration: Tomorrow We Mark International Day for the Prevention of Racial Discrimination.* Association for Canadian Studies. <http://www.acs-aec.ca/Polls/Openness%20to%20Immigration.pdf>, as of December 6, 2006.

Joppke, Christian (2007). Beyond National Models: Civic Integration Policies for Immigrants in Western Europe. *West European Politics* 30, 1 (January): 1–22.

Ley, David, and Daniel Hiebert (2001). Immigration Policy as Population Policy. *Canadian Geographer* 45, 1 (Spring): 120–25.

Lipset, Seymor Martin (1990). *Continental Divide: The Values and Institutions of the United States and Canada.* Routledge.

Martin, Don (2008, February 19). Tories Campaign on Ethnic Outreach. *National Post*: A4.

National Post (2007, October 23). Pauline Marois' Ugly Nativism. *National Post*: A14.

National Post (2007, December 5). Statistics Canada Counts Our Blessings. *National Post*: A24.

National Post (2007, December 7). And the Winner Is … *National Post*: A20.

Putnam, Robert D. (2007). E Pluribus Unum: Diversity and Community in the Twenty-first Century—the 2006 Johan Skytte Prize Lecture. *Scandinavian Political Studies* 30, 2: 137–74.

Qadeer, Mohammad A. (2003). *Ethnic Segregation in a Multicultural City: The Case of Toronto Canada.* CERIS Working Paper No. 28 (October). CERIS - The Ontario Metropolis Centre. <http://ceris.metropolis.net/Virtual%20Library/community/WP28_Qadeer.pdf>.

Quebec (2007). Pauline Marois dépose un projet de loi sur l'identité québécoise – Pour Donner des Assises Solides et Durables à L'Identité Quebecoise. Portail Québec, Fil de presse (October 18). <http://communiques.gouv.qc.ca/gouvqc/communiques/GPQF/Octobre2007/18/c5770.htm> as of April 8, 2008.

Reitz, Jeffrey G., and Rupa Banerjee (2005). Diversity, Inequality, and the Cohesion of Canadian Society: Research Findings and Policy Implications. Paper prepared for presentation at a conference on Diversity and Canada's Future: Recognition, Accommodation and Shared Citizenship, Institute for Research on Public Policy (IRPP), Montebello, Quebec (October 13–15).

Ridet, Philippe (2008, March 13). Nicolas Sarkozy reparle d'immigration pour rallier les abstentionnistes de droite. *Le Monde*: 11.

Robitaille, Antoine (2008, May 22). Constitution du Québec: Charest dit non. *Le Devoir*: A1.

Schain, Martin (2006). The Extreme-Right and Immigration Policy-Making: Measuring Direct and Indirect Effects. *West European Politics* 29, 2: 270–89.

Statistics Canada (2008) *Annual Demographic Estimates: Canada, Provinces and Territories, 2008*. Catalogue no. 91-215-X. Statistics Canada.

Termote, Marc (2008, January 30). Le français dans la tourmente. *Le Devoir*: B4.

Tsuda, Takeyuki, and Wayne A. Cornelius (2004). Japan: Government Policy, Immigrant Reality. In Wayne A. Cornelius, Takeyuki Tsuda, and Philip L. Martin, eds., *Controlling Immigration*, 2nd edition (Stanford University Press): 439–76.

United Kingdom, House of Lords, Select Committee on Economic Affairs (2008). *The Economic Impact of Immigration, Volume I: Report; Volume II; Evidence* (April 1).

United Kingdom, National Audit Office (2008). *Final Report: Costing of the New Asylum Model – NAO Asylum Study* (November 18).

United States, Congressional Budget Office (2006). *Cost Estimate: Comprehensive Immigration Reform Act of 2006, as passed by the Senate on May 25, 2006 (S. 2611)* (August 18).

Veugelers, John (2000). State-Society Relations in the Making of Canadian Immigration Policy during the Mulroney Era. *The Canadian Review of Sociology and Anthropology* 37, 1: 95–110.

Vorobyova, Anna (2006). Integrating Immigrants through the Policy of Multiculturalism as a State's New Response to the Sovereignty Challenge. *Review of European and Russian Affairs* 2, 3: 113–46.

Wattie, Chris (2005, May 5). Volpe Refuses to Apologize for Klan Remark. *National Post*: A9.

White, Marianne (2008, March 13). ADQ Urges Reducing Immigration. *National Post:* A6.

Chapter 10

Immigration and multiculturalism undermine culture and security in Canada

Salim Mansur

An immigrant society is generally reluctant to pose the question and examine how immigration over several generations might be changing its core identity. This reluctance might be even greater in an immigrant society whose future growth and prosperity are viewed as irreversibly tied to the flow of new immigrants, while efforts required to keep secure its core identity are considered to be of secondary importance. In such a situation, the core identity of an immigrant society is flexible and changing without any clear vision of what it will be in the future.

Canada is one of these immigrant societies. Over the past few generations, since the middle of the last century, Canadians in general have gradually come to the view their country's future growth and prosperity as being increasingly tied to keeping an open-door immigration policy and accepting of immigrants from around the world. It is a delicate question if Canada has reached a tipping point of dependency on immigration but the social indicators suggest that Canada is headed in that direction.

Given this fact, one question concerns the implications of such dependency in the light of the current demographic trend of an aging population and declining fertility rate among Canadians. A second question is how immigration that alters the ethnic profile of Canada might also alter the country's cultural identity as a unit of the West as a civilization distinct from other civilizations. In this paper, I offer a few propositions for consideration in weighing the pros and cons of an open-door immigration policy in the context of the current demographic trends in Canada and the politics of multiculturalism that came into vogue since the nineteen-sixties.

The West, immigration, and multiculturalism

Migration in the contemporary world is largely a unidirectional movement of people from non-Western societies and cultures to the West, which consists of advanced industrial democracies with shared values of politics and culture shaped by Christianity and the revolutions in science and philosophy of the Enlightenment, and resting on the inheritance of the ancient Greek and Roman civilizations: the countries of Europe, North America (excluding Mexico), Australia, and New Zealand. These countries have been the cradle of modern politics identified with democracy based on the notion of popular sovereignty; secularism as separation of church and state; liberalism as the idea of individual rights and freedom; equality as the principle of each individual, irrespective of gender or religion, being equal to another under the rule of law; and government deriving its legitimacy from, and accountable to, the people. These ideas emanating from the Western revolution in politics have travelled around the world and penetrated into other cultures in varying degrees but it is the sum total of these ideas and their further refinement over time that has defined the West as a civilization separate and apart from the Chinese, Indian, or the Islamic civilizations.

The important point to note in regard to the West as a distinct cultural unit or civilization is that the most effective contemporary assault upon this idea comes from within, through the politics of multiculturalism, as in Canada. The West is not monolithic in ethnolinguistic terms or, in religion, since the one universal church of Christianity splintered in the Middle Ages; and, moreover, the West divided into nation-states has meant modern politics spread unevenly within its civilizational boundaries. Yet, the distinctiveness of the West as a civilization has stood out since the early nineteenth century. Over this period, a large and growing gap in scientific and technological achievements and the level of income and wealth has developed between the West and the non-Western civilizations.

Unfortunately, the politics of Canadian multiculturalism is based on the notion that all cultures represented within an immigrant society are more or less equal, and deserve equal respect and treatment in politics and law. The idea of equality among individuals, a distinctly Western notion, has been changed to embrace equality among cultural groups. This change can be viewed as implying that the culture of the West is not distinctly better or more advanced than other cultures. The politics of multiculturalism in Canada discourages (if "prohibit" is too harsh a word) the majority population from demanding assimilation of minorities originating from a variety of non-Western cultures. Multiculturalism promotes and requires accommodation of ethnocultural minorities by the host society, a policy that has led in Canada to the encouragement and growth of *identity* politics. Consequently, multiculturalism together with an open-door immigration policy loosens the host society from its inherited culture.

Such a loosening is seen by some as a positive development. For example, John Ibbitson writes:

> Canada is the world's most successful country because it is profiting from the explosive creative forces that are unleashed when people of different races, cultures, and lifestyles live together and bond. Just as English has emerged as the world's most robust language by virtue of its being a mongrel tongue, so too are Canadians a mongrel people, a mélange. (2005: 3–4)

Similarly, Michael Adams sees Canada evolving as an "unlikely utopia" of ethnic diversity and multicultural harmony where there "is ample empirical evidence to suggest Canada *is* special, both in its social conditions and in the way its people (Canadians new and old) respond to those conditions" (2007: x).

However, some Canadians have found that multiculturalism and immigration have had negative effects by forcing them to change their own culture. Thus, recently the town of Herouxville in Quebec produced a charter in which its citizens declared that cultural accommodation is not a one-way street and that it is for immigrants to learn how to accommodate to the settled ways and lifestyle of the town. The existence of the Herouxville Charter was responsible in part for the creation of the Bouchard-Taylor Commission by the Quebec government to examine the public discontent concerning the concept of "reasonable accommodation." The Commission's report, *Building the Future: A Time for Reconciliation* (Bouchard-Taylor, 2008), acknowledged the existence of tensions within Quebec society between the majority Quebecois and the ethnic minorities and recommended that civil society and government make more efforts to ease tensions and to work towards reconciliation among cultures in the province.

A majority of Canadians appear to have accepted the notion that multiculturalism has positive effects on Canada, which in turn has allowed federal governments to commit the country permanently to an open-door immigration policy and no federal political party can afford to change it in the foreseeable future. Canadians sensitive to the negative impact of multiculturalism, like the proponents of the Herouxville Charter (Drouin and Thompson, 2007), tend to be viewed by politicians and the media as being at the margin of Canadian society. However, the critics of multiculturalism may well influence Canadian politics in the future. The debate over "reasonable accommodation" could be characterized as the prologue of the sort of public discussion waiting in the wings of Canadian politics, especially if there were more incidents of global terrorism like 9/11 in the United States, the subway bombings in London and Madrid, and others. Huntington (1996) in his seminal work had suggested that there would be a "clash of civilizations" that would lead to growing incidents of global terrorism and identity politics.

The West's vulnerability

During the seven years since 9/11, Canada has been spared terrorist attacks on her soil like those executed in the United States, Spain, and Britain. This could be due to luck and successful intelligence gathering by Canadian security forces; but it is no reason for complacency. The record shows that many terrorists reside in Canada and have exported terrorism abroad from Canadian soil (Bell, 2005).

In Canada, it has become very difficult to engage in open discussion of the impact on culture resulting from the open-door immigration and multiculturalism policies. It is similarly difficult to discuss critically whether these policies and the view of the equality of all cultures have made the country vulnerable to destructive forces within. Such difficulties are likely to increase as Canada becomes ever more dependent on immigration to sustain economic growth while the population is ageing and fertility declines even further.

The public discussion in Canada needs to come to terms with the threat to the country's cultural and civilizational character as secular, liberal-democratic, and predominantly Christian in origin is threatened by open immigration and multiculturalism. This discussion must consider the existence of attacks on the United States and other Western countries by Arab-Muslim[1] terrorists in the context of a global "clash of civilizations" while at the same time it must recognize that the contemporary process of globalization demands openness of society to an unprecedented pace of change and that multiculturalism can help Canada accommodate this change.

The West's demographic shift

The historic shift in the demography of the West, ageing population and declining fertility, which began around the second half of the last century, suggests that the populations of Western countries will decline severely and bring far reaching consequences for their civilization. Demographers estimate the "total fertility rate" (TFR)—or the average number of children born to women of childbearing age—needs to be 2.1 for a society to maintain a stable population over time. A TFR of less than 2.1 indicates declining population and a TFR of 1.3 or lower indicates that population will decline by half in 45 years. The recent compilation of TFR rankings by the United Nations places Niger with the world's highest TFR at 7.2 and Hong Kong with the lowest at 1.0. Among the Western countries, the United States scores 2.04; France, 1.88; the United Kingdom, 1.70; Germany, 1.35; and Italy, 1.29. Canada's TFR stands at present in the middle of the Western countries at 1.52 (United Nations, 2007) but Statistics

1 ◆ My use of the term "Arab-Muslim" refers to the ethnically diverse world of Islam. "Arab" in this usage indicates ethnicity by language since there are Christian Arabs, while "Muslim" signifies people of Islamic faith that include Afghans, Bengalis, Berbers, Javanese, Kurds, Punjabis, Malays, Turks, and so on.

Canada reported in 2004 that the age of mothers giving births has been steadily increasing over the past 20 years and that the fertility rate is likely to fall further (Statistics Canada, 2004, April 19). The case for immigration in Canada is based in part on the existence of these demographic facts and on the desire to maintain economic growth and to assure the financial viability of public pensions and health-care programs.

If fertility does in fact continue to decline and Canada's population falls dramatically, it will be an interesting question for historians in the future to understand why people in Canada and other Western countries made the decisions that brought them to these conditions. They will have to consider that, while technologically primitive cultures in the past have perished or been severely weakened when brought into contact with technologically superior cultures, Western countries went into demographic decline while they were at their civilizational apex, materially, culturally and technologically unthreatened by other cultures.

The paradox of liberal democracy

Liberal democracy, based on the notion of unalienable rights of the individual and the rule of law, is a product of the Western civilization. The basic idea and understanding of the workings of liberal democracy have spread throughout the world but its adoption has been very limited and where it has taken root it remains weak, needs protection, and can easily wither or be uprooted by people attached to their illiberal cultural values. For example, the rise and spread of Islamic fundamentalism or radical and militant Islam across the Arab-Muslim world have undermined any promise of liberal democracy. In its place, we find "illiberal" democracy and the rule of the majority based on cultural and religious values of traditional Islam.

Liberal democracy is the most beneficent and desirable political arrangement for the world and holds the promise of ending wars among nation-states that have marred Western history. However, liberal democracy is deeply vulnerable from the outside given its preoccupation with filling the needs of citizens through the improvement of living conditions and by upholding freedoms even in the face of those seeking to subvert them. As a result, reversals or defeats are due less to the superior power of external foes than to internal weaknesses. In *How Democracies Perish*, Jean-Francois Revel (1983) observed:

> Democratic civilization is the first in history to blame itself because another power is working to destroy it ... What distinguishes it is its eagerness to believe in its own guilt and its inevitable result. Democracy's predecessors hid such beliefs as shameful even when they thought, or knew, they were doomed. But democracy is zealous in devising arguments to prove the justice of its adversary's case and to lengthen the already overwhelming list of its own inadequacies. (1983: 7–8)

Revel belonged to the European generation that saw liberal democracies weaken themselves with mistaken guilt, and through the false choice of appeasement delude themselves with the expectation that hostile powers raging against democracies could be persuaded to opt for peace. His words have a powerful resonance in the post-9/11 world if we give credence to Huntington's thesis and acknowledge the Islamist-directed terrorism against the West is a civilizational war, and civilizational wars tend to be wars of religions and cultures.

Loss of traditional faith in the West

Religious or cultural wars are won and lost on the grounds of how confidently and tenaciously antagonists hold to their respective religious and cultural values. The Cold War was fought out between two ideological camps, and one reason the West won it is that it held more confidently and tenaciously to its principles of liberal democracy and capitalist market economy while the Soviet Union and its allies were less firmly committed to their socialist principles. It is undeniable that Christianity played a vital role in buttressing the liberal-democratic West in this war against Soviet Communism since the West, by acknowledging the place of religion in an open democratic society, stood in marked contrast to a Communist system based on militant atheism. It is uncertain how confidently the West holds its civilizational values in the post-9/11 world compared to the tenacity with which Islamists hold theirs while they pursue their declared war against the West. My sense is that this balance favors the Islamists.

The West's demographic decline is accompanied by a loss of traditional faith in Christianity. A 2002 survey by the Pew Research Center on the attitude of wealthy nations towards religion found that affluence is correlated with declining belief. The United States again was an exception. Nearly 60% of Americans reported religion being important in their lives. The comparative figures for Britain, Italy, Germany, and France were 33%, 27%, 21%, and 11%. The figure for Canada was 30% (Pew, 2002). If the downward trend over the past couple of generations continues, Christianity in Europe and Canada will cease to be a significant social institution. This decline of the role of Christianity in the West is likely to be accompanied by a decreased willingness to defend it and a greater openness to accommodate other faiths. This trend will be strengthened by the Western tradition of tolerance and freedom to pursue religious practices. However, since all major religions, including Christianity, have an in-built capacity for renewal, the declining trend is not certain to continue.

It is also important to note that in Europe the decline of Christianity will almost certainly be accompanied by the rise of other religions practiced by the many immigrants settling there. This process has already become quite pronounced and visible through the growth of Muslim communities in Britain, France, Italy, the Netherland, Denmark and other member states of the European Union.

The demographic bulge in the Arab-Muslim world and *jihad*

The "total fertility rate" in the Arab-Muslim world is the highest in the world and is only exceeded by that of sub-Saharan Africa. The TFRs of a few select countries from the Arab-Muslim world are as follows: Afghanistan, 7.48; Mali, 6.70; Somalia, 6.43; Yemen, 6.02; Palestine territories, 5.63; Iraq, 4.86; Sudan, 4.82; Pakistan, 3.99; Saudi Arabia, 3.81; Jordan, 3.53; Syria, 3.48; Egypt, 3.17; and Bangladesh, 3.22 (United Nations, 2007). This high fertility rate in the Arab-Muslim world has produced a demographic bulge of young people under the age of 25. A high proportion of young men in this age group are unemployed, under-employed, and unemployable due to lack of education and training for the modern economy.

This reservoir of young males has been estimated to number 25 million by 2010 (Spengler, 2005) and is the source of warriors for the Islamist cause. Many of these young men will migrate to Western countries and there some will join the already existing warriors of Islamist *jihad* (war) against the citizens and institutions of countries in Europe and North America. Interestingly, the large number of young men in the Arab-Muslim world has also fuelled conflict among countries in the region. These conflicts may well spill over into Europe and led Spengler (2005) to speculate that "[b]ecause of mass migration to Western Europe, the worst of the war might be fought on European soil."

Jihadist wars in Western countries involve not only terrorism but importantly also attacks on existing cultural institutions. For example, Islamists have demanded the creation of a parallel legal system based on Sharia law and changes in existing laws and traditions that interfere with Islamic practices such as unequal relationships between men and women, gender exclusion through dress codes, Islamic tradition of divorce and child custody, non-Western inheritance rules, Sharia financing, polygamy, and limits on free speech in discussing Islam. These demands are pushed by Islamist organizations in the West such as the Muslim Council of Britain (MCB), the Council of American-Islamic Relations (CAIR) in the United States and its counterpart or subsidiary in Canada (CAIR-Can), the Islamic Society of North America (ISNA), the Canadian Islamic Congress (CIC), the Muslim Student Associations (MSA), and a host of others that Daniel Pipes and Steven Emerson have documented (Pipes, 2002; Emerson, 2006).

Politics of identity and intercultural accommodation

In a world of accelerating change and mass movements of people, existing national identities are threatened and are replaced by new ones. In traditional society, identity has been developed over many generations and is mostly inherited. In a transient society, the search for new identities is deliberately crafted and formed on the basis of nostalgia, myths, and political demands. In the search for new national identities, Western countries have favored individuals over collectivities in the spirit of modernity. This quest threatens the continued existence of the values that are the base of Western identities. Replacement of these values by those of many ethnic groups fostered by the policy of multiculturalism leads to a "mongrel culture" (Ibbitson, 2005: 3–4) without strong and coherent values, except those used in Canada to justify multiculturalism itself. The rise of this "mongrel culture" threatens the existence of Canada's unique Anglo-French identity, history. and culture. This threat has been felt strongly by the residents of Herouxville and has driven them to develop a charter in an effort to combat this threat.

The recommendations by the Bouchard-Taylor Commission produced in response to the Herouxville initiatives and charter are that "reasonable accommodation" should allow immigrants from non-Western cultures to practice traditional customs like Sikhs wearing *kirpan* (dagger) and Muslim women wearing *hijab* (headscarf) in public. The acceptance of these recommendations is justified on the grounds that Canada has a tradition of tolerating minority cultures that is consistent with the broader policies stemming from the principles of multiculturalism.

The accommodation of non-Western cultures in Canada is based on domestic values and politics. The danger is that in the future, demands from foreign countries and religious organizations will also lead to the demand for, and granting of, accommodations to non-Western cultural values or norms. An example of such a development is found in the effort by member states of the Organization of Islamic Countries (OIC) to restrict free speech on Islamic issues in Canada and other Western countries. The instinctive response of Canadian society and governments to such responses is conditioned by real, imagined, or exaggerated guilt about the role of the West in the past development of Islamic countries. Concessions are made and foreign powers are appeased rather than opposed, encouraging them to increase their demands in the future knowing how weak liberal democracies are in their unwillingness and inability to protect their national identities. In Canada, assimilation is not demanded of immigrants and there is no required test of their loyalty, which encourages them to remain attached to their native cultures or faiths. These conditions can foster the making of homegrown terrorists, as occurred in Britain with the London suicide-bombers of Pakistani descent, bringing the risk that terrorism along the lines of the 9/11 events could be repeated in Canada and other Western countries.

Conclusion

The main proposition of this paper has been that open-door immigration from non-Western countries under Canada's multicultural policies and liberal-democratic values has resulted in a growing threat to the country's national identity and security. This threat has confronted the country with the difficult task of reconciling its desire to conserve the national identity and diffuse the threat of terrorism with the policy of multiculturalism and liberal desires for inclusion and individualism.

Unfortunately, these issues are getting very little attention from the public, media, or politicians, who prefer to treat the threats of global terrorism as questionable and treat open-door immigration policy and multiculturalism as "untouchable" pillars of the modern Canada that for demographic reasons is believed to require a steady influx of immigrants. Politicians as opinion makers and leaders are to be blamed for this absence of any serious discussion of these issues in Canada. Yet, given the nature of Canadian democracy, this behavior is understandable considering the voting power of the immigrant population. As is noted by David Harris, formerly Chief of the Strategic Planning of the Canadian Security Intelligence Service (CSIS): "Canada's immigration and refugee system has become largely a vote-importing mechanism designed to play on identity politics. It gives no consideration to the kinds and scale of terrorist threats, subversion, and disruption that such massive population movements can facilitate, even at the best of times" (2008: 139).

It would be good for Canada if politicians changed their behavior and encouraged a public discussion of the issues and possible changes to policies, rather than rushing into such a discussion after possible future terrorist acts in Canada or other Western countries or after there have been more militant domestic actions by Canadians bent on protecting their national identity in the spirit of the relatively restrained policies enacted by the citizens of Herouxville.

References

Adams, Michael (2007). *Unlikely Utopia: The Surprising Triumph of Canadian Pluralism*. Viking.

Bell, Stewart (2005). *Cold Terror: How Canada Nurtures and Exports Terrorism around the World*. John Wiley & Sons.

Bergesen, Albert J., ed. (2008). *The Sayyid Qutb Reader: Selected Writings on Politics, Religion, and Society*. Routledge.

Bouchard, Gerard, and Charles Taylor (2008). *Building the Future: A Time for Reconciliation.* Gouvernement du Quebec.

Drouin, Andre, and Bernard Thompson (2007). *Report Presented to Consultation Commission on Accommodation Practices Related to Cultural Differences.* <http://municipalite.herouxville.qc.ca/bouchardtaylorenglish.pdf>.

Emerson, Steven (2006). *Jihad Incorporated: A Guide to Militant Islam in the US.* Prometheus Books.

Habeck, Mary R. (2006). *Knowing the Enemy: Jihadist Ideology and the War on Terror.* Yale University Press.

Harris, David B. (2008). Is Canada Losing the Balance between Liberty and Security? In Martin Collacott and Alexander Moens, eds., *Immigration Policy and the Terrorist Threat in Canada and the United States* (Fraser Institute): 129–59.

Huntington, Samuel P. (1996). *The Clash of Civilizations and the Remaking of World Order.* Simon & Schuster.

Huntington, Samuel P. (2004). *Who Are We? The Challenges to America's National's Identity.* Simon & Schuster.

Ibbitson, John (2005). *The Polite Revolution: Reflecting the Canadian Dream.* McClelland & Stewart.

Lawrence, Bruce (2005). *Messages to the West: The Statements of Osama Bin Laden.* Verso.

Mansur, Salim (2008). Immigration and Muslim Extremists in the Post-9/11 World. In Martin Collacott and Alexander Moens, eds., *Immigration Policy and the Terrorist Threat in Canada and the United States* (Fraser Institute): 21–35.

Pew Research Center (2002). *Among Wealthy Nations ... U.S. Stands Alone in Its Embrace of Religion*. Washington, D.C.

Pipes, Daniel (2002). *Militant Islam Reaches America*. W.W. Norton.

Revel, Jean-Francois (1983). *How Democracies Perish*. Doubleday.

Statistics Canada (2004, April 19). Births, 2002. *The Daily*. <http://www.statcan.gc.ca/daily-quotidien/040419/dq040419b-eng.htm>.

Spengler (2005, August 23). The Demographics of Radical Islam. *Asia Times*. <http://www.atimes.com/atimes/Front_Page/GH23Aa01.html>.

United Nations (2007). *World Population Prospects: The 2006 Revision*. New York.

Wright, Lawrence (2006). *The Looming Tower: Al-Qaeda and the Road to 9/11*. Random House.

Political issues

Chapter 11

The politics of Canadian immigration policies

Gordon Gibson

As a political observer, it is interesting to me how rare a discussion of Canadian immigration policy is. In other areas of great importance for public policy—health care, say, or Afghanistan, or global warming—one sees lots of action and debate. True, it is often a dialogue of the deaf, in the sense that hard positions are taken and held, but at least there is a lot of talk. This enables members of the public to acquire some information to form their own thinking.

This is not the case in immigration policy. There has recently been a brief flare-up of mutual insults in the area, triggered by current government proposals hidden away in the fine print of the Budget, and even that has been all heat and no light. But the more usual condition is almost a conspiracy of silence on the basic questions. That is an important indicator. I know of only one other policy area of great importance where the same situation applies, and that is in Canadian Indian policy. I commonly refer to that as the most important moral issue in federal politics and yet the basics are never discussed by politicians and only rarely even by academics.

If Indian policy is Canada's greatest moral issue, I think it would not be unfair to refer to immigration as the most important political issue. The most important thing about Canada is who we are, and that goes immediately to the question of immigration. So why do we mostly ignore it? I suspect that a major factor behind the lack of public debate on these two topics is one of guilt. In the Indian case, it is a fact that we have much to be guilty for, and in the immigration case it is the background guilt of people who feel they have been very lucky in the lottery of life and wonder how they can deny such good fortune to others?

The fact that politicians do not talk about the basics in either of these areas also tells us something, namely that they see much more danger there than any possible upside in taking leadership. Intelligent politicians are looking for votes, not trouble. Therefore, the only aspect of immigration they discuss is that which might earn some votes without losing others, a topic I will return to later.

Other countries, especially in Europe, have begun a public debate about immigration. For example, Sir Andrew Green in chapter 12 describes a deep and growing anger in Britain. It is interesting to learn that the pollster, YouGov, found in an April poll that five out of six Britons feel an "immigration crisis" has hit them, with about the same number wanting to shut immigration down (YouGov®, 2008, April 7). The contrast between the public debate in Canada and Britain is all the more interesting given that, according to an estimate by the *Economist* (2008, January 5), Canada has almost double the fraction of foreign born as does Britain, with much less fuss. Are we doing some things right? In any event, we can surely learn from the problems of others. Thus the opening thought is this: this book stands out as a lighthouse illuminating generally dark and dangerous parts of our political landscape that seriously need attention.

Some of the chapters in this book directly address another of the reasons there is so little public discussion of immigration in this country, which is that most people do not feel well grounded in philosophy and principle and facts. They also are afraid of the almost automatic "racist" charge that accompanies the discussion of immigration policies, now that immigration has become largely non-white. Most Canadians find the subject too sensitive and lack the intellectual foundation to reject that accusation as nonsense.

Before I consider the politics and the institutional machinery that might make public discussion more open and rational, let me briefly present my own understanding of the main issues surrounding immigration policies in Canada. There are two approaches to immigration: one is about helping others; the other is about helping ourselves.

As to the first: Do Canadians have a moral or practical obligation to help other people in this world? I think overwhelmingly people would say, "Yes," but relative to our capacity. We are small and the world is large. There are two ways of helping the poor and disadvantaged in the poor countries of the world. One way is by importing people; the other is by exporting foreign aid. The latter is so much more effective and sustainable that there should be little debate—aid should be the focus. And yet, we spend only a small fraction on foreign aid per year as compared to the net costs of our immigration policy. Based on the work of Herbert Grubel (2005), a rough estimate would be that our direct net governmental subsidy costs attributable to immigration are five to ten times as much as what we send in foreign aid. On the face of it, we should dramatically change our priorities if what we have in mind is human welfare.

That does not exclude an obligation to assist with our share of genuine refugees. This must be noted and affirmed but, at the same time, it is not the topic of this conference and the numbers are much smaller. And, those numbers show no shame for Canada: most of the Western world accepts around 15% of refugee applicants; we accept about 50%.

The second question, helping Canadian interests, brings us to immigration policy and a consideration of the level and composition of the immigrant flow. It seems to me to be self-evident that once our moral obligations are discharged by way of accepting refugees and distributing foreign aid, our remaining study of migration policy should focus on its ability to provide the greatest net benefits to Canada. What are the broad options?

The first answer to this question comes from what I call the simplistic libertarian theory. (I will come to a sophisticated libertarian theory in a moment.) This is the idea of open borders and minimal influence with individual freedom of movement. It was in effect more or less 150 years ago and it worked. But since then we have seen two developments that have resulted in a dramatic increase in the number of potential immigrants: a reduction in mobility costs and the development of the welfare state offering major financial and social benefits to all residents, including new immigrants. If allowed, this increase in the number of potential immigrants would cause a tidal wave of movement across open borders that Canada's economy and society could not absorb without really serious disruptions. The idea of classical libertarian free immigration is clearly a practical and political non-starter in today's world.

The *Economist* looks on this issue a bit wistfully by concluding: "If labour flowed without restraint, social and political systems would be disrupted on a huge scale, but global poverty would be vastly relieved" (2008, January 3). Well maybe, but it is not going to happen and, besides, is it really obvious that the costs of lower incomes for Canadians and the disruption to their lives are smaller than the benefits to immigrants as a result of their enjoying reduced poverty?

The second idea that might guide Canada's immigration policy is the sophisticated libertarian theory, what I will call the "club" approach. Canada is a large club and its citizens own its stock of human and physical capital, either privately or through their government's ownership of infrastructure and social capital. These property rights, individual and collective, are not taken into account in the simplistic libertarian approach. New members are admitted to this and any private club only if in the long run they enhance the net satisfaction of the old members, including adding to or subtracting from their property. For Canada, the measurements of value or "net satisfaction" are many and subtle, involving the benefits of diversity, social dynamism, the costs of crowding and need for new infrastructure, the distribution of income, the level of economic output, the amount of capital (financial and human) brought by new members, and so on. The magnitude, timing, and speed of change, all need to be included in the measurements.

The third approach is what I will call the "political" one, which involves immigration policy, and which maximizes the returns to political decision makers. Here the measurements are much less subtle than in the "club" approach. The standard of value is reliable votes or other considerations useful to politicians. It is this third theory that governs our current immigration policy. That is not to say that the current policy need be corrupt just because it is political. It is true that the seeking of votes is often done by gathering support through giving large favors paid by public money to small groups but that must be done in such a way as not to offend the average voter. Indeed, as long as the average voter is well informed and takes the time to reflect upon policy issues, special-interest vote seeking cannot stray too far from acceptable norms.

But the problem is that the average voter is not well informed on immigration policy, where the language and data are confused, sometimes deliberately so. In this and other policy fields, therefore, the danger of political corruption is large, in the sense that politicians use the power of the state to buy selected votes. (That is not saying that the politicians themselves need be corrupt. In Canada, that is quite rare. They are simply following existing perverse rules and incentives that guide their behavior.)

As a classic example of the voters' not having information, consider the policy of supply management for dairy products. Any economist will tell you that supply management transfers wealth on a large scale from consumers to dairy quota holders. The key to making it work politically is that the large sums, which earn the gratitude and votes of quota holders, are extracted in small sums from the many consumers who do not know about the existence of the costs they are forced to pay. Poor parents and their children pay more for milk and never know it. So, one of the keys to political success is working with other people's money or property to confer favors on target groups. The old system of shoe quotas was another classic of this political game. Regional development schemes and Employment Insurance are large examples still in place. And, of course, a story of superficial justification can be spun in each of these cases. If other politicians do not contradict the spin—and they rarely do, as they all seek the same swing votes—then the scheme continues to work. That is why no politicians in or out of government talk about the realities of marketing boards or immigration.

But good things can happen in spite of our political system. The North American Free Trade Agreement (NAFTA) and the value-added tax (GST) are both examples of good economic policy in spite of being very bad politics. Unfortunately, those policies helped to destroy the career of the Prime Minister involved and because politicians are close observers of such things similar good policies face low prospects any time.

The superficial justification or spin in the case of immigration has three main parts. Part one of the spin is that immigration is necessary for economic prosperity. The lessons of this book and essentially all of the research going back to the McDonald Commission of the 1980s disagree with that, if by prosperity one means income and wealth *per capita*, which is the only sensible way to look at it. There is no point in having a large population and large GDP but low per-capita incomes. Indeed, a fruitful area for research would be to find better, quantified data showing to what extent the puzzling lack of growth in Canadian low and median incomes and labor productivity since 1980 is related to the high levels of immigration, which has increased the supply of labor relative to that of capital.

Part two of the spin is that immigration is needed to replace the demographic deficit of an aging population. That too has been discredited by chapters in this book and elsewhere, including the very recent and excellent report of the British House of Lords (United Kingdom, House of Lords, Select Committee on Economic Affairs, 2008). The fact is that immigrants age just like the rest of us and we import immigrants who are already old through the "family class" doorway. Immigration is not justified as an answer to an aging society. Much worse, the politicians do us harm by maintaining that stance, for the net result is that they and we are given an excuse not to talk about the even more serious fiscal problems of an aging society in our welfare state.

The obvious answers to the aging problem (in addition to higher fertility, unlikely these days) are growing productivity and a very gradual increase in the age of retirement. This gradually higher retirement age surely makes sense as we all live longer. To suggest that immigration solves this tough issue is just irresponsible. This issue is complicated by the idea that fertility is reduced as young families face high costs of living, especially of housing, and thus believe that they cannot afford to have children. Mass immigration, especially in Vancouver and Toronto, has caused housing prices and other living costs to be higher than they would have been otherwise. On the basis of this analysis, a reduction in future immigration rates and a slower increase in living costs would raise fertility and help ease the demographic problems facing Canada presently.

Part three of the spin is guilt: we owe the world somehow, because we are so lucky. We may owe something to the world, though there are questions about the role our efforts and hard work rather than luck played in our present condition and that of people in other countries. Whatever the answer to this conundrum, if we wish to be charitable, we should give more foreign aid. Immigration, again, is a very distant second-best solution to the issue. The refuting of these various spins is central to the public good.

Perhaps more interesting than the spin is the question of who the real drivers of policy are, because that exploration can point the way to necessary political reforms. The drivers of policy are those persons with a direct interest in the outcome. That does not mean that these interests are bad or good; the salient fact is that they benefit the interested party and not necessarily the public as a whole. Whether those special interests make for good or bad public policy is currently a matter of accident, not design. In the end, our challenge is to harness the interests so that good public policy does occur indeed by design, not accident.

The special interests are first and foremost the would-be immigrants and their relatives and friends in Canada. Their motives are what they are, and wholly human and understandable. Indeed, we are fortunate that many people would like to come here. However, the relatives and friends of potential immigrants should not determine immigration policy. Their goals and values may have little in common with those of Canadians already in the country.

The other policy drivers are less obvious. They are the Immigration Industry, which is a collection of lawyers, consultants, and settlement people whose work significantly depends upon immigrants coming to Canada and interacting with the social and legal system thereafter. For the economic interests of most people in this category, more immigration simply is good for business, the more so, the more problems the immigrants have for them to solve. One has in mind the interminable appeals embedded in our system and readily exploited by lawyers and consultants. The immigration industry is operated by a perfectly respectable group of people, and among them is to be found much expertise. They are, however, the wrong people to set policy because of clear conflicts of interest.

Another set of drivers of immigration policy are employers seeking labor for a variety of reasons. The simplest and best is a genuine lack of Canadian supply. Other reasons may be a desire for lower labor costs and for employees that may be more amenable, efficient, and reliable than Canadian workers. These employers too are simply following their own interests but, just like the immigration industry, they are not the appropriate setters of policy. Policies must serve the overall interest of Canadians, not just that of interest groups benefiting from them.

The design of such policies serving the interest of all Canadians is properly the responsibility of politicians. However, the issue is, to what extent do the politicians' incentives correspond to the public interest, and to what extent to special interests? We have already noted above the role in policy design played by the large gains politicians can confer on some while the costs are recovered from large numbers of others paying small sums. If the public at large knows and cares about the costs of the immigration policy imposed on them and votes accordingly, then the public interest will accommodated. However, if the knowledge and concern of the public about these costs is weak, the special interests will govern the design of policy.

It is important to appreciate the fact that special interests favoring mass immigration have a great deal to offer politicians. They can raise money in copious quantities and well-organized communities can turn out great numbers at election time as workers and voters. Historically, this use of the services offered by immigration interests has been a specialty of the federal Liberal party, but no party is immune to this practice. Politicians appreciate this kind of help and have been able to reward the immigrant interests with more open immigration policies. The rational interaction of immigration interests and politicians has brought us Canada's present immigration system. That is the way our system is designed, and that is the way it has worked, but it is noteworthy that there is one result quite special and unusual.

Most policies that benefit milk producers, the recipients of employment insurance in the Atlantic Provinces, and industries protected by tariffs involve transfers of money from some to others. They also induce changes in behavior that result in lower productivity and economic efficiency. However, immigration policies do much more by affecting social conditions. They can create new ethnic and cultural groups and shift the balance of power among existing ones. Over time, this shift can be—and in Canada has begun to be—especially significant because of its multicultural rather than integrating policy. This development of new patterns of cultural groupings and diversity may be considered to have positive effects on the well-being of Canadians but it raises significant problems for the integration of newcomers into Canadian society and their acceptance of fundamental Canadian values.

This problem is aggravated by the fact that immigrants today typically have higher fertility rates than Canadians and that they tend to be accompanied by parents, grandparents, and other relatives accepted under the "family class" reunification program. This propensity to demand family reunification is different for groups of immigrants from different ethnic origins, which in itself will add to divergent values and cultural standards among immigrant communities and Canadians.

The difference in fertility rates has important and powerful effects through time because of the power of compound interest. Most people are familiar with the "rule of 70," according to which one divides 70 by the annual percentage growth rate to obtain the approximate doubling time, in years. According to this rule, a 1% increase in Canada's population through immigration doubles the number of foreign-born every 70 years. These considerations imply that if the fertility of native Canadians remains at replacement levels, the share of immigrants in Canada's population rises very quickly. It rises even more quickly if these immigrants have high rates of fertility. The prospective effect of continued mass immigration on the ethnic composition of Canada appears to be behind the intense debate about "reasonable accommodation" in Quebec these days.

Whether the general public in the rest of Canada and possibly Quebec wishes the large present and forecast demographic changes going on in Canada, or the pace of change, I do not know. Whether they think immigration policy meets their idea of the public interest, I do not know. What I do know is that they have not been asked the question in those terms by their political representatives, most of whom would be utterly horrified by the prospect of having to deal with the issue. Politicians already have enough trouble dealing with other divisive problems and policies.

What we also know is that the overwhelming evidence is that immigration policy for the past generation has reduced per-capita income below what it would have been otherwise. The social cost to date has been surprisingly modest, perhaps because of useful screening aspects of the current admissions policy, felicitous country sourcing, and the success of public information campaigns about the alleged benefits from cultural diversity and the inhumanity of racism. However, we should not ignore the evidence from abroad that rapid demographic change can bring problems in spite of such public information campaigns. Nor should we ignore

Robert Putnam, the well-known Harvard academic, who to his dismay and in spite of himself found that greater diversity may lead to a short-term decline in social capital, in trust, cooperation, and shared values (Putnam, 2007).

While the preceding analysis implies that mass immigration and its effects on Canadians are important, the general public appears not to be aware of these facts and politicians have every reason to keep quiet. The key question, therefore, is how these conditions can be changed. We cannot expect politicians to act against their own interest. The only answer I can see is to bring about change through institutional reform, which would allow all politicians equally to hide behind it and quietly change the policies to be in the general public interest. Ideally this goal could be achieved through democratic reform. I think it is no accident that the European countries that first came to grips with this issue have proportional electoral systems. These systems yield smaller and more specialized parties, which often take up politically incorrect causes like opposition to mass immigration, as occurred in Denmark, the Netherlands, Austria, and France. But I think we may wait a long time to change our present first-past-the-post electoral system that would allow the development of such specialized parties in Canada.

This leads me to believe we need two things on the immigration file specifically. The first is to get the public to understand fully the facts surrounding the costs and benefits of mass immigration and, based on this information, public discussions to shape and build a consensus as to future immigration policies. I am aware that such studies and discussions are often used to bury issues but this one is too important not to gain attention and many Canadians would welcome and follow it, if the experience of Quebec's Buchard-Taylor Commission is any indication for the rest of Canada.

The second initiative involves the creation of a new immigration decision-making body that operates at arm's length from politicians but operates under principles laid down by them, much as the courts interpret the politician-made law or the Charter, for example. I referred earlier to the splendid study on immigration released a couple of months ago by the Select Committee on Economic Affairs of the British House of Lords, whose members included two former Chancellors, a former Governor of the Bank of England and distinguished economists. That is the kind of independent panel we need for the proposed study. I wish I could suggest that our Canadian Senate do the same thing here but fear it would not work. Many Senators, including the dominating Liberals, are too closely identified with the current system to fairly ask them to step back from it. Honesty in this area can convey partisan disadvantage. The interest of Canadians at this time would be best served by the creation of a Royal Commission to study Canada's demographic future, which includes not only immigration but also age of retirement and issues surrounding fertility.

Politicians would be responsible for setting the frame of reference and guidelines for the research and report of the proposed Royal Commission. In my opinion, these guidelines should be based on the "club" model with its emphasis on the "net self-interest of Canada" and the difference between the effects of immigration on aggregate national and per-capita incomes. The exact frame of reference and guidelines would have to be debated in parliament and in forums involving the general public.

I also recommend that the Commission consider the creation of a body for the daily administration of immigration policies that is independent of politicians in their routine administration of the law. In our existing democratic system, such independence is essential to assure the administration of policies in the public interest. The proposed body for the routine and daily administration of immigration laws should be made to be as transparent and accountable to the public as possible, with the ultimate oversight of operations and especially the determination of basic policies remaining the responsibility of politicians, who in addition should be required to review periodically the proposed body's work.

Conclusion

Let me conclude my study by introducing some sweeping thoughts about the present and future of Canada. In the last 50 years, Canadians have become the "nice" people of the world who are politically correct, relativistic, and tolerant with "whatever!" As a sort of political creed, they consider themselves privileged and feel a bit guilty about it. None of these characteristics make for the survival of Canadian society and the nation in the long run. Metaphorically speaking, we now have soft and smooth hands and soft and smooth minds: watching the tube and surfing the net, fixated on sports and celebrity, we belong to the "me" generation and are extremely risk averse. Some of these characteristics are good and some not but it is not a package that assures Darwinian survival in a competitive world. Are we to become what Stephen Gallagher in his chapter in this volume calls a mere "global suburb"? Maybe that is the future.

We have some hard questions to face. Immigration is only one of them but it is surely a litmus test as nothing is more important to a nation's future than "who we are." So, good luck to us all on that.

References

Economist (2008, January 3). The Long Term. Special report: Migration, from *The Economist* print edition. <http://www.economist.com/displaystory.cfm?story_id=10286111>.

Grubel, Herbert (2005), *Immigration and the Welfare State in Canada: Growing Conflicts, Constructive Solutions*. Public Policy Sources No. 84. Fraser Institute.

Putnam, Robert D. (2007). *E Pluribus Unum*: Diversity and Community in the 21st Century. The 2006 Johan Skytte Prize Lecture. *Scandinavian Political Studies* 30, 2: 137–74.

United Kingdom, House of Lords, Select Committee on Economic Affairs (2008). *The Economic Impact of Immigration. Volume I: Report.* HL Paper 82-1 (April 1). <http://www.publications.parliament.uk/pa/ld200708/ldselect/ldeconaf/82/8202.htm>.

YouGov® (2008, April 7). *YouGov/Juniper TV Survey Results.* [Topic: immigration; fieldwork: January 17–21, 2008.] <http://www.yougov.co.uk/extranets/ygarchives/content/pdf/Juniper%20Toplines.pdf>.

Chapter 12

The challenges of reforming immigration policy in Britain

Sir Andrew Green

The papers presented, and discussion at, the Canadian Immigration Policy Conference and found in this volume showed very clearly that the demography and economics of migration are very similar in the United Kingdom and Canada. However, public opinion and, therefore, the politics are very different. In Britain, immigration may well be the most serious problem of our generation, not only for its own sake but also because mistakes once made cannot be rectified.

MigrationwatchUK

It is important to be clear that Migrationwatch, the organization I founded and head, is not opposed to a sensible level of migration in both directions. This is a natural part of an open economy. Still less are we opposed to immigrants themselves. Our concern is with the *scale* of immigration, which is now 25 times higher than it has been in the past 1,000 years. People concerned about the impact of such immigration on their country's economy and society have a three-fold task: first, to alert public opinion; second, to propose solutions; third, to campaign for the adoption of these solutions.

Alerting public opinion

When we founded Migrationwatch in December 2001, we faced three fundamental problems that are almost identical to those existing in Canada: a general reluctance to discuss the subject; a widespread ignorance of the facts; an absence of solutions on offer.

Reluctance

In Britain there has been a deep reluctance to discuss immigration ever since an inflammatory speech by Enoch Powell in April, 1968 (Powell, 1968). This blatantly racist speech had the effect, presumably unintended, of placing the subject off limits for a generation. The key passage was a classical reference but was widely seen as a prediction of Britain's future: "As I look ahead, I am filled with foreboding; like the Roman, I seem to see the River Tiber foaming with much blood." People are also reluctant to raise the subject as it might offend immigrants and their families. Furthermore, the hugely influential British Broadcasting Corporation (BBC) has been deeply reluctant to address the subject.

Under that surface calm, however, there is a deep and growing concern. The public feels that our national culture is threatened and that, in some areas, our society is being changed beyond recognition without their ever being consulted. Successive polls show that almost 80% of the population does not believe that the Government has been open and honest about immigration. This is especially true of the working class, whether black or white, who feel that their interests have been ignored and that they have been condescended to. This goes a long way to explain the significant growth in support for the British National Party (BNP), which is running on an anti-immigration platform.

Ignorance of the Facts

From the outset, we in Migrationwatch decided to confine ourselves to making the facts known in the expectation that this would cause the political reform process to get under way. That is now beginning to happen. Our information is supplied through papers on a website and the provision of comments to newspapers and broadcasters. As we are the only body making a rational case against large-scale immigration, the BBC, who are obliged to seek balance, have to come to us for information and comment.

It was our ambition to become the first port of call for journalists and broadcasters on issues relating to immigration. Broadly speaking, that has now been achieved. Three factors have contributed to this success:

- We used extreme care in the presentation and verification of facts and we take care also never to exaggerate. In the past six years, the Government has not been able to discredit us on any of our facts.

- In our media work, we designate only a single spokesperson so that one cannot be played off against another.

- Our analysis has focused more widely than individual Government departments; this enables us to bring to public notice the whole range of ways in which large-scale immigration affects the economy and society.

Our efforts have also been helped by the sheer pace and scale of change. Net foreign immigration has trebled in the last 10 years to about 300,000 per year and public concern has risen correspondingly. In spontaneous public-opinion polls, the issues of race relations and asylum seekers have figured in the top four for several years and have often been at the very top.

The practical effects are also becoming more widely understood. On the Government's own projections, immigration will add seven million to our population in the next 25 years—this is seven times the population of our second largest city, Birmingham. Furthermore, one new household in three will be a result of immigration. This will require the construction of a new home every six minutes over a similar period.

Two particular developments have been very important. The establishment by the French government of an accommodation center for asylum seekers at Sangatte, near Calais, emphasized the extent to which migrants were crossing Europe in order to get into Britain. This development was publicized widely by television footage of migrants seeking to climb over wire fences and jump into trucks. The French Government has now closed Sangatte Camp but the televisual impact on public opinion was considerable.

Secondly, the arrival of a large number of eastern Europeans in a short period of time has attracted a great deal of attention, the more so as, unlike other migrants, they settled all over the country, including rural areas. It is estimated that approximately one million have arrived since May 2004, of whom perhaps half have since returned home.

Absence of solutions

The public debate has seen few positive proposals for changes in national immigration policies. The weakness of statistics on the size and economic and social impacts of immigration, and the inadequacy of border controls to record actual immigrant flows makes this a difficult area for policy formation. Furthermore, the government's very poor capacity to remove immigrants that the courts have ordered to leave the country undermines the credibility of any reforms that might be proposed. Canada appears to suffer from similar problems. In Britain, a start is being made under the pressure of public opinion but the tools are not yet in place for an effective immigration policy.

Proposing a solution

Now, however, is the time to propose constructive new immigration policies because under present conditions in the United Kingdom, immigration accounts for 70% of population growth and England has now caught up with the Netherlands as the most crowded country in Europe (apart from Malta) (United Kingdom, House of Commons, *Hansard*, 2008). This expected overcrowding of Britain is essentially why Migrationwatch has proposed that the policy aim should be "balanced migration." This means that immigration should be brought down to the level of emigration. More precisely, it means that foreign immigration should be reduced to the level of net British emigration, which is currently about 120,000 a year so that migration flows have a zero impact on the size of Britain's population. This zero impact is not equivalent to a zero population growth since that figure depends on the fertility rates and the age profile of the existing population. But, the effect of such a policy would be to stabilize the population of the United Kingdom at about 65 million by mid-century rather than the nearly 80 million now projected for 2056.

Promoting this solution requires a major effort to tackle the economic myths that have grown up around immigration. A recent report by the Select Committee on Economic Affairs of the House of Lords has been most helpful in this effort (United Kingdom, H.L., S.C.E.A., 2008). This Committee, which includes two former Chancellors of the Exchequer and a former Governor of the Bank of England found that there was "no evidence for ... significant economic benefits for the existing UK population" (2008: 5). It pointed out that the measure that mattered was not total national income but income per head and it found that the effects on the latter were small, especially in the long run. It also found that the fiscal benefit of immigration was likely to be small and it described the argument that immigration fills skills shortages as "analytically weak" and insufficient reason for promoting net immigration. All these points are likely to apply in similar measure to Canada.

Mounting a campaign

Any campaign for changes in Britain's immigration policies needs to be conducted on three levels: the public, opinion formers, and Government. Special-interest groups benefiting from immigration, such as UK fruit farmers and lawyers, would, of course, oppose it. So would the leaders of ethnic groups consisting mainly of relatively recent immigrants, despite the fact that a majority of their communities believe that there is too much immigration into Britain. Furthermore, the trades unions seem to oppose effective immigration control, despite the impact of immigration on the wages of their members with low wages. Some of the middle classes would also oppose immigration reforms on the grounds of self-interest; they benefit from cheap restaurants and affordable child care. Despite the opposition to immigration policy reforms from these opponents, the general public is strongly in favor of much tougher immigration controls, increasingly so in recent times.

Conclusion

As one speaker put it, "there is no expiry date on hope." Migrationwatch hopes that our work on the effects of massive levels of immigration on social and environmental conditions in Britain will continue to make the public aware of the facts and make politicians interested in appropriate policy reforms that will result in balanced migration. Our work has already begun to produce results but getting immigration reform adopted in Britain will inevitably be a long, hard slog. In the end, however, reform will have helped to preserve the high living standards, the environment, and social harmony of the British people for future generations. Other countries with high levels of mass immigration can learn much from Britain's past experiences and likely future changes in policies that are under way.

References

Powell, Enoch (1968). Like the Roman, I See the River Tiber Foaming with Much Blood. <http://www.sterlingtimes.org/text_rivers_of_blood.htm>.

United Kingdom, House of Commons, *Hansard*, 10 September 2008, col. 1831 W.

United Kingdom, House of Lords, Select Committee on Economic Affairs (2008). *The Economic Impact of Immigration. Volume I: Report.* HL Paper 82-1 (April 1). <http://www.publications.parliament.uk/pa/ld200708/ldselect/ldeconaf/82/8202.htm>.

About this publication

Publishing information

Distribution

This publication is available from <http://www.fraserinstitute.org> and <http://www.fraseramerica.org> in Portable Document Format (PDF) and can be read with Adobe Acrobat® 7 or later or with Adobe Reader® 7 or later. Adobe Reader® 9, the most recent version, is available free of charge from Adobe Systems Inc. at <http://get.adobe.com/reader/>. We encourage you to install the most recent version.

Ordering publications

For information about ordering the printed publications of the Fraser Institute, please contact the publications coordinator via:

- e-mail: sales@fraserinstitute.org
- telephone: 604.688.0221 ext. 580 or, toll free, 1.800.665.3558 ext. 580
- fax: 604.688.8539.

Media

For media enquiries, please contact our Communications Department:

- 604.714.4582
- e-mail: communications@fraserinstitute.org.

Website

To learn more about the Fraser Institute, please visit our website at <http://www.fraserinstitute.org>.

Disclaimer

ISBN

978-0-88975-246-7

Printed and bound in Canada.

Date of issue

August 2009

Editing, design, and production

Lindsey Thomas Martin

Cover design

Bill Ray

Image for front cover

Canada Customs Stamp ©Thorsten (Fotolia)

Supporting the Fraser Institute

To learn how to support the Fraser Institute, please contact:

- Development Department, Fraser Institute,
  Fourth Floor, 1770 Burrard Street,
  Vancouver, British Columbia, V6J 3G7 Canada

- telephone, toll-free: 1.800.665.3558 ext. 586
- e-mail: development@fraserinstitute.org.

About the Fraser Institute

Our vision is a free and prosperous world where individuals benefit from greater choice, competitive markets, and personal responsibility. Our mission is to measure, study, and communicate the impact of competitive markets and government interventions on the welfare of individuals.

Founded in 1974, we are an independent research and educational organization with locations throughout North America and international partners in over 70 countries. Our work is financed by tax-deductible contributions from thousands of individuals, organizations, and foundations. In order to protect its independence, the Institute does not accept grants from government or contracts for research.

菲沙研究所的願景乃一自由而昌盛的世界，當中每個人得以從更豐富的選擇、具競爭性的市場及自我承擔責任而獲益。我們的使命在於量度、研究並使人知悉競爭市場及政府干預對個人福祉的影響。

Nous envisageons un monde libre et prospère, où chaque personne bénéficie d'un plus grand choix, de marchés concurrentiels et de responsabilités individuelles. Notre mission consiste à mesurer, à étudier et à communiquer l'effet des marchés concurrentiels et des interventions gouvernementales sur le bien-être des individus.

تتمثل رؤيتنا في وجود عالم حر ومزدهر يستفيد فيه الأفراد من القدرة على الاختيار بشكل أكبر، والأسواق التنافسية، والمسؤولية الشخصية. أما رسالتنا فهي قياس، ودراسة، وتوصيل تأثير الأسواق التنافسية والتدخلات الحكومية المتعلقة بالرفاه الاجتماعي للأفراد.

Nuestra visión es un mundo libre y próspero donde los individuos se beneficien de una mayor oferta, la competencia en los mercados y la responsabilidad individual. Nuestra misión es medir, estudiar y comunicar el impacto de la competencia en los mercados y la intervención gubernamental en el bienestar de los individuos.

Editorial Advisory Board